BETTER LIVING THROUGH LITERATURE

HOW BOOKS CHANGE LIVES AND (SOMETIMES) HISTORY

ROBIN BATES

"Pages at Old Main Library, 1923." From the Collection of Cincinnati & Hamilton County Public Library.

Copyright © 2024 by Robin Bates

First Edition

Cover design and interior layout by Matthew J. Distefano
Cover image by Keith Giles
Author headshot photo by Rick Boeth

ISBN 978-1-964252-17-9
Printed in the United States of America

Published by Quoir
Chico, California
www.quoir.com

CONTENTS

I will tell you something about stories,
[he said]
They aren't just for entertainment.
Don't be fooled.
They are all we have, you see,
all we have to fight off
illness and death.
You don't have anything
if you don't have the stories.

— **Leslie Marmon Silko**, *Ceremony*

Every art contributes to the greatest art of all,
the art of living.

— **Bertolt Brecht**, "Appendices to the Short Organum"

Poets are the unacknowledged legislators of the world.

— **Percy Bysshe Shelley**, *A Defence of Poetry*

To Julia,

from the man who loves the pilgrim soul in you

PART ONE: The Power of Literature

INTRODUCTION

EVERYWHERE WE LOOK, LITERATURE appears to be losing ground. Colleges are slashing humanities programs, potential literature majors are choosing more "practical" programs that will land them jobs, and timeless literary classics suddenly appear timebound as they gather dust on library shelves. In middle and high school, meanwhile, the STEM disciplines of Science-Technology-Engineering and Math are all the rage, and the technical aspects of reading and writing take precedence over imaginative play.

Before we dismiss literature as a nice but unnecessary frill, however, consider the story of Mohamed Barud, a Somali political prisoner in the 1980s. As reported by Greg Warning's podcast *Rough Translation* and later aired on National Public Radio's *Morning Edition,* Leo Tolstoy's masterpiece *Anna Karenina* saved his sanity, his marriage, and possibly his life.[1]

Newly married in 1981, health care worker Barud was abruptly imprisoned. His crime? Naively believing that Somalia dictator Siad Barre wanted to hear about poor conditions in a local hospital. Instead, Barud was charged with treason and imprisoned to a lifetime of solitary confinement.

Cut off from all contact with the outside world and even other prisoners, Barud felt himself going insane. His tiny cell was three steps across and invaded by cockroaches, rats, flies, and millions of mosquitoes. In his solitude, he began to resent and even hate his wife Ismahan for not visiting him, even though he knew visits weren't allowed. He became frightened "of going to a certain area in my mind where I would commit suicide without knowing, without wanting to."

Barud's only solace was his neighbor in an adjoining cell, Dr. Adan Abokor, with whom he communicated through a system of taps. As he became proficient at the code, Barud would contact Abokor whenever he awoke from one of his ferocious nightmares.

Diagnosing Barud's condition as panic attacks, Dr. Abokor tried to counsel him but feared his efforts were hopeless. At this point, however, Tolstoy's novel came to the rescue.

After two years of imprisonment, Dr. Abokor had been allowed a change of clothes and, while retrieving the items from his suitcase, he asked the warden if he could take one of the books he had brought. In a moment of unexpected leniency, the man agreed, and Abokor chose *Anna Karenina* as the thickest of the lot. He then proceeded to tap out the entire book to Barud.

As reporter Warner notes, "*Anna Karenina* is about 800 pages, 350,000 words, nearly 2 million letters, each letter a set of taps." To protect his hand, Abokor wrapped a bedsheet around it. "Listening" to the novel proved to be a turning point in Barud's fragile condition.

Anna Karenina gave Barud a framework for processing his experience. For instance, he hated Anna's lover Vronsky at once, largely because he associated the military officer with his own military prison. At the same time, he identified intensively with Anna, especially when, after leaving her husband for Vronsky, she finds herself abandoned in an apartment and shunned by society. Like Barud, Anna both longs for her partner and wants him to suffer as she is suffering. She is crazily jealous yet hates herself for being jealous. Barud later said he identified with the sentence, "If he loved her, he would understand all the difficulties of her situation, and he would rescue her from it."

The novel offered yet more insights and more comforts. When Anna throws herself under the train, Barud saw his worst fears realized and found himself crying. He realized, however, that his tears were not for himself but for his wife Ismahan. He began asking himself whether he had been a good husband. Had he treated his wife as she deserved?

Why had he done something that had separated them? Wasn't she imprisoned by their situation as well? Perhaps she was suffering worse than he was. From hating his wife, he came to see the world through her eyes. Empathy replaced resentment.

The novel had at least one more role to play. Released six years later when the political climate changed, Barud discovered that Ismahan had remained faithful, despite intense pressure to divorce him. Reunited in a refugee camp in Germany, she wanted to rush into his arms. He, however, had forgotten how to love her and so maintained a distance.

Fortunately, the novel's other major storyline stepped in. Newly married to Kitty, landowner Levin is wracked with self-doubts about setting up a new life. Although Kitty is a wonderful woman who will prove a great wife, Levin is a restless soul. Only at the end of the novel does he learn to let her in.

Barud said that Tolstoy taught him how to love his wife again. He realized that, like Levin, he was hard to live with—solitary confinement does that to people—and having Levin as a model "made it easier for us to talk to each other. I knew that my heart wasn't quite working yet." In appreciation for its meaning-making and healing power, Barud declares in the podcast that he "should build a monument for that book."

In short, literature proved as essential to Barud's survival as food, shelter, and clothing.

If you haven't read *Anna Karenina,* perhaps you know *Little Women,* which saved 11-year-old Shamyla in a related way. As reported by Ira Glass's radio program *This American Life* in an episode entitled "Words Matter," the American-raised girl was essentially kidnapped by her birth parents when she returned to Pakistan for a visit.[2] While Shamyla's aunt had raised her in suburban Maryland, she could do nothing to bring her back as her guardianship had not been legally formalized.

Suddenly Shamyla's world was turned upside down. Her ultra-traditional Pakistani family confiscated her books and cassettes, kept her under virtual house arrest, and lectured her regularly about what her wifely duties would entail, including her sexual duties. Her hair had to be covered, she couldn't make eye contact with others, she was not allowed to speak English or Urdu, she had to eat after her brothers (one of whom sexually abused her), she was kept on small portions (so that she would stay slim), and she was occasionally beaten. She reports that, at different times, a squeegee, a cane, a golf club, and cleats were used.

At one point her father even determined that women shouldn't write, and he burned her journals in front of her. He also confiscated any books she smuggled into the house.

Through a friend, however, she managed to obtain a copy of *Little Women*, which she remembered reading while still in America. To hide it, she broke it into eight sections so that it wouldn't show under the mattress. Whenever the family left the house, she would grab whichever section of the book came to hand and read it. "It was the book of my life, the only book I had to escape," she says. She memorized parts of it.

She had multiple responses to Alcott's novel. Sometimes she fantasized about a Meg-Jo relationship, a friend she could confide in. When her Pakistani parents, hoping for an advantageous marriage, dressed her up and showed her off to other families, she thought of the "Meg Goes to Vanity Fair" chapter, where Meg too dresses up and parades before potential suitors and society guests. As the interviewer notes, *Little Women* functioned for Shamyla as both a "how-to" book and a survival guide.

Not surprisingly, Shamyla identified with the ambitious, rule-breaking Jo, which helped her hold on to the identity her family was trying to squash. She even had her own version of Jo writing stories in the attic, although her situation was more severe. When she was forbidden to write, she would go into the bathroom and write secretly before carefully washing the ink off the paper.

Because of her affinity with Jo, she was not fond of the book's second half, where the March sisters "let go of their wild ways to become good wives." She remembers thinking, "When Meg gets married, she loses her freedom. I said I don't want that to be my story–because that's what's expected of me." At a certain point, however, she began to surrender to her new identity. Her capitulation led her to fatalistically identify with the inevitability of Beth's death, especially Beth's image of the retreating tide. Even as she expresses her intense desire to live, Beth laments that "every day I lose a little, and feel more sure that I shall never gain it back." And then, "It's like the tide, Jo, when it turns, it goes slowly, but it can't be stopped."

Ultimately Shamlya convinced her parents that she had changed enough that it was safe to send her back to America, where they hoped she would learn certain skills, like swimming and driving, that would increase her bride price. As she left Pakistan, she knew she would never return. Although she suffered from severe culture shock and required much therapy to recover from her captivity, she is now, 30 years later, a therapist who specializes in trauma cases. Every year on her birthday she reads a chapter from *Little Women*.

Literature's Power

While Shamlya's and Barud's stories are extraordinary, they surprise only if we assume that literature is a mere diversion or pleasant interlude rather than a life-changing force. Maybe easy access causes us to take books for granted. I suspect, however, that if you were to look back over your own reading history, you could recall stories and poems that immersed you so deeply in their imagined universes that, at least for a short time, the world no longer seemed the same. Perhaps fond feelings of nostalgia wash over you as you recall them, or perhaps they have left behind disturbing images that haunt your nightmares. In either case, literature has left traces that can last a lifetime.

Over the centuries, poets, artists, philosophers, psychologists, cultural theorists, and others have sought to understand how literature influences audiences. This book surveys the most important of these thinkers, sharing their insights into how and why literature changes lives.

In the process, they have arrived at a wide variety of answers. In the upcoming pages, we will see them arguing that literature trains citizens, stiffens warrior spines, promotes virtue, civilizes nations, heals mental illness, galvanizes oppressed peoples, changes world horizons, etc. Among these thinkers we will meet principled conservatives who believe that literature staves off anarchy, conscientious liberals who contend it bolsters multicultural democracy, and enlightened activists who regard it as a force for social justice.

To be sure, we will also encounter thinkers (Plato for one) that believe literature encourages licentious behavior, poisons young minds, and undermines legitimate authority. Although they may differ about literature's effects, however, literature's friends and foes alike agree that it exerts a power that must be reckoned with.

So what has happened, we may ask, that allows people today to shrug off an activity that giants like Plato, Aristotle, Samuel Johnson, Karl Marx, and Sigmund Freud have regarded as momentous? A glance at literary history provides some answers and, in the process, provides ways for countering literature's skeptics. By highlighting the potential impact of good books, perhaps we can restore them to the prominence they have enjoyed for millennia.

Literature Marginalized

This prominence can be seen in the role that, throughout history, literature has played in civic life. Dramatic poetry was at the center of the Dionysian festivals in ancient Athens, and mystery plays featuring Biblical stories entertained and inspired medieval Europeans.

To be sure, the 16th century English courtier and poet Sir Philip Sidney sensed what was to come when he found himself entangled in a debate with an arts-skeptical Puritan, Stephen Gosson, who alternately attacked poetry as "unprofitable" and as dangerous.[3] In 1580 Sidney worried that "poor poetry," which once enjoyed "the highest estimation of learning," is "fallen to be the laughing-stock of children."[4]

For a time Sidney's worries proved premature as, in the following decade, large audiences flocked to see the plays of Christopher Marlowe and William Shakespeare. We can probably trace contemporary suspicions of literature to figures like Gosson, however, as the Puritans would grow in influence throughout the subsequent century. Suspicious of the arts in general and of drama and fiction in particular, they closed the English playhouses in the 1640s when they came to power.

Although Charles II, upon the return of the monarchy in 1660, reopened the theaters, the suspicion that literature was immoral remained. So did Gosson's charge that it was "unprofitable." As the pragmatic middle class challenged the more culturally engaged landed class, poetry found itself again under attack. In 1802, Romantic poet William Wordsworth worried that poetry was becoming "a thing as indifferent" as a taste for rope dancing or sherry. [5]

In 1820, poet Thomas Peacock appeared to confirm Wordworth's anxieties when, half-jokingly, he wondered whether "the progress of useful art and science" had made poetry obsolete. Calling verse-making "frivolous and unconducive," Peacock speculated that "intellectual power and intellectual acquisition have turned themselves into other and better channels, and have abandoned the cultivation and the fate of poetry to the degenerate fry of modern rhymesters." [6]

Peacock's comments triggered poet Percy Shelley's passionate *Defence of Poetry* (1821), but many since have shared Peacock's views. To be sure, Utilitarian philosopher John Stuart Mill tried to join poetry and utility in common cause. Poet and social critic Matthew Arnold, meanwhile, attempted to convince the middle class to add art's sweetness and light to their industrious, money-making lives. Nevertheless, literature's defenders too often appeared to be fighting an uphill battle.

The attitude seemed to be that literature, while nice, is not central. Looking back, contemporary theorist Terry Eagleton notes that English literature became an academic discipline in part because 19th century women's universities needed "harmless" subjects for their students.[7] Maybe literature makes one more genteel, people conceded, but it's not foundational to existence.

Rather than seeking compromises with their increasingly capitalistic society, some artists went to the other extreme, brandishing poetry's impracticality as a badge of honor. "All art is quite useless," Oscar Wilde provocatively proclaimed toward the end of the 19th century, speaking the language of the Art for Art's Sake movement.[8]

His defiant stance continued into the 20th century. W. H. Auden, for instance, declared that "poetry makes nothing happen" in his poem "In Memory of W. B. Yeats" (1939).[9] After all, he observed, Yeats's own poems about "mad Ireland" didn't end colonial rule or make Ireland any the less mad. Novelist Somerset Maugham, meanwhile, warned in 1946 against artists who try to get us to "swallow the powder of profitable information made palatable by the jam of fiction." Rather than turn to novels for information, he contended that "it is better not to know a thing at all" than to know it through the "distorted" lens of fiction.[10]

Twentieth century modernist American poet William Carlos Williams tried to reassert literature's relevance in his poem "Asphodel, That Greeny Flower" (1955). Although admitting that "it is difficult/to get the news from poems"—in other words literature doesn't impact our lives as newspapers do—he goes on to say, "yet men die miserably every day / for lack / of what is found there."[11] Authors like Williams engaged in a complicated dance with their practical society: while they didn't want practicality to define their enterprise, they also didn't want to see themselves as peripheral.

Yet by cordoning off life from literature, they ceded too much ground. By seeing poetry as only existential or spiritual, not pragmatic, they underestimated the many down-to-earth ways people use poems and stories to enhance their lives.

Some literary scholars, meanwhile, went even further than these authors in separating literature from everyday life. In 1949 during literary criticism's high formalist period (known as New Criticism), W.K. Wimsatt and Monroe Beardsley wanted to sideline the question of literature's impact upon readers altogether. To judge a work based on its emotional affect, they contended, was to commit "the affective fallacy."[12]

These New Critics influenced successive generations of literature professors and teachers. If (as they saw it) describing literary forms and interpreting symbols are the essence of literature, then don't bother to ask what poems and stories have to do with everyday affairs. New Criticism influenced literary scholarship for decades, and many high school teachers still demand that their students regard literary works as mainly aesthetic objects.

One can see why this would be a tempting option. It's easier to check whether students can distinguish between a metaphor and a simile than discuss with them, say, how young teens like Romeo and Juliet feel empowered when they discover sex. For their part, scholars often prefer problems they can pin down and measure rather than mucking around in the wide range of reactions to a work. How can one generalize when everyone seems to take away something different from a reading experience?

To be sure, the important thinkers featured in this book have generalized freely about literature's impact upon readers, but that didn't carry any weight with the post-World War II formalist scholars. Sure, they respected Plato's *Republic*, Aristotle's *Poetics*, and Horace's *Art of Poetry*, but at the same time they ignored what those figures said about literature's practical and societal applications. For instance, while they talked about Aristotle's definition of tragedy, they didn't mention how he saw tragedy helping train Athenians for citizenship duty. And although they looked at the poetic rules that Horace puts forth for creating a work, they paid no attention to how Horace saw heroic verse "animat[ing] the manly mind to martial achievements."[13]

While the academic debates of literary scholars may seem far removed from the general reader, they have had broad ramifications. When universities treated literature as a specialized discourse that is cut off from life, that perspective was passed along to those who teach literature to our children at all levels. Up to the early part of the

20th century, poems appeared daily in newspapers, but those poems eventually got laughed out of circulation by experts. Too often, even now, poems and stories are taught as something to be picked apart in boring analytical exercises, not as something people can use to make their lives better.

As a result, students too frequently come to experience literature as a set of grade hoops to jump through, not an essential resource.

An Alternate Way of Seeing Literature

Before writing literature's obituary, however, let's acknowledge that literature still packs a punch, and not only amongst Somali prisoners and kidnapped Pakistani girls. People regularly plumb literature's rich storehouse of narratives, characters, images, metaphors, and memorable phrases to help them name and negotiate everything that life throws at them.

For instance, we find literary allusions everywhere in the public arena, even if the sources aren't always identified. People talk of politicians selling their souls (the Faustus story), of political actors and policy makers creating an uncontrollable monster (*Frankenstein*), of reality-challenged individuals going down a rabbit hole (*Alice in Wonderland*), of Big Brother watching us (*1984*), or of authorities devising lose-lose situations for everyday men and women (*Catch-22*).

In recent years, I've seen certain passages applied to contemporary politics multiple times, especially the powerful lines, "Things fall apart, the center cannot hold" and "The best lack all conviction, while the worst are filled with passionate intensity" from Yeats's poem "The Second Coming."[14] F. Scott's Fitzgerald's novel *The Great Gatsby* makes frequent appearances in political discourse as well, especially the passage, "They were careless people, Tom and Daisy—they smashed up things and ... then retreated back into their money ... and let other people clean up the mess they had made."[15]

Often literature will languish forgotten on life's sidelines until we need it, at which point it steps forward and plays a starring role. For weddings, countless people have chosen Shakespeare's "Sonnet 116," which opens, "Let me not to the marriage of true minds / Admit impediments; love is not love / which alters when it alteration finds." Others cite Dylan Thomas's poem "Do not go gentle into that good night" when struggling with severe illness or death and Christina Rossetti's "Why cry for a soul set free?" when mourning a loved one. In the last two decades, the poetry of Black women has shown up powerfully in the public square at presidential inaugurations. Maya Angelou read "On the Pulse of the Morning" at Bill Clinton's swearing in, Elizabeth Alexander read "Praise Song for the Day" at Barack Obama's, and Amanda Gorman read "The Hill We Climb" at Joe Biden's.

In some ways literature resembles religion, proving its mettle in crunch time. Just as even the non-religious will flood into churches after a traumatic event, the non-poetic will turn to literature when life gets rough. During the London blitzkrieg, to cite one example, city bookshops sold out their poetry and their Jane Austen as well.[16] Artists have provided us with words and images for even the bleakest of occasions.

Censorship as an Acknowledgment of Literature's Power

Although indifference is perhaps literature's major enemy, another threat comes from those who would censor it. Paradoxically, however, these groups accord literature the kind of respect that the culture as a whole does not. Echoing Plato, who thought that Homer and Hesiod should be kept out of the hands of young people, those that would ban books are sometimes more attuned to how books can unsettle assumptions and alter perspectives than some of literature's defenders. It's therefore important to examine closely which books are under attack and why.

The novels of Toni Morrison, especially *The Bluest Eye, The Song of Solomon,* and *Beloved,* have appeared on many of the lists of rightwing censors. The closing Republican ad in a 2021 Virginia gubernatorial race, for instance, featured a mother complaining how her high school senior had been traumatized by Toni Morrison's *Beloved*—and that therefore voters should choose anti-woke candidate Glenn Youngkin, who went on to win the election and to set up a hotline to report teachers teaching supposedly nefarious content.[17]

Rather than casually dismissing Morrison's critics as cultural philistines (to apply an epithet that we will see used by Victorian critic Matthew Arnold), it's worth pointing out that they have reason to fear her novel, which touches on two of the most volatile issues in American politics, race and a woman's autonomy over her body. In the work, which earned Morrison the Nobel Prize, the pregnant slave Sethe is first sexually assaulted (White men suck milk from her breasts), then beaten savagely, and then, after she escapes and they come to reclaim her and her children, driven to kill the baby to save it from slavery. The novel is *meant* to be unsettling, and it can indeed challenge the worldview of those parents who don't want their children facing up to the ugly history of racism and sexism. For Morrison as for William Faulkner, one of the authors on which she models herself, the past is not dead nor even past, and we see it return in the form of the ghost baby that haunts Sethe.

Censorship is not limited to the right although it generally takes less virulent forms on the American left. For instance, there are liberal parents who fear that traditional princess fairy tales will sap their daughters' initiative. On race matters, meanwhile, *The Adventures of Huckleberry Finn* and *To Kill a Mockingbird* have sometimes been attacked for reenforcing racial stereotypes and, in the case of Atticus Finch, elevating the figure of the White savior. And then there are those liberals who want trigger warnings applied to works that they fear might unduly upset students with troubled histories.

In an ironic twist, some of the language used by college administrators in these trigger initiatives have been appropriated by rightwing supporters of book bans. Texas legislator Mike Krause, for instance, drew up a list of 850 books that he feared "might make students feel discomfort, guilt, anguish, or any other form of psychological distress because of their race or sex." The book ban included John Irving's *Cider House Rules*, William Styron's *Confessions of Nat Turner*, a graphic novel version of Margaret Atwood's *Handmaid's Tale*, and Tim Federle's young adult novel *The Great American Whatever*.[18] Krause's "psychological discomfort" language has since been recommended and occasionally adopted by other states, including Florida, Iowa, and Oklahoma.

Without weighing in on the political merits of any of these attacks, it's worth noting that they all assume that literature can have a significant influence on readers' lives. Some adults, either because they genuinely fear such viewpoints or because they wish to avoid controversy, confine children to anodyne stories and poems rather than have them read works that touch on pressing issues of the day.

It's not only contemporary works that raise controversial concerns, however. Although Shakespeare generally flies under the radar of conservative parents (with the exception of a Florida school district),[19] that's in part because many teachers fail to unleash his full potential to challenge various assumptions. If they did, the Bard might well join Morrison on banned book lists.

Imagine *Twelfth Night: or What You Will* (1601–02) being taught in such a way as to foreground its strong gender identity themes, which fascinate young people struggling to make sense of who they are. In the comedy, we encounter a man who discovers he has an inner woman, a woman who discovers she has an inner man, two men who are attracted to other men, and a woman who is attracted to another woman. Count Orsino gets to marry someone he once thought was a man; Lady Olivia makes overtures to another woman (although technically she thinks he's a man); Viola, under the flimsiest of pretexts, passes herself off as a man; and Orsino for a time mimics behavior that he regards as feminine. Understanding humans as well as anyone ever has, Shakespeare knew that we are more complex than the gender labels foisted upon us by tradition, and he found an artistic vehicle to explore our complexity. If teachers did more to advertise the play as a chance to explore gender identity, inviting students to explore their feelings about each of these characters, they could well generate new excitement amongst students, including some who would otherwise groan over a Shakespeare reading assignment.

Consider also a Shakespeare play that is often taught to high school juniors and seniors. While *Othello* may appear safe, it contains social dynamite, dealing directly with issues of race and interracial marriage that will challenge rightwing parents and perhaps some liberal parents as well. English teachers could generate powerful conversations if they taught Shakespeare's tragedy more intentionally as a case study in both White resentment (Iago) and Black insecurity (Othello). In expressing his hatred for Othello, Iago traffics in racist stereotypes of Black men as beasts threatening "the purity of White womanhood" ("an old black ram is tupping your white ewe," he informs Desdemona's father). At the same time, we see in Othello a status-conscious Black man who, while meritorious, desperately desires acceptance by his White peers, which helps explain why Iago can manipulate him so easily. Othello is both proud of having married a White wife (it's a sign that he's arrived) and insecure in the relationship (surely she must prefer a White man). These types of ambiguities are typical of real-life struggles, and the play's failure to find a satisfactory solution to them renders the story tragic. Black and White teens, who are coming of age in a society where these issues continue to swirl around us, will appreciate how the play provides compelling characters and a narrative that foregrounds their anxieties. Literature discussions could become life discussions.

One can understand why teachers might shy away from teaching Shakespeare this way. Who needs to add angry parents and (in Florida) the threat of lawsuits to an already long and overwhelming list of responsibilities? Why detonate a literary bomb in the classroom? It's a version of the choice African American poet Langston Hughes once described when his poetry became more political. "I have never known the police of any country to show an interest in lyric poetry as such," Hughes writes in "My Adventures as a Social Poet." "But when poems stop talking about the moon and begin to mention poverty, trade unions, color lines, and colonies, somebody tells the police."[20]

Unfortunately, when English teachers play it safe, they risk under-playing literature's fierce urgency and its ability to speak directly to our life struggles. Taming literature down to a boring irrelevancy leaves its potential untapped. Students go unchallenged in ways that could lead to real and exhilarating growth.

This is why it's useful to acquaint ourselves with stories of literature stepping up to the plate during tough times, often in the most unexpected of ways. Who could have predicted a Somali political prisoner falling in love with *Anna Karenina* or a kidnapped Pakistani girl turning to *Little Women*? Who could foresee Iranian women, banished from universities by fundamentalist mullahs, recognizing themselves in the character of Vladimir Nabokov's Dolores Haze? (In *Reading Lolita in Tehran*, Azar Nafisi reports that her students related to how "Lolita" is trapped in an older man's fantasies.)[21]

And then there are the South African freedom fighters who, when imprisoned by the apartheid regime, found purchase in the words of various Shakespeare characters. Nelson Mandela responded to Julius Caesar's "Cowards die many times before their deaths; / The valiant never taste of death but once"; his confidant Walter Sisulu saw himself in Shylock: "Still have I borne it with a patient shrug / For sufferance is the badge of all our tribe"; and future Parliament member Billy Nair saw a kindred soul in Caliban: "This island's mine, by Sycorax my mother / Which thou tak'st from me."[22] Why limit literature instruction to rhyme and meter when you could be preparing your students for life?

When I come across stories of people attacking and sometimes banning works of literature, I think of a scene from the Lawrence Kasdan film *Grand Canyon* (1991). Danny Glover, in the role of auto mechanic, is confronted by a gun-wielding gang leader while attempting to help stranded motorist Kevin Kline. Asked by the man whether he respects him or not, Glover replies, "You ain't got the gun, we ain't having this conversation."[23] These contentious conversations about literature are happening because literature wields the power of a loaded gun.

My Personal Search to Understand Literary Power

Since I part company with much of the scholarly community in emphasizing literature's practical import, I owe readers an explanation of how I have arrived at my views. Doing so also allows me to share how literature has changed my own life and how the thinkers I profile in this book have helped me develop my approach and methods.

I experienced literature's tremendous power at an early age. Born in 1951, I came from a reading family, with a father who taught French at the University of the South in Sewanee, Tennessee (he was also a published poet) and a mother who ran the town's weekly newsletter. We were one of the only families in town without a television—TV is unnecessary when one has books, my parents reasoned—and every evening my father would read novels and poems to me and my brothers, a chapter and a poem for each of us. We were also voracious readers on our own, of course, making no distinction between the good and the bad stuff. On the one hand, there were *Alice in Wonderland*, the Narnia series, *Wind in the Willows*, *The Secret Garden*, and *The Lord of the Rings*. On the other, the dreadfully written Hardy Boy and Bobbsey Twin series. Books, to quote W. B. Yeats, "had all my thought and love."[24]

Not until I was eleven, however, did I consciously realize that literature could help me handle real world pressures. At that age, *Huckleberry Finn* and *To Kill a Mockingbird* helped me negotiate the blowback we received from our involvement in a landmark civil rights case. The year was 1962 and my brothers and I were amongst the plaintiffs in a suit, brought by four Black families and four White and paid for by the NAACP, against the Franklin County Board of Education. At issue was our right to attend integrated schools in Tennessee, as mandated by the Supreme Court's 1954 Brown v. Board of Education ruling.

I got called "n*** lover" by some of my sixth grade classmates, but because Atticus discusses the phrase with his daughter Scout in *To*

Kill a Mockingbird (1960), I could see the epithet for what it is.[25] In *Huckleberry Finn*, meanwhile, I was touched to the core by the famous scene where Huck decides he will "go to hell" rather than betray his Black friend Jim.[26] I was inspired to stand up for what I believed was right, even as classmates and much of Tennessee thought otherwise.

While some activists critique the book for its use of the n-word and its portrayal of Jim (although not, incidentally, Toni Morrison, who is a strong defender),[27] it spoke to the possibilities of interracial friendship that I needed at the time. Therefore, when Ronnie Staten became the first Black student in our seventh-grade class, I made a point of reaching out to him.

Seeing literature as both a delight and a source of power, I went off to Carleton College in 1969, where I expected my literature courses to have some connection to the momentous events that were impacting us at the time. These included the 1968 shootings of Martin Luther King and Robert Kennedy, the urban race riots, the escalating Vietnam War, and the burgeoning anti-war movement. I was startled when my English classes barely acknowledged these occurrences. My composition instructor was even contemptuous of the anti-war marches and only begrudgingly allowed us to miss class to attend the October protest moratorium.

I was later to learn about formalism, which as I've noted downplayed or ignored historical context, the life of the author, and the responses of the reader. While my professors assumed that literature was good for us, they were vague as to how. Frustrated, I sought another major and settled on history, which at least had stories, characters, and politically active professors.

The decision to study history paid off in a medieval history class when I learned that literature did indeed have things to say about momentous events in real society. The work was *Beowulf* and I learned that, to its original readers, the monsters were real. That's because they symbolized medieval England's deepest anxieties. In warrior eyes, the Grendel trolls embodied murderous resentment, which could lead to catastrophic blood feuds, while the dragon shared traits with greedy and sullen kings. When warriors were loyal and kings were generous—the hero Beowulf is both—all went well. When they were not, the fragile societies disintegrated.

This revelation of literature's close connection with history was so powerful that I remember exactly where I was when I grasped it: in one of Carleton's all-night study rooms, where I used a blackboard to diagram an essay I would entitle, "The Social Role of Monsters in Barbarian Society." I've been pondering ideas on this topic ever since, and today I even write a daily blog on literature and culture entitled "Better Living Through Beowulf: How Great Literature Can Change Your Life."[28]

At that time, I did not yet have a full-fledged theory about literature's relationship with events in our lives, but I was so hungry to know more that I enrolled in Emory University's English PhD program. There I was fortunate to encounter two mentors who put me in touch with the ideas I needed. In his book *Before Novels: The Cultural Contexts of 18th Century Fiction,* my dissertation director J. Paul Hunter talked of the many ways that the genre of the novel spoke to the real-life needs and concerns of young people of the time.[29] For his part, Victorianist Jerome Beaty introduced me to the emerging field of Reception Theory, which emphasizes literature's impact upon its readers. Especially influential to my thought was University of Konstanz scholar Hans Robert Jauss, whom we will encounter later and who contends that great literature can shift an audience's "horizon of expectations."[30]

I wasn't the only young scholar at the time interested in literature's connection with pressing historical issues. Marxists, feminists, post-colonialists, queer theorists, African American, Latino, and Native American activists, and others were beginning to rethink revered works of literature. At the same time, they were discovering previously neglected works by oppressed or neglected populations. They saw literature playing a role in the struggle for equality and civil rights, either negatively (by perpetuating stereotypes) or positively (by opening up new human possibilities).

In my subsequent 37-year career as a full-time English professor at Maryland's public liberal arts college (St. Mary's College of Maryland), I continued to refine my theories about how literature impacts our lives. I generally took a moderate position so that, when the "culture wars" broke out over literary classics in the late 1980s and early 1990s, I refused to throw in my lot with either side. While I pushed back against those figures on the right who denigrated works by women and people of color, I also believed that the "canon" still had an important role to play in our lives and defended it against those leftwing purists who wished to jettison wholesale any authors that employed racist, sexist, classist, homophobic, or other demeaning tropes.

My middle positioning arose from my love of all literature. For me it was never (to quote a conservative slogan from the era) "Jane Austen, not Alice Walker" but always "Jane Austen AND Alice Walker." I found value in even "politically incorrect" works—say, in the hard-boiled detective novels of Dashiell Hammett, which contain misogynist, racist and homophobic elements—and was never willing to reduce literature to a subset of ideology or politics. Nevertheless, I learned a lot about literature's influence, including its dangerous side, as I struggled with the critiques.

How Students Expanded My View of Literature's Possibilities

While engaged in various theoretical debates, I was also discovering that my teaching needed to change. The generation following mine, I quickly learned, did not have the same grand vision of transforming the world. For many good reasons, which included the end of America's booming post-war economy and the end of the Vietnam War, my students were more practical and less idealistic. I came to realize that, if I was to convince them that literature can be a transformative force, I needed to listen to their concerns and adapt accordingly.

I therefore began reading psychological theory and even scientific studies about how literature affects readers, and I asked my students to connect the assigned class readings with their personal experiences. Their responses revolutionized the way I saw literature at work.

Take, for instance, Matt, an ex-Marine who rethought his war experiences after reading the medieval romance *Sir Gawain and the Green Knight*. Matt had become an enthusiastic English major after having served two deployments in Afghanistan, where he defused roadside bombs. In a classroom discussion about death, he remarked that he had learned to not care about dying when he was in the service.

While acknowledging that I was in no position to contradict him, I mentioned Gawain thinking he can shrug off his death fears, only to discover by the end of the poem that he can't. "In destinies sad or merry, / True men can but try," Gawain initially says, thinking himself calm as he prepares to keep a rendezvous with certain death.[31] By the end of the poem, however, the Green Knight reveals he has set up his challenges to teach Gawain a lesson: he wants the Camelot knight to acknowledge that he cares for his life after all.

As we weren't reading the poem for the class—I had mentioned it in passing—Matt went to the campus bookstore, bought a copy, blew off the *Jane Eyre* reading assignment, and spent half the night reading the fourteenth-century romance. The next day he told me how true the poem was. Even as he and his comrades had joked about death, he said, they were also careful to don their Kevlar vests whenever they went out on a mission. This he compared to Gawain secretly and somewhat dishonorably accepting a life-saving green girdle from the lady of a castle, where he is temporarily residing before journeying to meet the Green Knight. Gawain is ashamed that he wears it, especially after the Green Knight reveals that he knows of its existence. The poem helped Matt re-process his war experience in ways none of us could have predicted.

While most student "reading stories" (as I call them) are not as remarkable as Matt's, I have encountered hundreds of similarly insightful reflections over the years. For instance, I recall an essay on Samuel Taylor Coleridge's *Rime of the Ancient Mariner* from a lacrosse player, who identified with the wedding guest in the poem. The ancient mariner in the poem recognizes a youthful version of himself in the young man and tells him how he once gratuitously shot an albatross that his shipmates had befriended. He has been haunted by the action ever since. My student saw his lacrosse teammates doing their own versions of killing the large seabird—in their case, through meaningless acts of drunken college vandalism—and regarded the mariner's story as a wake-up call to start taking life seriously.

I remember another essay from Amanda, an Alabama student who had come to our Maryland school to escape the confines of her fundamentalist family and who found, in Christopher Marlowe's *Doctor Faustus,* her own struggle to reconcile Christian belief and secular humanism. Faustus has sold his soul to the devil in exchange for worldly knowledge and power but never feels at ease with his decision. Amanda reported feeling torn as Faustus feels torn and wrote that the play helped her find her own balance between faith and reason. Faustus's ambitions have some legitimacy, she wrote, but must be tempered with Christian humility. By engaging with the play, she articulated a more authentic and mature relationship to her faith.

I have learned that virtually every student essay proposal I receive, no matter how disjointed, has somewhere within it a precious insight. In Part III, I discuss my teaching practice and show how readers of this book can discover why this or that work had the impact it did—and by impact, I include the negative as well as the positive experiences. In some ways, my job resembles a dating service: I try to link each student up with the work I believe will lead to the most growth for him or her, given life circumstances, identity, and other relevant factors. To this end, I'm careful to provide a variety of works. Focus on the one, I tell each student, that most captures your imagination.

My teacher-student interactions proved invaluable when I underwent my own tragedy, my eldest son dying in a freak drowning. "I have always said that literature is there for when we need it," I said in desperation to the books of my life, "and I need you now." In Part III I tell the story of how *Beowulf* answered the call, providing me with images and a narrative that helped me to cope with the heartbreak

23

and, when the time came, to reconstruct my life and move ahead. I've also written at length (in my book *How* Beowulf *Can Save America*) about how the ancient saga of *Beowulf* can function as an extended guidebook or healing narrative for understanding our current social and political woes, along with providing possible solutions.[32]

Literature Teachers as Life Coaches

From the thousands of hours I have spent helping students understand their responses to literature, I have concluded that teachers should be regarded as life coaches. To them falls the responsibility of introducing this potentially life-changing material to impressionable minds that will grow from the contact.

Nor are classroom teachers the only ones who can be seen in this light. In the chapter on Utilitarianism, I mention the World War I librarians who used novels to comfort wounded servicemen. And then there's the Shared Reading organization in northern England, which has taken literature into community centers, hospitals, elder care facilities, prisons, and other spaces. Theater directors too have discovered that "Shakespeare in Prison" programs bring down recidivism rates. One can also turn to some fine books about how specific works have shaped individual lives, such as Alain de Botton's *How Proust Can Change Your Life* (1997), Rebecca Mead's *My Life in Middlemarch* (2014), and Adam Nicolson's *Why Homer Matters* (2014).

Granted, literature doesn't operate the way normal instruction manuals do. For one thing, literary works don't correspond in any one-to-one way with fixing our problems. In fact, one can't always tell ahead of time which work or which aspect of a work will hit paydirt. One person's life-changing work will leave someone else cold. A reading coach must be alert to any blips of engagement that show up on the student's radar screen.

For an enhanced reading experience, readers must take the work that generates an uptick in brain activity and immerse themselves in it. The deepest insights come when readers surrender themselves to the poem or story, losing themselves in its fiction and its language. While immersion sometimes comes naturally, that's not always the case, and the coach's greatest challenge can be finding ways to engage the reader. If you successfully hook the reader up to the power source and show him or her how to flip the switch, wisdom will flow.

The Power of Literary Immersion

Operating through images and stories, literature has the potential to invest us emotionally, intellectually, and spiritually in the situation put before us. For a famous literary example of the process at work, check out the scene in *Hamlet* where the prince encounters a troupe of actors. Hamlet marvels at how one of them can see himself in a literary character—and not only see himself but become emotionally involved. The character in this case is Hecuba, the queen of Troy, who sees the Greeks kill first her son Hector and then her husband Priam. Hamlet shakes his head in wonder at how the actor *becomes* Hecuba, asking, "What's Hecuba to him, or he to Hecuba, that he should weep for her?"[33]

It's not only actors who become immersed. Hamlet intends to use the play, to which he has added a scene, as a "mousetrap" that will "catch the conscience of a king." If Claudius can see, enacted on the stage, someone murdering a king, he will not be able to hide from Hamlet whether he has done the same to Hamlet, Sr.

And so it works out. Claudius, already fully immersed in the play, goes on to have the most intense theatrical experience of his life. Seeing himself in a staged fiction that knows him as well as he knows himself, he freaks out and rushes from the room. The trap has snapped.

Imaginary worlds, oral and written, have been immersing audiences since families sat around campfires in prehistoric times, and people have striven to document the experience ever since. In one of the world's great narratives, the Spanish novelist Cervantes famously shows his protagonist Don Quixote so moved by chivalric romances that he can no longer distinguish between them and reality. As a result, he ends up ludicrously attacking windmills, mistaking them for enemy giants. Quixote, of course, is an extreme example, but many works of literature, bad as well as good, have swallowed up readers. Philosopher Georges Poulet dramatically describes the phenomenon as follows:

> As soon as I replace my direct perception of reality by the words of a book, I deliver myself, bound hand and foot, to the omnipotence of fiction. I say farewell to what is, in order to feign belief in what is not. I surround myself with fictitious beings; I become the prey of language. There is no escaping this takeover. Language surrounds me with its unreality.[34]

The great Russian novelist Tolstoy once noted that we are "infected" with an author's ideas and emotions and opined, "The stronger the infection, the better is the art as art."[35]

As we will see, many thinkers have seen literary infection or literary immersion as a force for good. To give you a quick foretaste of what is to come, Romantic poet Percy Shelley contended that immersion in the works of Sophocles, Dante, and Shakespeare puts one in touch with revolutionary energies,[36] while Victorian poet and critic Matthew Arnold predicted that poetry would one day replace religion as the primary motivating moral force.[37]

Yet we must admit that not everyone has been positive. As Plato saw it, Homer-reciting rhapsodes were like demagogues, exerting a dangerous sway over audiences, which prompted him to ban them from his ideal rational Republic.[38] We've already mentioned the 16th century Puritan Stephen Gosson who, disturbed by the hypnotic power that Elizabethan drama exercised over audiences, complained that poetry infects us "with many pestilent desires, with a siren's sweetness drawing the mind to the serpent's tail of sinful fancies."[39] 18th century German parents, as they watched their children adopt the clothing and mannerisms of Goethe's protagonist young Werther, railed against

Goethe's novel out of fear that their young ones would also follow Werther's road to suicide.[40] And then there have been those modern parents and church leaders so worried about seeing young people disappear into the Harry Potterverse that they have attacked and, in a few instances, publicly burned J.K. Rowling's novels.[41]

Observing the dynamics at work in such encounters, novelist Iris Murdoch notes that "Art is close dangerous play with unconscious forces." If we enjoy art, she says, it is because "it disturbs us in deep often incomprehensible ways; and this is one reason why it is good for us when it is good and bad for us when it is bad."[42] Notice that she doesn't always say that literature is good for us: deep contact with unconscious forces can go multiple ways.

Indeed, because of the power of literary immersion, it's important to add reflection (and, I would add, application) to the coaching process. The best literature invariably encourages such reflection whereas, as we will discuss in the chapter on pop lit, lesser literature sometimes settles for an unreflective emotional high.

To highlight literature's power, I have focused on those genres that most take over our minds, conveying us into their worlds and, at least for a moment, persuading us to accept an alternate reality. In other words, I focus on drama, poetry, and fiction. (I could have added cinema, television, and even videogames but decided to limit myself to genres with a long history.) It so happens that, throughout the centuries, drama, poetry, and fiction are the three genres that have gotten the most attention, with different ages choosing one of the three to stand in for literature as a whole. In ancient Athens, heroic and tragic poetry commanded the most attention, in Elizabethan England drama, in the 19th century lyric and narrative poetry and the novel, in the 20th century again the novel. In each case, thinkers sought to understand some version (to use a modern example) of the literary immersion that Harry Potter fans experienced when, after having stood in bookstore lines at midnight to purchase *Goblet of Fire* or *Deathly Hallows,* they opened the volume and lost themselves in the world of Hogwarts.

The Structure of this Book

A fascinating world opens once we start looking into how literature transforms lives. In this introduction I've given a big picture view of how people have grappled—or not grappled—with the question. In "Hardwired for Story," meanwhile, I look at the importance of story, words, and images in our collective imagination, from the beginning of human time to the present.

Part II of the book examines how different thinkers throughout history have debated, sometimes heatedly, literature's impact upon individuals and society. Since time immemorial, literature has cast its spell upon audiences, and thinkers of each era have speculated on what this means for our lives. *Better Living through Literature* invites you to join that long-running debate because, like it or not, it is still going on.

In this survey, I first look at the authors of antiquity who began the conversations about literature's influence (Plato, Aristotle, and Horace); move on to Sir Philip Sidney and Samuel Johnson's theories of moral influence in the 17th and 18th century; and then turn to 19th century writers who saw the literary imagination as a powerful agent for social change. These include William Wordsworth, Samuel Taylor Coleridge, Percy Shelley, John Stuart Mill, and Matthew Arnold. In this section I also look at how Karl Marx and Friedrich Engels saw literature impacting the social order and Sigmund Freud and Carl Jung the psyche.

In the section on literature as "Voice for the Oppressed," I focus on what prominent activist intellectuals have said about how literature can sometimes aid and sometimes impede liberation. W.E.B. Du Bois, Chinua Achebe, and Langston Hughes show its influence on race, Bertolt Brecht on class, Frantz Fanon on colonialism, the Frankfurt School on capitalism, and feminist critics Rachel Blau DuPlessis, Sandra Gilbert, Susan Gubar, and Tania Modleski on gender.

The section on literature "Training Ground for Citizenship" looks at the role that literature teachers play in student socialization; explores literature's civilizing influence as cultural conservatives see it; and (following literary theorist Wayne Booth and philosopher Martha Nussbaum) discusses how great literature helps readers negotiate the complexities of a complex, multicultural world. I conclude by summarizing some of psychology's most recent findings about literary impact, especially how it fosters human empathy.

Part III contains several chapters that seek to apply the various theories of literary impact to individual works. "Has *Jane Eyre* Made the World a Better Place?" does a deep dive into the effect that Bronte's novel had both upon early readers and upon the 1970s feminist movement. To assess the differing impacts of great lit and pop lit, the chapter also contrasts *Jane Eyre* with Stephenie Meyers's gothic and teen sensation *Twilight* (2005-08).

The chapter "Jane Austen on Pop Lit: Enjoy but Be Wary" begins with a general discussion of the issues surrounding popular literature; touches on three popular but problematic novels that have had an outsized historical impact (Jean Raspail's *Camp of the Saints,* Ayn Rand's *Atlas Shrugged,* and Harriet Beecher Stowe's *Uncle Tom's Cabin*); and finally examines Austen's warnings about the limits of pop lit.

"Literature as Healing Narrative: How Beowulf Helped Me Grieve the Death of My Son" reflects more personally on my own life tragedy and how beloved and powerful literary works helped rescue me during the darkest period of my life. I also touch on the ongoing relevance of *Beowulf* as a way to talk about healing our current social and political woes.

"Assessing Literature's Personal and Historical Impact" invites readers to engage in a process of active reflection, showing how they can systematically assess the impact that intense reading experiences have had on their own lives. This chapter will also be of use to teachers, who can use the suggested assignments to have students explore how literature has influenced both their own lives and important historical events.

In the Conclusion—"Activating Literature's Power"— we return to the big picture questions of how poetry, fiction and drama continue to wield significant power and how the thinkers profiled here can help us harness that power.

HARDWIRED FOR STORY

Fiction has enabled us not merely to imagine things,
but to do so collectively. We can weave common myths
such as the biblical creation story, the Dreamtime myths
of Aboriginal Australians, and the nationalist myths of
modern states. Such myths give Sapiens the unprecedented ability to cooperate flexibly in large numbers.

— **Yuval Noah Harari**, *Sapiens: A Brief History of
Humankind* (2015)[1]

BEFORE TALKING ABOUT WRITTEN literature's influence, I turn to
the role that fiction has played in the evolution of the human species,
referencing the theories of Israeli historian Yuval Noah Harari. In
his ambitious *Sapiens: A Brief History of Humankind,* Harari argues
that narrative may have given homo sapiens an evolutionary advantage over other species. If Harari is right, the first humans essentially
weaponized stories, using them to triumph over the story-less Ne-
anderthals. Political theorists today talk about a candidate or party

"controlling the narrative," but in Harari's view, the ability to compose stories allowed humans to become the planet's dominant species. The idea that poets and novelists are harnessing a primal force lends credence to the anxieties of Plato and his heirs. If stories are at the very foundation of species being, then maybe we shouldn't so readily shrug off concerns about *Tom Jones, Madame Bovary,* and *Catcher in the Rye.* Maybe such works, as their detractors have contended, really *can* radically alter our lives.

In his argument, Harari says that it is not language alone that gave humans an advantage. True, language has certain side benefits, such as allowing humans to construct detailed plans of action (say, to hunt lions) and to gossip, which ensures social cohesion. When language is used for storytelling, however, even more becomes possible. Only Sapiens, he writes, "can talk about entire kinds of entities that they have never seen, touched or smelled."[2]

The ability to invent fictions, Harari elaborates, ushered in "the Cognitive Revolution." Pointing out that legends, myths, gods, and religions appeared for the first time with this revolution, he notes that *Homo Sapiens* moved beyond saying, "Careful! A lion!"—which many animals and human species can say—to "The lion is the guardian spirit of our tribe." This ability to speak about fictions, Harari says, "is the most unique feature of Sapiens language."[3]

Stories enable humans to "cooperate in extremely flexible ways with countless numbers of strangers"[4] and, furthermore, to collectively handle whatever reality throws at them. This is not the way other species evolve. "Since large-scale human cooperation is based on myths," Harari says, "the way people cooperate can be altered by changing the myths—by telling different stories. Under the right circumstances myths can change rapidly."[5]

Harari cites, as an example, the 1789 French Revolution, when "the French population switched almost overnight from believing in the myth of the divine right of kings to believing in the myth of the sovereignty of the people."[6] Because of the Cognitive Revolution, humans can revise their behavior rapidly in accordance with changing needs.

Harari says that narrative has "opened a fast lane of cultural evolution, bypassing the traffic jams of genetic evolution."[7]

We should be cautious about Harari's French Revolution example since revolutionary beliefs did not materialize out of thin air, nor did everyone in France abandon their belief in monarchy after 1789, as France's subsequent history makes clear. Indeed, when we come to Karl Marx and Friedrich Engels, we will see that the relationship between the realm of ideas and the realm of social and economic reality is complex and that one can't willy-nilly change reality by changing the narrative. Nevertheless, Harari has a point when he says that, with the Cognitive Revolution, history "declared its independence from biology"[8] and that, from thenceforth on, "historical narratives replace biological theories as our primary means of explaining the development of *Homo sapiens*."[9]

Literary scholar Jonathan Gottshall, in *The Storytelling Animal: How Stories Make Us Human* (2012), makes a related point. Humans, he notes, can't help but think in terms of narrative so that, even when we are given random sentences or encounter random events, our natural inclination is to weave them into stories. That's how we make sense of the world and how we bond as communities. Like Harari, he notes we have been doing this for thousands of years.

Stories and literature, to be sure, aren't synonymous. We'll be talking a lot about stories that rise to the level of high art and stories that don't, about stories that reveal deeper truths and stories that mislead. For the moment, it's enough to emphasize once again the centrality of story to the human experience.

Still speaking in the guise of anthropologist, Gottschall moves from oral to written storytelling in a chapter entitled "Ink People Change the World." As he sees it, storytelling is a force that can be used for good or for ill, as he makes clear by using fascist dictator Adolph Hitler as his example. He examines how Hitler was shaped by story, how he used story in his rise to power, and how he suppressed countervailing stories.

Starting off with the Fuhrer at 16, Gottschall says that Hitler's megalomania was triggered by Richard Wagner's opera *Rienzi* and that he relied on Wagner ever after. The opera tells a story about a populist hero who rises to power and then is betrayed by his former allies and dies in a glorious last stand. In other words, Wagner's work operatically fed both Hitler's megalomania and his narcissistic self-pity. Gottschall argues that Hitler essentially "ruled through art, and he ruled *for* art."[10] Citing Frederic Spotts's *Hitler and the Power of Aesthetics*, he notes that Hitler's goals were more "broadly artistic" than military or political. According to Spotts, "Hitler's interest in the arts was as intense as his racism; to disregard the one is as profound a distortion as to pass over the other."[11]

This helps explain why Hitler and his propagandist Joseph Goebbels focused so much on books that they claimed were "un-German in spirit." They had to ensure that their own story would prevail. By consigning to the flames such writers as Heinrich Mann, Bertolt Brecht, Ernst Glaser, Erich Kastner, Jack London, Theodore Dreiser, Ernest Hemingway, Heinrich Heine, and Thomas Mann, the Nazis implicitly acknowledged that "ink people are among the most powerful and dangerous people in the world."[12]

Since many of the thinkers in this study emphasize literature's power to do good, Hitler's toxic use of the arts in his rise to power provides a useful caution. We will see distinctions made between classics and pop lit, with many arguing that the first has good effects while the latter has bad. For the most part, however, Gottschall doesn't wade into this area, focused as he is on the raw power of storytelling. He mentions a few works that he believes have been good for humanity, including Harriet Beecher Stowe's *Uncle Tom's Cabin*, Charles Dickens's *Christmas Carol*, George Orwell's *1984*, Arthur Koestler's *Darkness at Noon*, Ralph Ellison's *Invisible Man*, and Harper Lee's *To Kill a Mockingbird*. He does this, however, only to make the point that stories can move readers in profound ways.[13] In his view, the power of stories comes through their ability to circumvent our intellectual guards and move us emotionally (which, as we will see, is Plato's major objection to literature).

Gottschall does express some concern toward the end of his book that junk stories are swamping our culture. Unlike culture critics such as Samuel Johnson, Matthew Arnold, Harold Bloom, and Allan Bloom, he does not directly advocate reading great literature to counteract their effect. Nevertheless, he shows the damage that bad stories can wreak, making a comparison between "our craving for story and our craving for food." Although overeating "served our ancestors well when food shortages were a predictable part of life," he says, we presently face a different reality:

> But now that we modern desk jockeys are awash in cheap grease and corn syrup, overeating is more likely to fatten us up and kill us young. Likewise, it could be that an intense greed for story was healthy for our ancestors but has some harmful consequences in a world where books, MP3 players, TVs, and iPhones make story omnipresent—and where we have, in romance novels and television shows such as *Jersey Shore*, something like the story equivalent of deep-fried Twinkies. I think the literary scholar Brian Boyd is right to wonder if overconsuming in a world awash with junk story could lead to something like a "mental diabetes epidemic."[14]

We will see that Reception Theory proponent Hans Robert Jauss also utilizes a food analogy to differentiate between great literature and "culinary literature," which is to say between literature that challenges our existing horizon of expectations (like healthy food) and literature that simply confirms what we already believe (like junk food). Gottschall appears to have culinary literature in mind when he observes that, as digital technology, our stories will become ever more attractive, even dangerously so. "The real threat," he warns, "isn't that story will fade out of human life in the future; it's that story will take it over completely."[15]

Peter Brooks's recent book *Seduced by Story: The Use and Abuse of Narrative* (2022) makes a similar point, opening with a quotation from *The Game of Thrones*: "There's nothing in the world more powerful than a good story. Nothing can stop it. No enemy can defeat it."[16]

Brooks also points to a short story by Argentinian author Jorge Luis Borges, "Tlön Uqbar, Orbis Tertius," where an "ascetic millionaire" commissions the creation of an imaginary planet, complete with its own 40-volume encyclopedia. This invented planet so captures the public's fancy that, by the end of the story, the narrator is predicting that "the world will be Tlön."[17] "Swamped in story as we seem to be," Brooks writes, "we may lose the distinction between the two, asserting the dominion of our constructed realities over the real thing."[18]

The danger of authoritarians imposing their own stories, a central drama in George Orwell's *1984,* has come to seem particularly pressing in recent years as rightwing billionaires take over news outlets and social media sites. Meanwhile politicians talk of creating "our own reality" (an anonymous George W. Bush official) and resorting to "alternative facts" (senior Donald Trump advisor Kellyanne Conway).

Brooks's solution is to use literature instruction to develop in students "a more critical attitude" toward narrative. Years ago Brooks designed an "Introduction to Literature" class at Yale where students studied fictionality itself. Key works included Borges's short stories and *Don Quixote*. In *Seduced by Story,* Brooks also recommends Charlotte Bronte's *Villette,* Proust's *In Search of Lost Time,* and the novels of Henry James and Honoré de Balzac. For instance, Lucy Snow in Bronte's novel struggles against attempts by others to impose limiting fictions upon her. At the heart of James's works, meanwhile, nefarious characters attempt to manipulate others by means of narrative.

Laudable though Brooks's goal is, using challenging stories such as these to develop critical thinking skills in elite students will take the country only so far.

Another recent work exploring how fiction rewires us, and thereby changes our behavior, is Angus Fletcher's *Wonderworks: The 25 Most Powerful Inventions in the History of Literature* (2021). The Ohio State "Professor of Story Science" takes us on an anthropological-psychological tour of literary history, proposing that we think of literary techniques the way we think of tools that address our physical needs. The needs addressed by literature, however, are not hunger, shelter, travel, communication, etc. but "the problem of being human in a nonhuman world."[19]

Whereas Harari talks about primitive humans weaponizing story to become the predominant species and Gottschall and Brooks point to the dangers of story in the hands of demagogues and dictators, Fletcher shows us how literary inventions have benefited humankind. Following in the tradition of Horace and Sir Philip Sidney, who as we will see contended that different genres have different beneficial effects, Fletcher starts with the earliest known instances of each technique and then provides later examples. Drawing on advances in both the study of narrative and neurobiology, he charts the interaction between audience and text.

As he sees it, from the inventions of such literary elements as omniscient narration, intimate point of view, ironic distancing, foreshadowing, stream of consciousness, literary rule breaking, and others flow invaluable gifts:

> Some of these inventions target what modern psychiatrists have identified as common forms of mental distress: grief, grudges, pessimism, shame, heartbreak, rumination, reactive thoughts, self-doubt, numbness, loneliness. Some impart what modern psychologists have identified as well-being boosters: courage, love, curiosity, belief, energy, imagination. And some indirectly support our mental health and well-being by nurturing practical life skills: freethinking, problem solving,

de-biasing, counterfactual speculating, cognitive flexing, relearning, introspecting.[20]

For instance, Fletcher credits the ancient Greek poets Homer and Sappho for the literary inventions of, respectively, omniscient heroic narrative and first-person love lyrics. Storytellers broke important new ground thousands of years ago when they realized they could speak in a "God Voice." ("Let there be light" in *Genesis* is an example, and one also finds the God Voice being used to instill wonder and fear in the Sumerian epic *Gilgamesh* and the Egyptian *Book of the Dead*.) Homer took this invention, Fletcher contends, and added recognizable human emotions. When he opens *The Iliad* with "Sing, goddess, of the anger of Achilles," for instance, the bard brought the voice down to earth. The perspective is no longer "a divinity aloof" but "an 'Almighty Heart' that echoes our emotional response to the spectacle of war and death."[21]

By blending mortal sentiment and cosmic scope, Fletcher says, Homer found a new way to engender courage in listeners and readers. And indeed, Homer has been used to educate young men, both in 5th century BCE Athens and in 19th century Britain. Fletcher claims that there are also physiological and neurological effects. "When that feeling of vaster humanity is combined with the neurochemicals stimulated by our primary fear response," he writes, "the result is a threefold chest heat: the blood-pumping warmth of adrenaline, the pain-dulling warmth of our native opioids, and the social-bonding warmth of oxytocin. This neurochemical elixir makes us feel energized, impervious to harm, and willing to sacrifice ourselves. It's the heart flame that we hail as courage."[22]

In contrast to Homer's omniscient voice, Sappho pioneered a private first-person voice to invent literary love. Then, in a further development, she combined this private perspective with Homer's omniscient voice to enter the mind of Helen of Troy, thereby transforming *The Iliad* from a warrior epic into a love story. Helen, she concludes in one poem, is the real hero of *The Iliad*:

Some say that horsemen,
or soldiers, or ships,
are the most beautiful things on earth—
but I say it's your love.
Isn't that why
Helen, the most beautiful
of women,
left the best of men
and sailed to Troy?[23]

The literary invention of Sappho's personalized love poetry, Fletcher says, means that we no longer require another person to experience love. We can find it instead in books, say in Jane Austen's story about Darcy and Elizabeth.

Poetry's undoubted power brought it to the attention of the early philosophers. They realized, as Native American novelist Leslie Marmon Silko puts it in her novel *Ceremony*, that stories "aren't just entertainment."[24] Plato, witnessing poetry's emotional power, called for philosopher guardians to regulate it while Aristotle embraced its cathartic effects. Neither doubted, however, that poetry could rock the worlds of those it touched.

PART TWO: Literature's Impact—in Theory

THE DEBATE BEGINS

PLATO

POETRY, A THREAT TO JUSTICE AND VIRTUE

All poetical imitations are ruinous to the understanding
of the hearers...

— **Plato**, *The Republic* (c. 375 BCE)[1]

IT SEEMS STRANGE TO begin a book that generally celebrates literature's good influence with a thinker who warns of its dangers. No survey of what great thinkers have written about literature's impact, however, would be complete without Plato. His criticism of Homer and Hesiod, poets from 300 years earlier, represents philosophy's most famous attack on literature. As Plato saw it, the emotions unleashed by poetry threaten to overwhelm rational thought.

Poetry in Plato's day was at the heart of the raucous Athenian festivals that attracted thousands, with dramatic presentations of *The Iliad* and *The Odyssey* by gifted rhapsodes taking audiences on emotional roller coaster rides. There were also elaborate theatrical competitions, held in conjunction with a major Dionysian feast day, in which some of theater history's greatest playwrights competed for an Athenian version of the Oscars. Authors transformed familiar myths into spell-binding melodrama, composing three tragedies and a comedy. These were performed over several days by actors and choruses that had been practicing for months.

The productions, which featured elaborate set designs and expensive costumes, drew audiences from all over the Greek world. When, in his philosophic masterpiece *The Republic,* Plato announced his ideal society would ban poets, he would have been taking a wildly unpopular stand. It would be like someone today suggesting that we outlaw film and television.

Born to Greek aristocrats, Plato (c. 427–c. 347 BCE) encountered the philosopher Socrates as a young man and was inspired by the old man's search for the true and the good. Although Plato fought briefly in a war between Athens and Sparta and was drawn to politics, he focused solely on philosophy after Socrates was executed for "impiety" and "corrupting the young" in 399. He founded the first philosophical school twelve years later and is now considered the first systematic philosopher.

Plato discusses literature most extensively in his dialogues *The Ion* and *The Republic* although observations also surface in *The Apology, The Phaedrus,* and *The Symposium.* In his dramatic dialogues, which came to be called "the Socratic method," he imagines an idealized version of his mentor Socrates questioning various people in an attempt to uncover truth. In other words, Plato uses the figure of "Socrates" as a literary device to express his own thinking, and I use the two figures interchangeably here.

To understand literature's power over us, in one dialogue Plato has Socrates question Ion, a prize-winning rhapsode specializing in Homer. It's worth noting that Plato knows his Homer well and has Socrates quote numerous passages verbatim as he cross-examines the rhapsode. Elsewhere, Socrates expresses an "awe and love of Homer,"[2] and in *The Ion* he appears to appreciate Ion's performances of the great epics.[3] Nevertheless, the elder philosopher is wary of Homer's ability to immerse us in his fictions. When a rhapsode is inspired and when audiences are caught up in a rhapsode's performance, they are not (as Socrates sees it) "in their right mind."

Socrates uses the analogy of a magnet to make his point. Artistic power originates in Calliope, the muse of epic poetry, and moves through Homer to rhapsodes like Ion and through Ion to the audience:

> The gift which you possess of speaking excellently about Homer is not an art, but, as I was just saying, an inspiration; there is a divinity moving you, like that contained in the stone which Euripides calls a magnet, but which is commonly known as the stone of Heraclea. This stone not only attracts iron rings, but also imparts to them a similar power of attracting other rings; and sometimes you may see a number of pieces of iron and rings suspended from one another so as to form quite a long chain: and all of them derive their power of suspension from the original stone. In like manner the Muse first of all inspires men herself; and from these inspired persons a chain of other persons is suspended, who take the inspiration.[4]

This image of the rhapsode as an inspired artist tickles Ion, but for Socrates it's a problem. If philosophy considers itself a rational search for truth, then anything that elevates emotion over reason will be suspect. This becomes clear when Socrates, dissatisfied with the somewhat static magnet analogy, supplements it with dynamic images of possessed dancers:

> For all good poets, epic as well as lyric, compose their beautiful poems not by art, but because they are inspired and possessed. And as the Corybantian revelers when they dance are not in their right mind, so

47

> the lyric poets are not in their right mind when they
> are composing their beautiful strains: but when falling
> under the power of music and meter they are inspired
> and possessed; like Bacchic maidens who draw milk and
> honey from the rivers when they are under the influence
> of Dionysus but not when they are in their right mind.[5]

We moderns, influenced by the 19th century Romantics' celebration of artistic genius, probably have few problems with this dynamic. Isn't it good to be moved by divinity, even by a god as dangerous as Dionysus, the lord of divine disorder and frenzy? One thinks of how Samuel Taylor Coleridge, perhaps alluding to Plato's passage, describes the poet figure as something dangerous in his poem "Kubla Khan": "Then close your eyes in holy dread / For he on honey dew hath fed / And drunk the milk of paradise."[6]

Keep in mind, however, that Dionysus's followers, when possessed, could rip people apart, as they do in Euripides's *The Bacchae*. Plato sees his ideal republic functioning smoothly only if its subjects see the right relations of things, not if they are driven by divine ecstasy or other bouts of passion. For Plato, all must go soberly about their business if things are to proceed well: the philosopher guardians rule the state, the auxiliaries or warriors guard it, and the producers provide its necessities. If the auxiliaries were to become emotional and imitate the quarreling gods in Homer and Hesiod—Ion's powerful performances of these poets could put ideas in their heads—then chaos would ensue. Plato had witnessed such chaos firsthand when demagogues whipped up the Athenian Assembly to embark on a ruinous war and, later, to execute his beloved teacher.

Plato's concerns about poetry anticipate the many censorship battles that will erupt over the centuries, in which moralists will worry about misbehaving literary characters leading their readers astray. As Plato sees it, stories are so dangerous that they shouldn't even be (as we now call it) commercially accessorized:

> Neither, if we mean our future guardians to regard the habit of quarrelling among themselves as of all things the basest, should any word be said to them of the wars in heaven, and of the plots and fightings of the gods against one another, for they are not true. No, we shall never mention the battles of the giants, or let them be embroidered on garments...[7]

So no battling gods printed on tee-shirts.

Because stories bring the gods down to earth, making them relatable, Plato worries that audiences will disrespect God, the transcendent being that uses eternal forms or archetypes to fashion the universe. Even though mature readers can separate higher from lower—the true and the good from chaotic narrative—Plato is concerned that young people cannot. The philosopher here sounds like modern parents worried about their children reading *Harry Potter* or *The Perks of Being a Wallflower.* He also brings to mind those 20th century Soviet censors who believed that farmers and factory workers required black and white versions of the class struggle. Any socialist realist drama displaying nuance, they feared, would only confuse audiences.

For his part, Plato believes that a young person cannot judge "what is allegorical and what is literal" in the Hesiod episodes where Hephaestus binds his mother Hera and where Zeus pushes Hephaestus off Mount Olympus for taking Hera's part when she is being beaten. "These tales must not be admitted into our state," Socrates declares, because anything that a young person "receives into his mind at that age is likely to become indelible and unalterable." Instead, the young should only be exposed to tales that are "models of virtuous thoughts."[8]

Plato would undoubtedly disapprove of how, when I read *The Iliad* as a child, I thrilled to the gods fighting each other in the Battle of Troy. What I saw as a game involving imaginative toy soldiers, Plato regards as a threat to our reverence for divinity. He has in mind the passage in book 20 where we see Poseidon mixing it up with Apollo, Athena with Ares, Artemis with Hera, Leto with Hermes, and Hephaistos with the local river god Skamander.[9]

Exciting though this may be, Plato cares more about public morality than about what constitutes a compelling work of art. "Let this then be one of our rules and principles concerning the gods," Socrates states, "to which our poets and reciters will be expected to conform—that God is not the author of all things, but of good only."[10] Gods in these old tales cannot be authors of good if they are fighting on both sides of a battle and exhibiting very human bloodlust as they do so.

Along with depictions of misbehaving gods, Plato also worries about epic heroes voicing fleshly appetites. He fears such literature will enflame base desires rather than elevating the spirit. In the 18th century novel *Tom Jones,* Henry Fielding describes *The Odyssey* as "that eating poem,"[11] and Plato picks up on this theme as well. For instance, Plato alludes critically to Odysseus's speech as he sits down to eat after escaping from Calypso's island. In the poem Odysseus declares,

> There is no boon in life more sweet, I say,
> than when a summer joy holds all the realm,
> and banqueters sit listening to a harper
> in a great hall, by rows of tables heaped
> with bread and roast meat, which a steward goes
> to dip up wine and brim your cups again.
> Here is the flower of life, it seems to me![12]

Rather than being charmed by this scene, stern Plato worries that young men, upon encountering the passage, will choose to get drunk rather than seek glory in battle. We can hear Plato's disapproval in Socrates's rhetorical question. "When the tables are full of bread and meat, and the cupbearer carries round wine which he draws from the bowl and pours into the cups," he asks, "is it fit or conducive to temperance for a young man to hear such words?"[13]

Socrates is even more offended by a passage in which Odysseus confesses to being ruled by his stomach. Such imagery undermines Plato's insistence that we should prioritize ideal forms over base material reality:

You will indulge me if I finish dinner—?
grieved though I am to say it. There's no part
of man more like a dog than brazen Belly,
crying to be remembered—and it must be—
when we are mortal weary and sick at heart;
and that is my condition.[14]

It's difficult to imagine a more anti-Platonic sentiment.

Another Homeric passage that Socrates/Plato fears will corrupt young men, one that he would like to "obliterate" for being "obnoxious," occurs in the Underworld scene where Achilles tells Odysseus he would rather be poor and alive than famous and dead:

Let me hear no smooth talk
of death from you, Odysseus, light of councils.
Better, I say, to break sod as a farm hand
for some poor country man, on iron rations,
than lord it over all the exhausted dead.[15]

Socrates cites this passage, along with other doleful descriptions of Hades, as potentially harmful. After all, if death is depicted as so terrible, young men will do anything to escape it, including run away in battle.

Many have puzzled over Plato's apparent attack on poetry given his own poetic talents. Classicist Julia Annas points out how superbly Plato has crafted his Socratic dialogues, creating memorable characters, carefully guiding the discussions, and finding ways to keep the reader involved.[16] Plato also exhibits a subtle humor and has compelling metaphors, most famously the Allegory of the Cave. Plato's style contrasts dramatically with the dry and analytical way that most philosophers write (including drama enthusiast Aristotle), leading Annas to ask, "How can so literary a writer be against what literature does?"[17] Sir Philip Sidney will ask the same question in *Defence of Poesy* (c. 1580), where he describes Plato as "the most poetical" of all philosophers and the one "most worthy of reverence." Why, he wonders, would Plato "defile the fountain out of which his flowing streams have proceeded?"[18]

This apparent contradiction makes sense, however, if we see Plato attacking poetry, not because he dislikes it, but because he fears he loves it too much. Like Shakespeare's Othello, perhaps he sees himself as one who loves "not wisely, but too well." In the final book of *The Republic*, we see Socrates expressing his enormous regard for Homer before going on the attack. He tells his interlocutor,

> Although I have always from my earliest youth had an awe and love of Homer, which even now makes the words falter on my lips, for he is the great captain and teacher of the whole of that charming tragic company; but a man is not to be reverenced more than the truth, and therefore I will speak out.[19]

Socrates here mentions the "ancient quarrel between philosophy and poetry," which he regards as essentially a quarrel between reason and emotion. Since, as Plato sees it, philosophical reason is the way to truth, then poets must be banished, all the more if we love them. We must cut them out of our lives the way we give up a cherished mistress who is not good for us. Plato says this after having given poetry a chance to defend herself:

> If her defense fails, then, my dear friend, like other persons who are enamored of something, but put a restraint upon themselves when they think their desires are opposed to their interests, so too must we after the manner of lovers give her up, though not without a struggle.[20]

Socrates goes on to describe our love of poetry as akin to a "childish love" which "captivates the many." When one becomes a man, however, one must put away childish things (as St. Paul puts it). Then, gendering poetry as female (as contrasted with masculine Reason), Socrates calls poetry a seductress. The mind is a city that should be governed by Reason, he says, and "he who listens to her [poetry], fearing for the safety of the city which is within him, should be on guard against her seductions and make our words his law."[21]

To further accentuate his argument, Socrates puts love of poetry in the same category as love of social position, wealth, and power. "Will anyone be profited," he asks, "if under the influence of honor or money or power, aye, or *under the excitement of poetry,* he neglect justice and virtue?" (my italics).[22] While we will see Plato's student Aristotle embrace the intense emotions unleashed by tragedy, Socrates dismissively says such emotions are "deemed to be the part of a woman."

Perhaps he is thinking of the moment when Odysseus weeps upon hearing a Phaeacian bard sing of the Trojan War. Or of audience members crying at the conclusion of the great tragedies (say, over the death of Antigone). Such crying Plato sees as "unmanly." Perhaps he recalls times when he himself has wept over the sorrows of Trojans Andromache, Hecuba and Priam, scenes from *The Iliad* that Ion has communicated with feeling.[23]

When men weep over such scenes, Plato complains, they express emotions they would normally strive to suppress: "The feeling of sorrow which has gathered strength at the sight of the misfortunes of others is with difficulty repressed in our own," he warns in Book 10.[24] When he links crying with poetry, insulting both, Plato also manages to insult women. In his hierarchy, which hasn't entirely left us, reason and philosophy are male and therefore understood to be superior to emotion and literature, which are gendered female.

Given the immense popularity of both Homer and the Greek tragedians, Plato's Socrates knows that he is bucking popular consensus with his attacks. He sees himself as challenging those "eulogists of Homer"—let's call them Homer groupies—who go overboard in their love of the bard. Somewhat sarcastically, Socrates says these groupies declare that their idol "has been the educator of Hellas, and that he is profitable for education and for the ordering of human things, and that you should take him up again and again and get to know him and regulate your whole life according to him."[25]

To be sure, Socrates admits that "Homer is the greatest of poets and the first of tragedy writers." However, if we allow ourselves to be swayed by the "honeyed muse," whether in the form of epic or of drama, then we yield to a false authority. Instead, we should listen to "law and the reason of mankind, which by common consent have ever been deemed best." Reason, not emotions generated by artistic "pleasure and pain," should be the right ruler in our state.[26]

These restrictions mean that Homer, no matter how much Plato or the rest of Greece loves him, will be forbidden entrance to the idealized Republic. The only poetry that Socrates will allow in are "hymns to the gods and praises of famous men."[27]

If such plain-minded poetry sounds boring, it is. Literature suffers when people narrowly censor it for moralistic purposes. If Plato were to "obliterate many obnoxious passages" from *The Odyssey*, as he threatens to do in Book 3 of *The Republic*, Homer would not be Homer.[28] (Something similar happened in the 19th century when Thomas Bowdler "cleaned up" Shakespeare for popular consumption.) Aristotle will later observe that characters who are all good or all bad lack dramatic force and that only a flawed hero can profoundly move us—but then, rational Plato claims he is against being profoundly moved at all.

The emotions unleashed by poetry are not the only danger Plato sees. If poetry is to benefit society, he says, then it must be closely aligned to truth, and Plato regards poets as deceivers, not truthtellers. Whereas philosophy seeks to uncover the real nature of things, Plato sees poetry and the arts providing us with a mere imitation of an imitation of an imitation.

Since we will see thinkers like Aristotle, Sidney, Shelley, Marx, Engels, Du Bois and others all claim that truth is literature's greatest gift to us, it's important to understand why Plato regards poetry as false. In his view, we can never directly see the eternal forms that exist in the mind of God. Instead, what we see on earth are but shadows of these forms. First we have a mental image of, say, a chair (already one step removed from the ideal in the mind of God) and then we have a carpenter's physical version of a chair (two steps removed). The artist, however, in depicting a chair, is *three* steps removed: he or she only imitates the carpenter's imitation (two steps removed) of our mental version (one step removed) of the eternal form. Or to mention other examples cited by Socrates, a poet's rendition of a charioteer or a general or a doctor must be inferior to actual charioteers, generals, and doctors. While Homer's depictions of these professions may be compelling, Socrates says, they are inferior to the real thing, mere imitations. They "copy images of virtue and the like, but the truth they never reach."[29]

Socrates pushes his point home by contrasting actual leaders with Homeric depictions of leaders. After all, Homer never helped a leader better govern a state or conduct a military campaign.[30]

Although parents generally do not have Plato in mind when they demand that their children major in engineering, pre-med, or accounting rather than the arts, they share his assumption that vocational education comes closer to reality than literature, theater, and music. (Then again, they don't want their children majoring in philosophy either.)

If Plato's logic casts doubt on poetry, why, he asks, do we still accord it credibility? Why are we so drawn to mere imitations of imitations?

Plato has Socrates answer that poets are "deceivers" who deck out their illusions with meter, harmony, and rhythm. They bamboozle us with beauty, in other words. If we were to strip away their poetic aids, however, poets would make "a poor appearance" and we would see poetry for the fraud it really is.[31]

Socrates seems to give poetry one last chance as *The Republic* nears its end. Anticipating a distinction that the Roman poet Horace will later make, he invites poetry's defenders to "show not only that she is *pleasant* but also *useful* to states and to human life [italics mine], and we will listen in a kindly spirit; for if this can be proved, we shall surely be the gainers—I mean, if there is a use in poetry as well as a delight."[32] If poetry's defenders want to argue that poetry *serves* us as well as *delights* us, Plato will listen. He adds, however, that they must make their case in prose. Were they to resort to beautiful poetry to argue for poetry, they might subvert our rational capacities and bamboozle us once again.

To sum up Plato's outlook, literature prompts us to behave as irrationally and as dangerously as bacchic dancers in a Dionysiac frenzy, thereby leading us away from truth. Perhaps because Plato himself responds to the "honeyed muse" at such a gut level, he is even more aware of its dangers than those who feel less deeply. Dreaming of a controlled and rational utopia as he engages in philosophic dialogues, Plato sees the explosive power of poetry as potentially gumming up the works. He therefore concludes, perhaps reluctantly, that he must sacrifice his own pleasure by banishing poets from his ideal society in the interests of social order.

ARISTOTLE

POETRY, TRUER THAN HISTORY

> Poetry, therefore, is a more philosophical and a higher thing than history: for poetry tends to express the universal, history the particular. By the universal, I mean how a person of a certain type will on occasion speak or act, according to the law of probability or necessity...

— **Aristotle,** *The Poetics* (c. 335 BCE)[1]

UNLIKE PLATO, ARISTOTLE SAW dramatic poetry as a social good. And because he could not let his teacher's criticisms go unanswered, he authored *The Poetics,* which has earned him the title "Father of Literary Criticism." Whereas the older thinker worried about the emotions unleashed by drama, his protégé would embrace them.

Plato's junior by 45 years, Aristotle (384–322 BCE) was a student at Plato's academy for two decades. He left after Plato died, later tutored the young Alexander the Great (Aristotle's father had been the personal physician of Alexander's grandfather), and returned eventually to Athens to set up his own school, the Lyceum, which featured Europe's first library. Aristotle's systematic examination of, well, pretty much everything under the sun—from biology to politics to rhetoric to the soul—established the blueprint followed by the great medieval universities, which in turn have served as models for our own modern studies of the sciences and liberal arts.

It's clear from reading *Poetics* that Aristotle was thoroughly familiar with the tragedies, comedies, and satires of his day. Classicist Edith Hall speculates that he positioned the Lyceum so that it would be close to the Athenian theater of Dionysus, and she imagines him excitedly discussing the latest dramas with his students as he returned to the Academy at nightfall.[2]

Aristotle regards the arts as critical to producing an educated citizenry. As Hall puts it, "Athenian drama was designed not only to enthrall its spectators but to train them in the cognitive, moral and political skills they needed to run a healthy city."[3] Aristotle agrees with Plato that people are likely to imitate what they encounter in literature, noting that man "is the most imitative of living creatures, and through imitation learns his earliest lessons."[4] He focuses, however, on the positives of imitation rather than on its potential pitfalls so that, while Plato accuses poets of merely imitating imitations of imitations of the eternal forms—three steps removed from eternal truth—Aristotle believes that great poets have a special handle on truth. Homer, Aeschylus, Sophocles, and Euripides, he believes, grasp truth at a deeper level than historians because, in his words, "poetry tends to express the universal, history the particular."

Historians, he says, merely record the acts of quirky individuals (Aristotle mentions by name Alcibiades, the eccentric Athenian general who defied classification) while poets look to the "law of probability and necessity" when they have their characters speak or act. "It is this universality," Aristotle writes, "at which poetry aims in the names she attaches to the personages."[5] Whereas Plato would regard, say, Odysseus as simultaneously unworthy of imitation and unrealistic (what can Homer know about actual kings?), in Aristotle's view

Homer provides a brilliant depiction of and therefore an invaluable window into leadership in action.

Aristotle contends that different forms of literature imitate different sorts of universalities. Epic and tragedy (Aristotle mentions Homer and the playwright Sophocles) imitate "higher types of character." Comedy, such as that composed by the playwright Aristophanes, imitates lower types. As Aristotle puts it, "The graver spirits imitated noble actions, and the actions of good men. The more trivial sort imitated the actions of meaner persons."[6]

In other words, rather than seeing audiences as led astray by theatrical performances, Aristotle claims that art brings spectators closer to the essential nature of reality. His argument, familiar to defenders of the liberal arts, is that poetry grasps truths that literal approaches overlook. Unlike Plato, Aristotle thinks that a statesman would learn a great deal from reading *The Iliad*. Because a great tragedy understands "how a person of a certain type will on occasion speak or act,"[7] we can imagine Aristotle pointing out valuable Homeric insights into human behavior. For instance, a statesman will learn from Agamemnon's quarrel with Achilles that leaders should avoid personal pique if they want to succeed.

Classicist Edith Hall observes that the tragedies of Aeschylus, Sophocles, and Euripides had a function particular to Athenian society given how dependent it was on its popular council, which required common citizens to spend vast amounts of time and attention on a "breathtaking" range of responsibilities. As she sees it, the tragedies offered a training in deliberate decision-making, from "the Persian Queen's request for advice from her elders on how she should react to her dream and the omen she has seen in *Persians*, to Iphigenia's articulation of her limited alternatives (i.e., whether to die willingly or unwillingly) in *Iphigenia in Aulis*."[8]

Deliberation as a mental process, Hall notes, was particularly important for the dramatist Sophocles, the one tragedian among the big three who held public office. It's not accidental then that his tragedies are often "precipitated by the inability of a character in a quandary to listen to good counsel, to discount bad, or simply to spend sufficient time considering potential outcomes." For example, "Oedipus fails to hear Tiresias, neither Ajax nor the Atridae demonstrate much ability to anticipate the consequences of their actions, and Creon substitutes bluster for deliberation when faced with cogent arguments framed by both Antigone and Haemon."[9] Hall concludes that, as Aristotle saw it, Greek tragedies "had the potential massively to enhance the emotional and moral life of both individual spectators and the community as a whole."[10]

Contemporary philosopher Martha Nussbaum agrees. Her book *The Fragility of Goodness: Luck and Ethics in Greek Tragedy and Philosophy* regards Aristotle's *Poetics* as a direct answer to Plato. Whereas Socrates wants to limit poetry in the Republic to "hymns to the gods and praises of famous men," Nussbaum says that Aristotle prefers stories of "good human activity." "The concrete and complex stories that are the material of tragic drama," she writes, are vital to the philosopher, who believes that "a detailed account of a complex particular case will have more of ethical truth in it than a general formula."[11] If Aristotle understands so well how we respond to external pressure, Nussbaum says, it's because he has been schooled by such plays as Sophocles's *Antigone* and Euripides's *Hecuba*.

While Aristotle believes tragedies influence audiences by providing compelling models to imitate and learn from, what makes the lesson stick is the emotional purging or purification they undergo while watching. This is the famous and much debated theory of catharsis, which Aristotle says is caused by a mingling of "pity and fear": we are drawn closer to the tragic hero through pity while, at the same time, we pull back out of fear, relieved that it is happening to someone else.[12] Think of it as a dance of approach/avoidance. The better the play, the deeper the catharsis.

In Hall's view, catharsis is a particularly effective teaching tool because it "elict[s] a response that it both emotional and intellectual."[13] "While representing an instance of suffering in dramatic form," she writes, Tragedy "always asks *why* it occurred."[14] The genre, therefore, is a "dramatic expression of an *enquiry* into suffering, an aesthetic question mark performed in enacted pain."[15] This focus on poetry as intellectual exploration further differentiates Aristotle from Plato, who sees poetry as only appealing to the emotions and therefore at war with philosophy. Aristotle, by contrast, thinks tragedy explores the dynamic tension between emotion and reason.

Incidentally, that distinction will figure largely in our later discussions about lesser and greater literature, with some arguing (as I do) that lesser literature works primarily on our emotions while greater literature works on emotion and reason both. Horace's distinction between poetry that only delights and poetry that delights *and* instructs is a variant of this pattern.

We can imagine emotion and reason warring in the mind of Aristotle himself as he watched *Oedipus*, which would explain why it is his prime example of tragic catharsis. If, as one of the smartest people who ever lived, Aristotle thinks that the intellect can handle all that life throws at us, he might well have identified with Oedipus, who thinks the same. After all, Oedipus knows he has solved the riddle of the sphinx and he is sure he can unravel the mystery of Laius's murder, which is necessary to stop the plague that is decimating Thebes. Aristotle must have recognized in Oedipus both his own confident assurance in his reasoning powers and his realization that arrogance, accident, fate, and the gods can limit even the most intelligent. As he wept for the hero, whose tragedy is partly of his own making and partly not, he wept for himself.

While Plato decries weeping as contrary to "the manly part," for Aristotle catharsis is central to tragedy's educational effectiveness. Aristotle believes that the emotional engagement feared by Plato will strengthen society, not undermine it. Intense involvement with such plays as *Antigone* and *Hecuba* guided audiences toward the deeper understanding needed to handle citizenship duties and other life challenges—deeper, Aristotle would argue, than is available from a mere rational understanding.

We recognize the difference between the two philosophers in the censorship battles that have followed. In the mid-20th century, for instance, Plato's successors feared that young people reading *Catcher in the Rye* would behave like Holden Caulfield, who uses bad language, disrespects authority, runs away from school, and hires a prostitute. Aristotle's successors, meanwhile, counterargued that adolescents gain new insight into themselves as they interact with a character such as Holden, finding a language and a narrative for their own confusion, their fears, and their longings. Platonists worry that such stories will ruin people for the world while Aristotelians hope they will help people better handle the world's difficulties.

The difference here is that, while Plato worries that disturbing literary images will corrupt our values, Aristotle assumes that our values are already on solid ground. It's why Plato talks about poetry misleading young people and the warrior class—he believes only the philosophic guardians can make fine distinctions—whereas Aristotle talks as if everyone can tell right from wrong. Aristotle starts with the premise that theater spectators are already fully formed moral beings whereas Plato sees them as still developing.

This becomes clear when Aristotle, in his discussion of catharsis, describes how different dramas will affect spectators. He's assuming everyone will respond the same way to tragedies in which a virtuous man is brought low or a bad man is elevated:

> It follows plainly, in the first place, that the change of fortune presented must not be the spectacle of a virtuous man brought from prosperity to adversity: for this moves neither pity nor fear; it merely shocks us. Nor, again, that of a bad man passing from adversity to prosperity: for nothing can be more alien to the spirit of Tragedy; it possesses no single tragic quality; it neither satisfies the moral sense nor calls forth pity or fear.[16]

What seems plain to Aristotle, however, is precisely what is at issue. While perhaps people with the same background will respond roughly the same way, what happens when one changes the background? As we will see, such 20th century thinkers like W.E.B. Du Bois, Bertolt Brecht, and Rachel Blau DuPlessis will show that marginalized people may respond very differently to a work than the privileged do. Aristotle comfortably assumes that we will recognize, from the first, who is virtuous and who is vicious and we will respond appropriately: we will rejoice if virtue is rewarded and vice is punished.

But what if (this is Plato's point) poetry has misled us into accepting and even approving certain behaviors that we should view with abhorrence? What if we find ourselves cheering for the bad guys?

This question goes to the heart of censorship battles. The fear that literature can muddy the line between good and evil is why Vladimir Nabokov couldn't initially find American publishers for his novel *Lolita,* now considered one of the 20th century's masterpieces. Publishers knew that society would object to a sympathetic treatment of a pedophile (sympathetic in part because Humbert Humbert tells his own story), forcing the author to settle for a French publisher specializing in pornography. If a novel normalizes such behavior, might not impressionable souls follow suit, finding a permission structure for their own pedophilia?

Or take a contrary example, one that (in Aristotle's words) "merely shocks us" by bringing a virtuous character "from prosperity to adversity." The 19th century writer Thomas Hardy certainly shocked audiences with his novel about "a pure woman" (so reads the subtitle of *Tess of the d'Urbervilles*) dying on the gallows for murder. As the protagonist, Tess is a thoroughly engaging character who has a horrific story: she is raped by her employer, lives with him for a few months, loses her child, loses the husband she loves, and (now destitute) returns to and then murders her rapist. As critics saw it, either Hardy was mocking traditional Christian values by describing a fallen woman and murderess as pure, or he was questioning divine providence by showing fate meting out unjustified punishment to an innocent. Either was a horrifying prospect. By blurring a clear line between virtue and vice, both Nabokov and Hardy challenged the conventional "moral sense" of the audiences of their day, thereby shocking the guardians of decency. By Aristotle's criteria, such dramas do not allow for traditional catharsis or rise to the level of great art.

We can find other examples that strike even more directly at Aristotle's view of the world. Since he regarded women and slaves as inferior to male Athenian citizens, what would he think of Margaret Atwood's dystopian novel *The Handmaid's Tale* (1985), where men are depicted as tyrannical for drastically curtailing women's rights as they reestablish traditional patriarchy? Or what about John Steinbeck's *Grapes of Wrath* (1939), which elevates lowly dust bowl refugees to heroic stature? Aristotle no doubt couldn't foresee that scenario. For that matter, how would he view Arthur Miller's project to turn an out-of-work, adulterous salesman into an Aristotelian tragic hero. Aristotle might see Miller's protagonist Willie Loman in *Death of a Salesman* (1949) as a fit subject for comedy but not for tragedy.

I frame the issues this way to show how much Aristotle's literary views are based upon certain social assumptions. When Aristotle sees plays performing an educational function, he has in mind educating property-owning Athenian male citizens only. As we will see, poets like Horace and Sir Philip Sidney will also see literature as upholding patriarchal social values. It will not be until the Romantic poets, writing in the wake of the American and French Revolutions, that we will witness thinkers contending that great literature should challenge the social status quo, not uphold it. Poet Percy Shelley will even argue that the great Greek tragedies have aspects that support the liberation of women and the freeing of slaves, an interpretation that would have surprised Aristotle.

Over the centuries, Plato's and Aristotle's different views of literary impact have returned in debates over whether certain works are good or bad for us. Their heirs have argued over such controversial and challenging works as Christopher Marlowe's rip-roaring Renaissance tragedy *Doctor Faustus,* Moliere's satiric comedy *Tartuffe,* Goethe's steamy melodrama *The Sorrows of Young Werther,* Emily Bronte's tempestuous love story *Wuthering Heights,* Henrik Ibsen's feminist play *A Doll's House,* Albert Camus's existentialist masterpiece *The Stranger,* and countless others. Social and political conservatives have feared that readers will be induced to misbehave when encountering certain of these works whereas progressives have counterargued that they help us navigate moral complexities.

Because they are more confident that readers can find their own way to virtue, Aristotle's heirs are less likely to ban books. This also means, however, that they sometimes underestimate the power of literature to upend lives. When conservative parents complain bitterly about school reading lists, liberals—like Aristotle with Plato—wonder what all the fuss is about.

HORACE

INSTRUCTING WHILE DELIGHTING

The tribes of the seniors rail against everything that is
void of edification: the exalted knights [young men]
disregard poems which are austere. He who joins the
instructive with the agreeable, carries off every vote, by
delighting and at the same time admonishing
the reader.

— **Horace,** *Art of Poetry* (c. 19 BCE)[1]

WE HAVE SEEN PLATO distinguish between poetry that is useful and
poetry that is merely delightful—he banishes the latter from his ideal
Republic—but it was the Roman poet Quintus Horatius Flaccus
(Horace) who got the world to focus on it. While there are some poets
who "wish either to profit *or* to delight," Horace wrote in *Art of Poetry*,
the best poets "deliver at once both the pleasures *and* the necessaries of
life" (italics mine).[2] For him, poets should unite practical instruction
and entertainment.

Although famous for his easy-going ways, Horace (65-8 BCE) lived
a surprisingly eventful early life. The son of a freed slave, as a young
man he fought with Brutus and Cassius against Mark Antony and
Augustus and saw his family farm confiscated. Fortunately, he later
reconciled with Augustus when the latter became Caesar and was rewarded for his odes and satires, many of which would go on to become

poetic models for centuries afterwards. In *Horace and Me: Life Lessons from an Ancient Poet,* arts writer Harry Eyres says the poet shows us how to slow down the pace of life. Living the ideal, Horace turned down an administrative post offered by Augustus, and he would coin the phrase "carpe diem" or "seize the day" as he advocated living a life that balances work and play. In a society that was "pragmatic, increasingly instrumental and money-driven," Eyres notes, Horace managed to "carve out a space for lyric poetry."[3]

What Horace has to say about poetry's utility occupies only a few sentences of *Art of Poetry,* which is mostly concerned with providing advice to active poets. In fact, the rules that Horace set forth were used as a poetic blueprint for centuries, falling out of favor only with Romanticism's celebration of poetic originality. Horace's discussion is useful for our purposes, however, as time and again we will see thinkers returning to the tension between delight and usefulness, with some worrying that literature is spoiled when it has a serious agenda and others worrying that literature is frivolous when it does not.

Horace, however, contends that we don't have to choose. To make his point, he contrasts "the tribes of the seniors" with "the exalted knights." The grumpy old men frown on anything that is not edifying whereas the young bucks "disregard poems which are austere." By "austere" he probably means preachy and moralistic.

We saw Plato raise concerns about impressionable young people in *The Republic,* and we will see Samuel Johnson write about them again in the 18th century. As often as not, our own censorship battles concern readings assigned to young people in school or over the summer. Horace's young "exalted knights" at first seem impervious to instruction, especially after they shake free of their guardians. At this point in life, as characterized by the poet, they are lazy, useless, and irresponsible spendthrifts, fickle in love and "pliable as wax to the bent of vice":

The beardless youth, his guardian being at length discharged, joys in horses, and dogs, and the verdure of the sunny Campus Martius; pliable as wax to the bent of vice, rough to advisers, a slow provider of useful things, prodigal of his money, high-spirited, and amorous, and hasty in deserting the objects of his passion.[4]

Horace believes we can penetrate such minds, however, if we set aside long-winded advice and "superfluous instructions" and instead give them poetry. After all, poets can teach and entertain at the same time. Or as Horace puts it, the one "who joins the instructive with the agreeable carries off every vote."

Later thinkers will second Horace's advice. In his *Defence of Poesy* (c. 1580), poet Sir Philip Sidney says that those who "despise the austere admonitions" of moralists may nevertheless "be content to be delighted" by poetry. Therefore, the poet can use beauty to lure them into goodness, "ere themselves be aware, as if they took a medicine of cherries."[5] Meanwhile, satirist Jonathan Swift, in his *Battle of the Books* (1704), characterizes Horace's dual properties of literature as "sweetness and light." Swift employs the symbol of the honeybee, which makes both honey (literary delight) and wax (for wax candles, by which one can study).[6]

Even after reassuring us that delightful poetry can be useful, however, Horace predicts—probably accurately—that skeptics will still be "ashamed of the lyric muse, and Apollo the god of song." These are probably Rome's practical citizens, as well as today's practical parents. To bring the naysayers around, therefore, he ramps up his argument, piling up one poetic accomplishment upon another.

The legendary poet Orpheus, he says, "deterred the savage race of men from slaughters and inhuman diet"—Orpheus supposedly taught cannibals how to subsist on fruit—and he tamed tigers and "furious lions." Amphion, another figure from Greek mythology, built the walls of Thebes with his music ("was said to give the stones motion with the sound of his lyre"). Other poets taught people civic responsibility; created a sense of the sacred; regulated sexual behavior ("prohibit[ed] a promiscuous commerce between the sexes"); taught civilization how to conduct marriages; designed cities; and established laws. Homer and the Spartan poet Tyrtaeus, meanwhile, "animated the manly mind to martial achievements with their verses."[7]

Nor should we forget, Horace says, that oracles deliver their pronouncements in poetry and that poetry can be used as a guide to life and a way to praise princes. Oh, and one final thing: think of the delight we take in attending a play at the end of a long day of tedious work. Case closed!

Whether Horace actually believes the strains of a lyre can shift stones, his list of poetry's worldly accomplishments points to the power he senses in it. He knows that poetry has moved him, and he marshals a host of examples to prove that it works on others as well. He's the first of many thinkers to recognize that poetry needs defending against accusations of frivolity—we're about to see Philip Sidney grapple with the issue head-on—and he is the first to explicitly assert that literature can be simultaneously serious and delightful, at once a practical tool and a source of pleasure. The balancing act becomes a major issue in the 19th century, when figures like Percy Shelley, John Stuart Mill, and Matthew Arnold battle with pragmatic middle class "Philistines" (Arnold's word) who want to dispense with poetry altogether.

The classic trio of Plato, Aristotle and Horace would set the basic terms for discussions about how literature shapes us for the next 2000 years. While Plato warned that literature is too emotional, causing audiences to misbehave, Aristotle countered that this emotional power can be a force for good. Instead of debauching young people, it creates ethical and effective citizens, moving them in ways that other ways of writing cannot.

For his part, Horace assured us that one doesn't have to choose between literature that entertains us and literature that makes us better people. The best works do both.

FORCE FOR MORAL TRANSFORMATION

SIR PHILIP SIDNEY

POETRY AS A GUIDE TO VIRTUE

So that the ending end of all earthly learning being
virtuous action, those skills that most serve to bring
forth that have a most just title to be princes over all
the rest; ...the poet is worthy to have it before any other
competitors.

— **Sir Philip Sidney,** *Defence of Poesy* (1579)[1]

LIKE HORACE, WITH WHOM he was well familiar, Sir Philip Sidney
(1554–86) believed that poetry inextricably intertwines delight and
instruction. And while, like Aristotle, he saw literature as essential to
forming good citizens, his primary emphasis was on morality: poetry
instructs us in how to be virtuous. He put forth these views in *Defence
of Poesy* (1579), one of England's great works of literary criticism. Poetry needed defending, Sidney decided, after Puritan moralist Stephen
Gosson attacked it as both useless and immoral.

No one was better positioned to defend poetry's value to society.
Sidney, after all, balanced the vocations of poet and warrior as few

people have. The living embodiment of the Renaissance man, Sidney was a courtier, soldier, diplomat, author, and patron of the arts in the age of Elizabeth I. By the age of 32, along with *Defence of Poesy* he had authored an influential sonnet cycle and a significant work of prose fiction (*Arcadia*). He then died heroically, leading a doomed Dutch charge against the Spanish in support of the Protestant cause.[2]

Drawing heavily upon Aristotle and Horace and even trying to enlist Plato (this is more difficult), Sidney in *Defence* contends that all earthly learning should lead toward "virtuous action" and that no form of learning accomplishes this more powerfully than poetry. Gosson's tract was the prod he needed to put his already existing views into print.

Gosson was an unsuccessful playwright and actor who then turned against the theater, writing the prodigiously titled *The School of Abuse: Containing a pleasant invective against Poets, Pipers, Players, jesters and such like Caterpillars of a commonwealth; Setting up the Flag of Defiance to their mischievous exercise, and overthrowing their Bulwarks, by Profane Writers, Natural reason, and common experience: A discourse as pleasant for Gentlemen that favor learning, as profitable for all that will follow virtue.* Further goading Sidney into a response was the fact that Gosson dedicated this unctuous tract to him directly.

Gosson draws on Plato's major arguments against the arts, arguing that poetry:

- is "unprofitable" and a waste of time;

- is untrue ("the mother of lies");

- is "effeminate" (Plato called such tears "unmanly"); and

- infects us "with many pestilent desires, with a siren's sweetness drawing the mind to the serpent's tail of sinful fancies."[3]

In reply to this screed, Sidney acts like a good defense attorney, marshaling every instance that comes to mind where poetry can be shown to have made lives better. Citing Horace, he finds poetry to be superior to moral philosophy because it is more fun to read. Sidney essentially argues that a spoonful of poetry makes the moral instruction go down. Or as he puts it, readers can be lured into goodness "ere themselves be aware, as if they took a medicine of cherries."[4]

Quoting Aristotle, meanwhile, Sidney also contends that poetry is superior to history because it makes clear what should be shunned and what should be emulated whereas history merely gives us facts. Sidney, however, makes a slightly different argument than Aristotle. Recall that Aristotle believes that poets help us better understand human beings through depicting "probability and necessity." Sidney, by contrast, is interested in virtue, not realism *per se*, and he lauds poetry for its ability to focus on the realm of virtuous relationships and duties.

Through feigning, Sidney says, poets can set out virtue "in her best colors" whereas historians, unless they become "poetical"—unless they make it clear how God's will works through history—are "manacled" to random facts. (Arnold Toynbee, the famous chronicler of civilizations, reportedly derided such prosaic history as "one damned thing after another.")[5]

In his focus on the ideal rather than the real, Sidney is closer to Plato than to Aristotle, and he has been called a Neoplatonist. In a rather remarkable turn, he uses Platonic arguments to refute Plato, saying that poetry will inspire us to become virtuous, not (as Plato argued) cowardly and debauched. Whereas Plato thinks it is philosophy's job to lead us to the good, Sidney sees it as poetry's. After all, who wants to read those moral philosophers "whom, me thinks, I see coming toward me with a sullen gravity, as though they could not abide vice by daylight"?[6]

Given his life as warrior and courtier, Sidney's contention that poetry inspires us to act virtuously carries weight. So does his claim that real men like poetry. Contra Plato, he insists that poetry is *not* "an art of lies, but of true doctrine; not of effeminateness, but of notable stirring of courage; not of abusing man's wit, but of strengthening man's wit..."[7]

Sidney's essay then provides specific examples. Each literary genre, he says, leads us to act virtuously in its own way.

For instance, **pastoral poetry**, with its scenes of simple folk in rural surroundings, dramatizes the plight of the oppressed, encouraging those "that sit highest" to minister to them. Such poetry also teaches us to be patient in the face of suffering. Meanwhile, **elegiac poetry**, where the speaker expresses grief, sadness, or loss, has a therapeutic function, allowing us to emote when there are "just causes of lamentation." For its part, **satire** shames villainy and, by laughing at folly, deters us from behaving villainously or foolishly ourselves.[8]

Comedy, like satire, represents the "common errors of life" in "the most ridiculous and scornful sort that may be; so as it is impossible that any beholder can be content to be such a one." **Tragedy**, on the other hand, "openeth the greatest wounds, and showeth forth the ulcers that are covered with tissue," with the result that kings, if they watch tragedies, will fear to be tyrants and tyrants will refrain from acting tyrannically. Furthermore, tragedy makes us realize just how uncertain the world is, thereby prompting us to turn towards God.[9]

Lyric poetry, which expresses personal emotion and was Sidney's own specialty, reinforces virtue by praising it. ("Look in thy heart and write," he instructs in one sonnet.) It also teaches moral precepts and brings us closer to God when we use it to sing God's praises. **Heroic poetry**, which Sidney regards as "the best and most accomplished kind of poetry," "makes magnanimity and justice shine through all misty fearfulness and foggy desires." His major example is Virgil's *Aeneid*, which gives us a hero that "inflames" our minds with the desire to be like him and instructs us in how to do it:

> Only let Aeneas be worn in the tablet of your memory, how he governs himself in the ruin of his country; in the preserving his old father, and carrying away his religious ceremonies; in obeying the god's commandment

to leave Dido, though not only all passionate kindness, but even the human consideration of virtuous gratefulness, would have craved other of him; how in storms, how in sports, how in war, how in peace, how a fugitive, how victorious, how besieged, how besieging, how to strangers, how to allies, how to enemies, how to his own; lastly, how in his inward self, and how in his outward government; and I think, in a mind most prejudiced with a prejudicating humor, he will be found in excellency fruitful...[10]

Aeneas, in short, is Sidney's ultimate role model, and he's probably thinking of *The Aeneid* when, in his essay's opening, he finds poetry more inspiring than the sight of a gallant man astride a horse. I suspect he channeled Aeneas when, against the wishes of the crown, he went to Holland to fight against the Spanish.

If, in *Defence of Poesy*, Sidney functions as literature's defense attorney, citing every instance where his client has done good, one can imagine a prosecutor going to work. We can find many instances, for example, where satire has failed to persuade fools not to act foolishly, prompting satirist Jonathan Swift's observation that satire "is a sort of glass wherein beholders do generally discover everybody's face but their own, which is the chief reason so few are offended by it."[11] Similarly, do we really think that tragedy will persuade tyrants not to act tyrannically? For that matter, even heroic verse may fail in its intended effect. What would Sidney have made of 20th century Italian fascist Benito Mussolini using *The Aeneid* to bolster his imperial ambitions, including the conquest of Ethiopia and Slovenia?[12]

In *Defence* Sidney appears to think that the rest of the world ascribes to his own high standards. As he sees it, if every form of literature contributes to making *him* a more virtuous man, then literature must clearly be good. In this way Sidney is like Aristotle, who believes that audiences, even potential tyrants, have a moral compass well in place when they view a tragedy. We already have an urge toward virtue, both men appear to believe, which literature only reenforces.

Sidney can't altogether ignore Plato's counter argument about literature's potential to corrupt, however, and he makes one key concession: if literature is the powerful force that he thinks it is, then it can indeed be used for ill as well as good. Since no use of words "can both teach and move [towards virtue] so much as poesy," the opposite must also be true—a poetic use of words could also potentially move people towards vice. Or as Sidney puts it, "by the reason of [poesy's] sweet charming force, it can do more hurt than any other army of words."[13] He may have in mind here Plato's warning that poetry can dupe us with its beauty.

Because he is defending poetry, Sidney must therefore qualify his endorsement. It is not poetry itself that is at fault but those who misuse it, and Sidney contrasts poetry that is abused with poetry that is "rightly used." He says that just as a physician can use his knowledge of physic to poison or to cure, just as a preacher can use God's word to breed heresy or to raise people up, just as a man can use a sword to kill his father or to defend his prince, so one can use poetry for bad or for good.[14]

Sidney's analogies—medicine, God's word, swords—indicate, contra Plato, that poetry is itself essentially good. Sidney would definitely want poetry in his own ideal republic. But he also would only want citizens who use poetry rightly, and his concession plays into Plato's hands. Sure, Plato might say, the guardian philosophers will rightly use poetry. But what about the military auxiliaries and the class of people who produce society's necessities? What about teenagers? If poetry is so vulnerable to misuse, we can imagine Plato asking, then shouldn't it be tightly regulated and, in certain instances, even banned?

Sidney doesn't seem concerned by this theoretical problem because, acquainted as he was with the upper-class men of his time who read poetry, he is confident in how they would respond. While he might acknowledge that a few will misuse poetry, the ones who matter will, like himself, be inspired by heroic verse and strive to emulate Aeneas and other literary heroes. If the poem is beautiful and powerful enough, why would one do anything other than embrace the virtue it affirms? And for the holdouts, maybe his own *Defence of Poesy* will push them in the direction of right reading.

Would Sidney have been less idealistic could he have foreseen Moll Flanders, Pamela Andrews, Tom Jones, Tristram Shandy, Humphry Clinker, Evelina, and other protagonists of a "novel" genre that would come into being a little over a century later? Sidney's aristocratic ideal no longer seemed as convincing once Plato's producing class, having learned to read in massive numbers, began demanding characters who looked like themselves and had values and concerns alien to a 16th century courtier. The heroic narratives of Daniel Defoe, Samuel Richardson, Henry Fielding, Laurence Sterne, Tobias Smollett, and Fanny Burney would feature, not the dukes and princes of Sidney's *Arcadia,* but solidly middle- and lower-class characters. Suddenly the literary scene would be filled with models seemingly unworthy of imitation.

Not that everyone in the 18th century will embrace the new literature. Critic Samuel Johnson will pen his own version of Gosson's diatribe against "sinful fancies," describing "comedies of romance" as "unjust prejudices, perverse opinions, and incongruous combinations of images." He and others will still see certain forms of literature as immoral and dangerous. Now, however, they will focus on the novel, which came into ascendency in the early modern era.

SAMUEL JOHNSON

SHAKESPEARE INSTRUCTS, NOVELS SEDUCE

Shakespeare is above all writers, at least above all modern writers, the poet of nature; the poet that holds up
to his readers a faithful mirror of manners and of life...

—Samuel Johnson, *Preface to the Plays of William
Shakespeare* (1765)[1]

ALTHOUGH MIDDLE CLASS READERSHIP skyrocketed in 18th century Britain, not everyone saw the new encounters with print as beneficial. As in previous eras, social guardians had concerns about literature
leading young people astray. And not only young people. Scholar J.
Paul Hunter recounts how husbands were unnerved when their wives
would disappear for days into Samuel Richardson's million-word
melodrama *Clarissa,* neglecting household responsibilities.[2]

Given how we ourselves have been thrown off stride by global-
ization and social media, we can certainly relate to what the British
were undergoing at the time. The country was rapidly changing from
an agricultural to a mercantile society, with power shifting from the

landed gentry to the middle class. International trade and technical innovations were ushering in a new prosperity that was at once exhilarating and disorienting, a discord captured in Tobias Smollett's epistolary novel *The Expedition of Humphry Clinker* (1771). While Smollett's grumpy and gout-ridden Matthew Bramble writes letters complaining about the classes intermingling, his niece and nephew revel in the variety and energy of the emerging social order. In this new environment, many parents and other members of the public expressed a need for public counselors who could guide them through the confusion, both in the real world and in its literary output.

Into that vacuum strode powerhouse critic Samuel Johnson (1709–84), who aimed to (among other things) teach people what to read, what to avoid, and how to judge what they read. As Johnson saw it, Shakespeare was must-reading for the masses because he so masterfully shows us the truth of our condition. On the other hand, Johnson recommended shunning modern romance novels for the way they pander to our baser instincts.

The last third of the 18th century is sometimes known as "the Age of Johnson," and it's easy to see why. A man of vast intelligence, Johnson, working virtually alone, created the first comprehensive English dictionary, an achievement that, in the words of biographer Walter Jackson Bate, "easily ranks as one of the greatest single achievements of scholarship."[3] Johnson was also the author of a magnificent long poem ("The Vanity of Human Wishes"); a dazzling philosophical novel (*The History of Rasselas, Prince of Abyssinia*); an important critical edition of Shakespeare; an in-depth survey of England's contemporary poets; and two sets of groundbreaking essays (the *Rambler* essays, published twice a week from 1750–52, and the *Idler* essays, published weekly from 1758–60).

In addition, Johnson presided over regular gatherings of the leading lights of the day. Meeting with him in coffee houses and over bowls of rum punch to discuss everything from art to science to politics were figures like painter Joshua Reynolds, legendary actor David Garrick, political theorist Edmund Burke, historian Edward Gibbons (*The De-*

cline and Fall of the Roman Empire), author and playwright Oliver Goldsmith (*Vicar of Wakefield, She Stoops to Conquer*), and James Boswell, whose account of Johnson's life would become one of the world's great biographies.

According to Walter Jackson Bate, another great Johnson biographer, Johnson considered himself above all as a moralist.[4] While Johnson is generally regarded as a Tory conservative, Bate says he is more complicated than such a label suggests. Johnson was certainly suspicious of grandiose claims of progress being made by the mercantile classes, not to mention by America's founding fathers. He knew well how humans fall short of their ideals and so was unwilling to jettison time-honored traditions, including class hierarchy and colonial rule. His Shakespearean dedication to capturing the truth about human beings, however, led him to reject facile political bromides coming from any party. He refused to reduce people to ideological caricatures.

Echoing Aristotle, Johnson believes the poet, in contrast to the historian, expresses the universal rather than the particular. As he sees it, no modern poet does this better than Shakespeare, whose plays shook Johnson to his core. (*King Lear*, he writes, "fill[s] the mind with a perpetual tumult of indignation, pity and hope,"[5] and the death of Cordelia so affected him that he couldn't return to the play for years after reading it.)[6] In his *Preface to Shakespeare*, which Bate describes as "one of the landmarks in the history of literary criticism,"[7] Johnson tells us that those who wish to operate more effectively on the world should read Shakespeare, who captures the essence of people rather than their surface characteristics:

> His persons act and speak by the influence of those general passions and principles by which all minds are agitated, and the whole system of life is continued in motion. In the writings of other poets a character is too often an individual; in those of Shakespeare it is commonly a species.[8]

In Johnson's formulation, Shakespeare is a rich treasure trove that is to be mined for his insights. After quoting Horace that "the end of poetry is to instruct by pleasing," Johnson says that Shakespeare's plays provide "much instruction":

> It is from this wide extension of design that so much instruction is derived. It is this which fills the plays of Shakespeare with practical axioms and domestic wisdom. It was said of Euripides, that every verse was a precept; and it may be said of Shakespeare, that from his works may be collected a system of civil and economical prudence.[9]

Like Aristotle, Johnson thinks that literature's profound understanding of human nature helps us become better people. Or as he says of Shakespeare later in *Preface*, "From his writings indeed a system of social duty may be selected."[10]

As we look to the Bard for guidance, Johnson cautions us not to limit ourselves to individual quotes (what we would today call soundbites). Shakespeare's "real power," he says, "is not shown in the splendor of particular passages, but by the progress of his fable, and, the tenor of his dialogue." To limit oneself to memorable passages," Johnson observed, would be to resemble one who, "when he offered his house to sale, carried a brick in his pocket as a specimen."[11]

In other words, don't quote Polonius's "to thine own self be true" advice if you want to do justice to Shakespeare's insights. Rather, watch how Polonius and Laertes and Hamlet and other characters respond to the pressures of the moment and how they talk to others. Johnson could well have Aristotle's law of probability and necessity in mind when he writes,

> Shakespeare has no heroes; his scenes are occupied only
> by men, who act and speak as the reader thinks that

he should himself have spoken or acted on the same occasion: Even where the agency is supernatural the dialogue is level with life...Shakespeare approximates the remote, and familiarizes the wonderful; the event which he represents will not happen, but if it were possible, its effects would be probably such as he has assigned; and it may be said, that he has not only shown human nature as it acts in real exigencies, but as it would be found in trials, to which it cannot be exposed.[12]

According to Johnson, by reading Shakespeare's "human sentiments in human language," a hermit could figure out what is going on in the world and a religious confessor could predict where the human passions will lead.[13] Taking advantage of Shakespeare's insights will, in turn, help us live better lives.

So far, so good. Something bad starts to happen, however, when young people read "comedies of romance." Although Johnson may echo Aristotle as he discusses Shakespeare, when it comes to novel-reading teens he sounds like Plato worrying that military auxiliaries will be corrupted by Hesiod's quarreling gods and goddesses. These pernicious novels, Johnson says in one of his *Rambler* essays, target "the young, the ignorant, and the idle, to whom they serve as lectures of conduct, and introductions into life." Because youthful minds are "unfurnished with ideas," Johnson writes, they are "easily susceptible of impressions; not fixed by principles, and therefore easily following the current of fancy; not informed by experience, and consequently open to every false suggestion and partial account."[14]

Because young people are eager to learn by imitation (as Aristotle too observed), they turn out badly when they choose bad models. Johnson notes that when an adventurous character "is leveled with the rest of the world, and acts in such scenes of the universal drama, as may be the lot of any other man," then "young spectators fix their eyes upon him with closer attention, and hope, by observing his behavior and success, to regulate their own practices, when they shall be engaged in the like part.[15]

Johnson's argument here sounds very much like the account given by psychologist Melanie Green in our upcoming psychology section on how readers are transported into fictional characters. Given these dynamics, Johnson says that parents and society's moral guardians must intervene to protect young people from dangerous content. Citing Horace's concerns about young people, he writes that "nothing indecent should be suffered to approach their eyes or ears." Parents must exercise caution in everything that is laid before young people in order "to secure them from unjust prejudices, perverse opinions, and incongruous combinations of images."[16]

Literature is particularly dangerous, Johnson believes, because it is so insidious. Sounding again like Plato, who worries about audiences getting caught up in the rhapsode Ion's Homeric performances, Johnson fears that dubious fictional characters will "take possession of the memory by a kind of violence, and produce effects almost without the intervention of the will."[17] Once again, because of fiction's power, he says that "the best examples only should be exhibited,"[18] a sentiment reminiscent of Plato banning all poetry except "hymns to the gods and praises of famous men."

Johnson, however, isn't entirely against minds being so seized—he is different from Plato in this regard—and indeed, like Horace and Sidney, he sees the delight we get from literature as potentially a powerful means to inculcate virtue. For instance, he describes Richardson's *Clarissa*, where one weeps when the virtuous heroine dies after escaping from her abductor and rapist, as "the first book in the world for the knowledge it displays of the human heart."[19] But if the right ends are to be achieved, Johnson stresses, the right tools must be employed.

The right tools do not include the bawdy *History of Tom Jones, a Foundling*. When, in 1750, Johnson wrote about novels leading young people astray, he particularly had in mind Henry Fielding's runaway sensation among the young the previous year. That Fielding gives his hard-drinking, hard-loving protagonist a good heart and a noble spirit makes the novel all the more dangerous in Johnson's eyes:

> Many writers, for the sake of following nature, so mingle good and bad qualities in their principal personages, that they are both equally conspicuous; and as we accompany them through their adventures with delight, and are led by degrees to interest ourselves in their favor, we lose the abhorrence of their faults, because they do not hinder our pleasure, or, perhaps, regard them with some kindness, for being united with so much merit."[20]

In other words, Tom's good qualities lure us into overlooking his faults so that we may think it permissible to get drunk and womanize ourselves. Johnson fears that Fielding (as we would put it today) normalizes such behavior.

Johnson is not entirely consistent here. What he says about free-spirited characters like Tom could just as easily be said about, say, Shakespeare's Falstaff. Even while Johnson acknowledges Falstaff to be "a thief and a glutton, a coward and a boaster, always ready to cheat the weak, and prey upon the poor," he admires his gaiety and wit.[21] (At least Falstaff doesn't kill anyone, he says in the character's defense.) Johnson excuses Shakespeare by noting that Falstaff can be held up as a cautionary tale, teaching the lesson that "no man is more dangerous than he that with a will to corrupt hath the power to please." But the same could be said about Tom Jones. Certainly Plato would not allow Shakespeare into his Republic.

Johnson's inconsistency may lie in the fact that novels gripped the young people of his day while Shakespeare did not. As in every era, when the young become engrossed in fictional worlds, certain of their elders become concerned.

FORCE FOR SOCIAL TRANSFORMATION

ROMANTICS AND UTILITARIANS

CONNECTING THROUGH THE POETIC IMAGINATION

> I pass, like night, from land to land;
> I have strange power of speech;
> That moment that his face I see,
> I know the man that must hear me:
> To him my tale I teach.

— **Samuel Taylor Coleridge,** *The Rime of the Ancient Mariner* (1798)[1]

IN THE 18TH AND early 19th centuries, a new vision of literature's power to impact lives arose. The creative power that an anxious Plato once compared to wild Bacchanalian dancing was suddenly celebrated. Various philosophers, social scientists, political activists, and above all poets ardently believed that the human Imagination could transform the world.

It's hard to overstate the importance placed on the Imagination at this time. "Seldom in Western culture," writes James Engell in his landmark study *The Creative Imagination: Enlightenment to Roman-*

ticism, "has one idea excited so many leading minds for such a stretch of time. It became the impelling force in artistic and intellectual life..."[2] Applied to everything from William Wordsworth's "meanest flower that blows" ("Intimations of Immortality") to Percy Shelley's "light whose smile kindles the universe" (*Adonais*), the Imagination came to be seen as the key that would unlock the secrets of creation. In his essay "Poetry and the Imagination," American Transcendentalist philosopher Ralph Waldo Emerson wrote that poetry "is the perpetual endeavor to express the spirit of the thing, to pass the brute body and search the life and reason which causes it to exist..."[3]

In these exciting times, Engell notes, "literature and art were elevated to a height and popularity they had never enjoyed and from which they have yet to descend." Poets and critics came to see themselves as having a mission, "not only to fabricate a new worldview, a reappraisal of man and nature, but even more to swaddle this thought and energy around human feelings in the forms, colors and sounds of a rediscovered natural world."[4]

Amongst the many attempts to define the Imagination, for the purposes of this study I focus on a simple description favored by the English essayist and literary critic William Hazlitt: "Imagination is another name for an interest in things out of ourselves."[5] As Hazlitt saw it, our feelings of empathy spur us to step beyond self and imagine ourselves in the place of another. If this sounds like a modest accomplishment compared to Romanticism's grand claims, recall that the Imagination's ability to take us out of ourselves and immerse us in other worlds panicked Plato and exhilarated Aristotle, sent Dante's two famous lovers Paulo and Francesca to hell and showed Sir Philip Sidney the way to heaven. I suspect the power of the Imagination to take us into perspectives not our own motivates many of America's book banning efforts, including such children's stories as Peter Parnell's *And Tango Makes Three,* Lesléa Newman's *Heather Has Two Mommies,* George M. Johnson's *All Boys Aren't Blue,* and Ben Franks's *The Boy Who Wore a Dress.*

Among the tangible effects of the Imagination, which we see in Wordsworth's "Preface to *Lyrical Ballads*," are a new appreciation of both the lower classes and nature. Wordsworth's vision helped accelerate a revolutionary perspective that had immense historical ramifications. Once literary celebrations of oppressed peoples and of the natural world took hold, reality never looked the same way again. Indeed, if we are to address today's problems of severe inequality and catastrophic climate change, we should take our cue from the Romantic era, when the problems of social injustice and industrialization came fully to the forefront. Our challenge is to imagine and bring to life other possibilities.

Wordsworth (1770–1850) and fellow poet Samuel Taylor Coleridge (1772–1834) were key figures in spreading general excitement about the Imagination, their collection *Lyrical Ballads* (1798) being arguably the most influential book of poetry in English history. As a young man, Wordsworth was an enthusiastic supporter of the French Revolution. Visiting revolutionary France in 1791, he fell in love with and had a child by Annette Vallon but was forced to return to England the following year because of political tensions between France and England. Wordsworth would become disillusioned with the Revolution during the reign of terror, and in later life he became a reactionary Tory.

That was later, however. When he returned to England in 1795, he met Coleridge, and three years later they published their collection. In his famous 1802 preface to the second edition, Wordsworth described poetry as "the spontaneous overflow of powerful feelings" and "emotion recollected in tranquility."[6] Coleridge made his own important contribution to literary theory in 1817 with his *Biographia Literaria*, where he explored different levels of the creative Imagination. The two broke up over Coleridge's opium habit but they reconciled years later. Though their poetic output ceased in later years, their early poems ensure their immortality, with Wordsworth's "I Wandered Lonely as a Cloud" heading many English "favorite poem" lists and Coleridge's "Kubla Khan" often regarded as the quintessential Romantic lyric.

In his "Preface" Wordsworth writes that in "low and rustic life, our elementary feelings co-exist in a state of greater simplicity, and, consequently, may be more accurately contemplated, and more forcibly communicated." Wordsworth believes that choosing the gritty reality of low and rustic life as one's subject matter—an unheard-of idea before this time—gets the poet closer to the essential nature of reality because the passions of rural workers "are incorporated with the beautiful and permanent forms of nature."[7] The poet thus finds deep truths in people who would have once been ignored, such as leech gatherers, farm workers, and vagrants. In "Resolution and Independence" Wordsworth says that an old leech gatherer is "like one whom I had met with in a dream; / Or like a man from some far region sent, / To give me human strength, by apt admonishment."[8] Meanwhile his character Michael, a shepherd, embodies nobility in how he goes about his work. Our hearts are torn when he loses his son to urban decadence.

Of course, Wordsworth risks sentimentalizing both peasants and nature. Romanticizing unrealistic shepherds and shepherdesses had long been characteristic of British pastoral poetry, and it didn't entirely end with the Romantics, including Wordsworth. Nevertheless, the door had been opened for poets and writers to use the Imagination to step beyond their own narrow class boundaries in ways that would have been, well, unimaginable in earlier times. Through literature authors have entered the lives of the marginalized (Walt Whitman), the urban poor (Charles Dickens), American slaves (Harriet Beecher Stowe), Dorset dairy maids (Thomas Hardy), French coalminers (Émile Zola), Nebraska pioneers (Willa Cather), Harlem residents (Langston Hughes), African American sharecroppers (Jean Toomer), African American homosexuals (James Baldwin), bankrupted Oklahoma farmers (John Steinbeck), Laguna Pueblo war veterans (Leslie Marmon Silko), transplanted Pakistanis (Hanif Kureishi), West Indian immigrants (Zadie Smith), American lesbians (Alison Bechdel), and on and on. While we can see fiction introducing readers to the poor and the outcast as early as 1554 with a rollicking Spanish novel about a street urchin (*Lazarillo de Tormes*), and while Daniel Defoe's early 18th century novels featured shipwrecked sailors, prostitutes, and thieves, the Romantic Imagination elevated lower-class figures to new levels of importance. In the process, it inspired generations of social and political idealists and changed conversations about public policy.

With these expanded horizons came new debates over how previously overlooked populations should be depicted. For instance, when *Uncle Tom's Cabin* appeared in 1852, the editor of the abolitionist newspaper *North Star* Frederick Douglass praised it for opening White eyes while his co-editor, Black nationalist Martin Delany, accused Stowe of stealing from black authors and complained that "Mrs. Stowe knows nothing about us."[9] We can see versions of these debates resurfacing today, both over the ethics of appropriating other people's stories and the question of whether the creative Imagination can bridge demographic differences. These sometimes-heated arguments show us the importance of the issue: it's no small matter how people imagine themselves and how others imagine them.

A comparable process occurs with how the Romantics handled nature. The scientific and technological advances of the 17th and 18th centuries, which allowed humans to control nature in unprecedented ways, also separated them from nature. It's easier to sentimentalize the elements when they're not starving, freezing, or otherwise killing you, and once poets had turned nature into an object of ecstatic contemplation, they attacked the technology that was subduing it. Poet William Blake, for instance, complains about "dark Satanic mills" befouling England's "green and pleasant land" (in "Jerusalem"),[10] and Wordsworth laments how the triumph of capitalism means that we are no longer in tune with nature. Declaring that by "getting and spending we lay waste our powers" and that "little we see in nature that is ours," he dreams of a closer connection such as that experienced by pre-industrial pagan society:

Great God! I'd rather be
A Pagan suckled in a creed outworn;

So might I, standing on this pleasant lea,
Have glimpses that would make me less forlorn;
Have sight of Proteus rising from the sea;
Or hear old Triton blow his wreathèd horn.[11]

The best Romantic work for exploring how the Imagination can transform humankind's relations with nature may be Samuel Taylor Coleridge's *Rime of the Ancient Mariner*. This long narrative poem also presents us with a new picture of the imagining poet: the Mariner is a prophetic figure verging on madman who serves as a conduit for visionary truths. Responding to the breach that has opened between humans and nature, he grabs public attention with oracular pronouncements and hallucinatory narratives. In the poem, we see the Mariner picking out a random young man who serves as a proxy for the audience, telling him a story that is so powerful that he "cannot choose but hear."

I examine the poem closely because it serves as a model for how the poetic Imagination can help us save the planet—and how, without that Imagination, we are lost. The Mariner begins by recalling when, as a young man, he was caught up in the excitement of the age over exploring new lands, including the Antarctic. Despite this apparent openness to new experience, however, he instead opts for domination, gratuitously killing an albatross that the sailors have befriended. Because he is at odds with the natural order, he comes to see aspects of nature as alien and loathsome:

The very deep did rot: O Christ!
That ever this should be!
Yea, slimy things did crawl with legs
Upon the slimy sea.[12]

The separation he feels also brings about a sterility of soul, so that he finds himself living a nightmarish "life-in-death." Unable to connect, he says his heart was "as dry as dust." The albatross, meanwhile, has been hung around his neck, both as a punishment by his shipmates and a sign of the internal weight he is carrying.

After much suffering, however, the Mariner is saved by a sudden epiphany. Even the foulest of Nature's creatures, he realizes, are kin. In this moment of spontaneous identification, he no longer sees the water snakes as slimy things. Instead, they have become marvelous creatures moving in shining tracks, a realization that frees him:

> Within the shadow of the ship
> I watched their rich attire:
> Blue, glossy green, and velvet black,
> They coiled and swam; and every track
> Was a flash of golden fire.
>
> O happy living things! no tongue
> Their beauty might declare:
> A spring of love gushed from my heart,
> And I blessed them unaware:
> Sure my kind saint took pity on me,
> And I blessed them unaware.
>
> The self-same moment I could pray;
> And from my neck so free
> The Albatross fell off, and sank
> Like lead into the sea.[13]

Having experienced the joy of rejoining nature, he feels compelled to share his insight with others:

> Since then, at an uncertain hour,
> That agony returns:
> And till my ghastly tale is told,
> This heart within me burns.
>
> I pass, like night, from land to land;
> I have strange power of speech;
> That moment that his face I see,
> I know the man that must hear me:
> To him my tale I teach.[14]

In the context of the poem, the Mariner knows that a callow youth intent on drinking and carousing at a wedding needs to hear him. His message has a Sunday school simplicity to it as it emphasizes the sacred connection with nature:

> Farewell, farewell! but this I tell
> To thee, thou Wedding-Guest!
> He prayeth well, who loveth well
> Both man and bird and beast.
>
> He prayeth best, who loveth best
> All things both great and small;
> For the dear God who loveth us,
> He made and loveth all.[15]

The Mariner's message could well fall flat, however, were Coleridge to convey it without story or poetry. The poet shows, through the interaction between Mariner and young man, that the poetic Imagination is needed if human behavior is to change:

He holds him with his glittering eye—
The Wedding-Guest stood still,
And listens like a three years' child:
The Mariner hath his will.

The Wedding-Guest sat on a stone:
He cannot choose but hear;
And thus spake on that ancient man,
The bright-eyed Mariner.[16]

The proof of poetry's transformative power shows up in the guest's response at the end of the poem:

The Mariner, whose eye is bright,
Whose beard with age is hoar,
Is gone: and now the Wedding-Guest
Turned from the bridegroom's door.

He went like one that hath been stunned,
And is of sense forlorn:
A sadder and a wiser man,
He rose the morrow morn.[17]

A powerful story has changed the young man's relationship with nature, getting him to see the world around him in a new light. In other words, the Imagination expands what it means to be a natural being, just as we've seen it expanding what it means to be a social being.

In the years since the Romantic movement, the rich tradition of nature literature and the exciting field of ecocriticism has moved beyond Wordsworth's picturesque daffodils and Lord Byron's soul-stirring storms to an "earth-centered approach."[18] This new type of nature writing no longer makes simple distinctions between the environment and culture, between the natural and the human. Now the focus is on their complex intersection, with contemporary authors such as Wendell Berry, Barbara Kingsolver, and Margaret Atwood using the Imagination to explore human/nature interdependence as they grapple with the challenges of human-caused climate change.

The issue is so urgent that it's worth noting some of the ways these authors use their poetry and fiction to push past our narrow confines of thought and understand the full scope of our relationship with nature. In his poem "The Sycamore," for instance, Berry shows how nature and humans are engaged in a complicated dance. Even as the tree bears the scars of humans— "Fences have been tied to it, nails driven into it / hacks and whittles cut in it"—it has a resilience "that I would be ruled by." In "the warp and bending of its long growth," Berry writes, "it has risen to a strange perfection."[19]

Atwood, meanwhile, uses her dystopian or speculative fiction to imagine our nightmarish future if current trends of environmental degradation and growing income disparity continue. Feminist sci-fi author Ursula K. Le Guin has noted that, in science fiction, the future is a metaphor for the present,[20] and Atwood draws on the power of the Imagination to capture our plight. Her compelling *Oryx and Crake* trilogy, set in a dystopian future, functions as a diagnosis and a call to action.

Given 18th and 19th century excitement about the social and environmental potential of the creative Imagination, we might ask why literature has dwindled to the peripheral social position it occupies today. While there are multiple answers, some of which we will explore in upcoming chapters, two stand out: a growing emphasis on work and the heightened importance of practicality. Many at the time regarded literature as unserious and impractical. So do many today.

Nor can we put the entire blame on rapacious capitalists desiring to maximize profits by requiring long hours and stultifying labor from their workforce. The new focus on utility extended to philosophy, and England saw the rise of Utilitarianism, a material approach to ethics and morality. While many capitalists regarded their workers as so many numbers on a financial ledger, Utilitarians had their own calculus for tabulating moral good, in which process they excluded subjective human emotion. For Enlightenment atheist Jeremy Bentham, the measure of right and wrong is not religious morality but "the greatest happiness of the greatest number." Seeking to make pleasure and pain the foundation of social policy—that which brings pleasure is "good" and that which brings pain is "bad"—Bentham and his disciple James Mill did the math to arrive at their practical policy prescriptions. In the process, they didn't differentiate between kinds of pleasure. Referring to a child's game, Bentham famously (and chillingly) declared, "Prejudice apart, the game of pushpin is of equal value with the arts and sciences of music and poetry. If the game of pushpin furnish more pleasure, it is more valuable than either."[21]

We will see, however, a third-generation Utilitarian philosopher, James's son John Stuart Mill, break with his predecessors and attempt to reconcile poetic pleasure with utility. First, however, let's look at Utilitarianism's goals, which were generally laudable. Bentham, for instance, advocated for equal rights for women, the decriminalization of homosexuality, the ending of slavery, the ending of the death penalty, the ending of physical punishment (including for children), the protection of animal rights, and the development of social safety nets for the poor and the destitute. James Mill, meanwhile, pushed hard for prison reform while his son, J.S. Mill, was one of the first members of Parliament to advocate for women's suffrage (in 1867). J.S. Mill also wrote eloquently in favor of liberty and against despotism and warned against "the tyranny of the majority."[22]

Because the spirit of Utilitarianism still pervades western democracies, J.S. Mill's effort to reconcile poetry and utility is important to our study. Indeed, this book owes a debt to the philosopher in that it too argues for literature's social usefulness. The Utilitarians, by focusing on actions that would lead to better living conditions for humankind, made immense contributions to public happiness.

Nevertheless, various authors took understandable umbrage at Utilitarianism, especially in the stringent form as practiced by Bentham and the elder Mill. For instance, Charles Dickens, the most famous novelist of the Victorian era, skewered Utilitarian themes in his novel *Hard Times* (1854), where he sets the government and factory world against the seemingly useless world of the circus. Employing suggestive and humorous names, he shows the facts-obsessed Parliament member Thomas Gradgrind and the literal-minded teacher Mr. M'Choakumchild attempting to snuff out imagination in their children, who as a result grow into self-absorbed adults. Grandgrind, meanwhile, is associated with the ruthless capitalist Bounderby although, ultimately, the men separate when Grandgrind rediscovers his heart and sees the errors of his philosophy.[23]

Nor was Dickens the first artist to critique the Utilitarian impulse. Even before Bentham and the Mills duo formulated their philosophy, intellectual currents were already moving in their direction, as we can see from satirist Jonathan Swift's attack in "A Modest Proposal" (1729). Pushing the concept of utility to its logical extreme, Swift's proposer argues with a straight face that eating Irish babies will raise the living standards of everyone else, thereby proving to be a public good.[24] The supposed author of the essay has done the Utilitarian math and arrived at a logical conclusion.

Similarly, in Swift's fanciful novel *Gulliver's Travels* (1726), his practical-to-a-fault horses (the Houyhnhnms) seek to exclude passion and the Imagination from their society. As a result, they can coldly contemplate the genocidal slaughter of the passionate Yahoos (humans). For his part Gulliver, having internalized the Houyhnhnms' rational perspective, foreshadows Nazi concentration camps by using the skin of Yahoo babies to fashion sails for his boat and Yahoo fat to stuff the cracks.[25] This is the stuff of nightmares.

Pushback against society's emphasis on practicality intensified as the 19th century progressed. English essayist Walter Pater and the Aesthetic Movement adopted French novelist Théophile Gautier's slogan "art for art's sake" (*"l'art pour l'art"*), contending that art should be judged for its aesthetic qualities rather than for its social, political, or moral values. Along with his "all art is quite useless" declaration, late Victorian writer Oscar Wilde also stated, "Art never harms itself by keeping aloof from the social problem of the day: rather by so doing, it more completely realizes for us that which we desire."[26] Although Wilde always intended for his pronouncements to spark debate rather than be taken at face value (as he himself would be the first to point out), one can once again see the conflict between literary delight and literary utility that J. S. Mill would seek to reconcile.

Mill turned to poetry during a prolonged experience of depression, caused by his realization that his highly rational philosophy was missing an essential ingredient. Asking himself whether he would experience joy if Utilitarianism were to achieve all its humanitarian goals, he could not answer yes. Instead, at this point in his intellectual trajectory he saw life as meaningless. Mill describes his existential crisis in chapter 5 of his autobiography:

> During this time I was not incapable of my usual occupations. I went on with them mechanically, by the mere force of habit.... Two lines of Coleridge, in whom alone of all writers I have found a true description of what I felt, were often in my thoughts, not at this time (for I had never read them), but in a later period of the same mental malady:

> Work without hope draws nectar in a sieve,
> And hope without an object cannot live.[27]

In his depressed state, Mill turned to poetry in a search for answers. His first choice was Lord Byron, who suffered from a depression resembling his (although for different reasons). Unfortunately, Mill discovered that Byron's poetry only articulated the condition whereas he wanted ways to address it.

Fortunately, the poetry of Wordsworth came to the rescue, providing Mills with a way forward. While, like Byron, Wordsworth suffered from feelings of emptiness, his poetry taught Mill how to use nature's beauty to reconnect with his emotions. As Mill puts it, "What made Wordsworth's poems a medicine for my state of mind, was that they expressed, not mere outward beauty, but states of feeling, and of thought colored by feeling, under the excitement of beauty. They seemed to be the very culture of the feelings, which I was in quest of. In them I seemed to draw from a source of inward joy, of sympathetic and imaginative pleasure, which could be shared in by all human beings..."[28]

Mill could see Wordsworth working through his own depression in a poem like "Intimations of Immortality." Initially, the poet experiences a disconnect with the world. Although there once was a time, he writes, when "every common sight" seemed "appareled in celestial light, / The glory and freshness of a dream," that has all changed. "The things which I have seen I now can see no more," Wordsworth cries out and falls into despair.

When he listens closely to the human heart, however, he receives intimations of a creative force beyond the self, thereby reconnecting with the emotional richness he has lost:

> Thanks to the human heart by which we live,
> Thanks to its tenderness, its joys and fears,
> To me the meanest flower that blows can give
> Thoughts that do often lie too deep for tears.[29]

J.S. Mill went through a similar journey. When he emerged from his funk, however, he did not abandon his Utilitarian philosophy. Instead, he folded human feeling and aesthetic beauty into it, basically arguing that we will work more effectively on the world *with* poetry than without it. Oh, and we'll be happier too, which after all is Utilitarianism's goal. The philosophy is not an abstract calculation but must be joined with human emotion. As he writes of his revelation in his autobiography, "The maintenance of a due balance among the faculties now seemed to be of primary importance. The cultivation of the feelings became one of the cardinal points in my ethical and philosophical creed."[30]

Reading poetry, Mill came to believe, was the best way to cultivate those feelings since it arouses feelings of benevolence. Like the Romantic critic William Hazlitt, he appreciated how poetry's empathetic imagination could develop in readers the capacity of taking on the emotions or mental states of others. As Mill saw it, this is particularly important if we are to persuade society as a whole to commit to the welfare of everyone.

Later in life, Mill was able to put his ideas into practice. When he became head of St. Andrews University in Scotland, he provided a blueprint for today's liberal arts education by requiring students to study the arts along with mathematics and science.

In his inaugural address, Mill posed the question of how to convince the businessman, "whose ambition is self-regarding," to commit to improving the lives of his fellow creatures. How, he asked, are we to get him to experience virtue "as an object in itself, and not a tax paid for leave to pursue other objects?" How are we to develop in him an "elevated tone of mind" and a recognition of "the miserable smallness of mere self?" The answer is poetry, which both instills in us lofty ideals and calms the soul. That's because poetry "brings home to us all those aspects of life which take hold of our nature on its unselfish side, and lead us to identify our joy and grief with the good or ill of the system of which we form a part."[31]

Sounding very much like Sir Philip Sidney, only with social utility rather than Christian virtue as his aim, Mill then cites beloved authors. "Who does not," he extolled the faculty and students gathered for his inauguration, "feel himself a better man after a course of Dante, or of Wordsworth, or, I will add, of Lucretius or the Georgics, or after brooding over Gray's "Elegy [Written in a Country Churchyard]" or Shelley's "Hymn to Intellectual Beauty?"[32]

One can imagine Jeremy Bentham and J.S. Mill's father spinning in their graves—or in Bentham's case, inside the glass box at University College London, where at his request his body sits embalmed—in seeing their intellectual heir citing the opening lines from "Hymn to Intellectual Beauty": "The awful shadow of some unseen Power / Floats though unseen among us."[33] Suddenly their materialist philosophy has taken a spiritual turn. J. S. Mill, however, perceives the power of the poetic Imagination to be a vital ally. Without it, people (as we have seen with Dickens) will regard Utilitarianism's humanitarian goals as dull and lifeless.

One logical outgrowth of Mill uniting literature and utility is the practice of bibliotherapy, a 20th century development that seeks practical applications for literature. Bibliotherapy took on a scientific aura during World War I when, following the Library of Congress establishing the Library War Service, librarians began distributing books to wounded veterans, noting the books they chose and recording the therapeutic effects.[34] As Theodor Wesley Koch observed when visiting hospitals on the front, "Stories are sometimes better than doctors."[35]

Since then, many have examined literature's healing potential for depression, drug use, prisoner recidivism, and other problems. A noteworthy effort is Jane Davis's "Shared Reading" movement in northern England, which each week brings together thousands to discuss great literature. Shared Reading reaches out into various public spaces, including prisons, hospitals, and retirement centers.

Although bibliotherapy is proving to have many benefits, a few cautions are in order. First, as we have discussed, different readers take away different things from a work. Koch noticed this in his visits to war hospitals, observing that "a novel with a happy ending is not necessarily a stimulant to the depressed patient, who may be tempted to contrast his own wretched state with that of the happy hero. Nor is every tragedy a depressant." Elaborating on the latter, he observed that "a serious book may prove to be better reading for a nervous patient than something in a lighter vein – he may get new courage and a firm resolve to be master of his fate and by reading of another's struggle against adverse circumstances.[36]

A book can also lose some of its effectiveness if it is prescribed rather than discovered. Many, not only Horace's young knights, bridle at attempts to impose a life lesson upon them. After all, one of literature's greatest delights is how it can surprise us with unexpected revelations, and the joy dissipates if we see ourselves being steered to a predetermined breakthrough. In such instances, Sidney's "medicine of cherries" is more medicine than cherries. We have seen how the Art for Art's Sake Movement, Oscar Wilde, W. H. Auden, William Carlos Williams, and Somerset Maugham kick back when people yoke a practical agenda to poetry.

Yet the idea of poetry having a practical impact has never gone away. True, current poets and thinkers no longer proclaim poets as "the unacknowledged legislators of the world," as second-generation Romantic poet Percy Shelley did, or predict like Victorian poet and social critic Matthew Arnold that society will one day turn from religion to poetry to instill basic moral and social values in the populace. But if today's literature advocates are less ambitious, they continue to point out ways in which poems and stories make our lives better. The creative Imagination, announced with great fanfare by Wordsworth and Coleridge two centuries ago, is still seen as having a tangible impact on our well-being.

PERCY BYSSHE SHELLEY

POETRY AS A FORCE FOR LIBERATION

> It exceeds all imagination to conceive what would have
> been the moral condition of the world if neither Dante,
> Petrarch, Boccaccio, Chaucer, Shakespeare, Calderon,
> Lord Bacon, nor Milton, had ever existed; if Raphael
> and Michael Angelo had never been born; if the He-
> brew poetry had never been translated; if a revival of the
> study of Greek literature had never taken place.

— **Percy Bysshe Shelley,** *Defence of Poetry* (1821)[1]

REPRESENTING THE GENERATION OF Romantic poets following
Wordsworth and Coleridge, Percy Bysshe Shelley (1792–1822) was
even more ambitious than his predecessors in what he thought poetry could accomplish. While the French Revolution disillusioned
Wordsworth, prompting him to turn inward, it fueled Shelley's radical
pronouncements. In *Defence of Poetry* he argues that literature does
more than influence individuals. It can change history itself.

Although Shelley drew on the literary theories of Plato, Aristotle, Horace, Sir Philip Sidney, and Samuel Johnson, they might not have recognized themselves in the new uses to which he put them. Before the Romantics, thinkers believed that literature worked within the framework of the existing social order, and they were blind to their class and gender privilege. Literature, as Plato and Aristotle saw it, was the special province of Athenian male citizens, not women or slaves, while Horace wrote for Roman citizens and Sidney for the Elizabethan upper class. In contrast, Shelley saw literature as providing a potential voice to the voiceless. The greatest works, he believed, liberate untapped human potential.

In this shift we can trace two contrasting theories on how literature impacts human lives, one progressive, the other conservative. These two strains have dominated conversations about how literature affects us ever since.

In the progressive strain, literature partners up with history to support human freedom, which is however thwarted by various oppressive systems: patriarchy thwarts the liberation of women, class society thwarts the liberation of the working class, sexual restrictions thwart LBGTQ+ rights, colonialism thwarts the liberation of the colonized, and so forth. Great literature, as Shelley sees it, is always on the side of human fulfillment. If it isn't, then it's not great literature.

In the conservative vision, by contrast, literature aids civilization as it fights a continuous battle against the forces of chaos. We're always in danger, as 17th century philosopher Thomas Hobbes saw it, of slipping back into perpetual war, where humans are subject to "continual fear and danger of violent death"—a world, in his memorable summation, where the life of man is "solitary, poor, nasty, brutish and short."[2] A figure like Samuel Johnson regarded revolutionary idealism with suspicion and embraced conservative traditions because he saw only too clearly the human capacity for sin. If he had lived to see the French Revolution, he would have focused on the reign of terror and attacked Thomas Paine's *Rights of Man*. Meanwhile Matthew Arnold, as we will see, looks to literature and the arts as a bulwark against working class barbarians, who are storming the gates of enlightened middle-class values.

Shelley's and Arnold's heirs continue to fight these culture battles. Marxists, feminists, queer theorists, post-colonialists, and others assume the mantle of progressives while figures like Allan Bloom, Harold Bloom, and other proponents of the Western canon speak for traditionalists.

Although he was born while the French Revolution was still underway, Shelley came of age during a time of conservative reaction. Once describing himself as "a lover of humanity, a democrat and an atheist," he was expelled from Oxford for writing "The Necessity of Atheism" and had to tread carefully for much of his life to avoid political prosecution for his revolutionary views. He wrote "Song: To the Men of England" in support of the working class and the verse drama *Hellas* in support of the 1821 Greek revolution. His free-spirited personal life came up against traditional family values, leading him and family members into various messy tangles and heartbreak. Ultimately he would marry Mary Godwin, daughter of Mary Wollstonecraft (author of *A Vindication of the Rights of Women*), who would go on write the ur-sci-fi novel *Frankenstein* and the dystopian *Last Man*. Percy Shelley himself wrote some of Romanticism's great poems, including "Ozymandias," "Ode to the West Wind," "To a Skylark," and *Adonais*.

Shelley's *Defence of Poetry* was triggered by his friend Thomas Peacock, who in "The Four Ages of Poetry" had light-heartedly argued that poetry was in decline, bypassed by new scientific and technological breakthroughs. Shelley found Peacock's reasoning too close to the pragmatic views of many of their countrymen, who, as noted in the last chapter, attached more importance to making money than cultivating artistic sensibilities. Shelley's defense therefore went far beyond an immediate response to Peacock. Examining poetry's historical impact, it argued that the arts made possible the scientific breakthroughs responsible for Great Britain's prosperity.

Although a radical, Shelley doesn't entirely disagree with conservatives about literature's civilizing role. For instance, he sounds very much like Sidney when he talks about the salutary effect of reading Homer:

> Homer embodied the ideal perfection of his age in human character; nor can we doubt that those who read his verses were awakened to an ambition of becoming like to Achilles, Hector, and Ulysses: the truth and beauty of friendship, patriotism, and persevering devotion to an object, were unveiled to the depths in these immortal creations: the sentiments of the auditors must have been refined and enlarged by a sympathy with such great and lovely impersonations, until from admiring they imitated, and from imitation they identified themselves with the objects of their admiration.[3]

Shelley shows that the process works with Aeschylus and Sophocles as well. When immersed in these works, he writes, audiences sensed, and still sense, unplumbed depths. As we watch Orestes, Oedipus, Antigone, and others command the stage, we go beyond the "tumult of familiar life" and find ourselves in touch with all that we love, admire, and "would become":

> The imagination is enlarged by a sympathy with pains and passions so mighty, that they distend in their conception the capacity of that by which they are conceived; the good affections are strengthened by pity, indignation, terror, and sorrow; and an exalted calm is prolonged from the satiety of this high exercise of them into the tumult of familiar life.... In a drama of the highest order there is little food for censure or hatred; it teaches rather self-knowledge and self-respect.[4]

As Shelley sees it, when literature experiences a glory moment—as in fifth-century Athens, when civilization attained "moral and intellectual greatness"—it captures the essence of what it means to be human. This includes all the grandeur that is possible.

Having celebrated how the ancients depict royalty, however, Shelley then proceeds to expand the franchise. As he sees it, history is about *all* humans becoming all that they can be, not just the upper-class. History's two most momentous developments, in Shelley's view, have been "the abolition of personal and domestic slavery, and the emancipation of women."[5]

If (in Shelley's famous formulation) poets are "the unacknowledged legislators of the world," it's because they help us imagine an all-inclusive and egalitarian social order. As Shelley puts it, the poet can pierce the veil of historical prejudice, seeing beyond oppression to the true relations between things. The poet "not only beholds intensely the present as it is, and discovers those laws according to which present things ought to be ordered, but he beholds the future in the present, and his thoughts are the germs of the flower and the fruit of latest time."[6]

Since literature grasps the underlying dynamics of history, Shelley thinks, it can provide a guide for activists involved in political and social work. Their challenge is to create institutions and pass laws that will fulfill literature's vision.

We should note that the ancient Athenians, despite their insightful poets, couldn't pull this off. After all, they were a patriarchal slave-owning society whose notion of perfectibility didn't extend beyond the land-owning men who ran things. Shelley is playing a long game, however, and says that it can take millennia for social systems to catch up with great literature's insights. In his view (to borrow Martin Luther King Jr.'s phrase), the arc of history bends inexorably towards justice, even though the bending may take some time. Poets are an integral part of that process.

Occasionally history does not bend slowly but advances dramatically, as it did with the American and French revolutions. At such times, poetry has a more immediate impact. On the other hand, history sometimes regresses into dark times. In those instances, poetry functions as a repository of dreams of a freer world.

Writing in the wake of history-bending revolutions, Shelley is most interested in history's breakthrough moments. Expanding his definition of "poet" to include certain historians, philosophers, religious visionaries, and scientists, he finds his egalitarian beliefs at the core of Plato, Herodotus, Plutarch, Jesus, Livy, Sir Francis Bacon, and others he enumerates.

Shelley's inclusion of Plato is unexpected and would have startled that philosopher given his suspicion of democratic rule and his insistence on social hierarchy. Furthermore, Shelley's Platonic-sounding contention that "a Poet participates in the eternal, the infinite, and the one" has the effect of replacing Plato's philosopher kings with poets, whom Plato regarded as liars. Furthermore, as if to add insult to injury, Shelley classifies Plato *himself* as a poet. Re-envisioning *The Republic* so that it sounds like a Marxist text, the poet applauds Plato's vision of all humans working together for the common good, with each contributing his or her special talents.

After Plato, Shelley turns his attention to Jesus. Shelley may have been an atheist, but he likes how Jesus called for us to love all humankind, not just people like us. Shelley writes that "the great secret of morals is love; or a going out of our nature, and an identification of ourselves with the beautiful which exists in thought, action, or person, not our own." Jesus opened the way for people to be "greatly good" since, to be so, they "must imagine intensely and comprehensively," putting themselves "in the place of another and of many others." It is for humankind as it was for Jesus: "The pains and pleasure of [the] species must become [their] own."[7]

We have seen John Stuart Mill, a Shelley fan, make a similar argument. In an upcoming chapter, contemporary philosopher Martha Nussbaum too will argue that a literary education produces good citizens, enabling them to understand people unlike themselves. Shelley believed that literature's mind-expanding powers helped change the way the world viewed women, raising them from household drudges to figures of respect. Thus Chrétien de Troyes's Camelot stories, Petrarch's love sonnets, and Dante's *Divine Comedy* (with the vision of Beatrice as a spiritual guide) played a vital role in gender progress:

> Love became a religion, the idols of whose worship were ever present. It was as if the statues of Apollo and the Muses had been endowed with life and motion, and had walked forth among their worshippers; so that earth became peopled with the inhabitants of a diviner world. The familiar appearance and proceedings of life became wonderful and heavenly, and a paradise was created as out of the wrecks of Eden. And as this creation itself is poetry, so its creators were poets; and language was the instrument of their art.[8]

What, one might ask, are we to make of the fact that neither Plato's *Republic* nor medieval love poetry has a particularly egalitarian view of women? In reply, Shelley would say that we must distinguish between poetry's core and its external trappings. He acknowledges that every epoch, "under names more or less specious, has deified its peculiar errors." He adds, however, that despite an author being mired in these peculiar errors—say, sexism or classism—the author's *creation* can break free of them. That's because the creation is in touch with the deepest currents of history, which point toward equality. The great poets may need to clothe their poetry in the customs and values of their time, but Shelley says that we are able in their works to see through these outer vestments to the truth underneath:

> But a poet considers the vices of his contemporaries as the temporary dress in which his creations must be arrayed, and which cover without concealing the eternal proportions of their beauty. An epic or dramatic

personage is understood to wear them around his soul, as he may the ancient armor or the modern uniform around his body; whilst it is easy to conceive a dress more graceful than either. The beauty of the internal nature cannot be so far concealed by its accidental vesture, but that the spirit of its form shall communicate itself to the very disguise, and indicate the shape it hides from the manner in which it is worn. A majestic form and graceful motions will express themselves through the most barbarous and tasteless costume.[9]

Because distinguishing between a work's topical or local concerns and its core meaning is so important—some activists dismiss certain great works for politically incorrect depictions of this or that demographic—it's worth delving into examples. Since Shelley believes the poetry of ancient Greece glimpses "the principle of equality," despite the culture's reliance on slavery and female subjugation, perhaps Shelley would point to how Homer creates three-dimensional portraits of slaves in *The Odyssey* (the pig keeper Eumaeus and Odysseus's nurse Eurycleia). After reading the work, it's difficult to see them simply as beasts of burden.

Likewise, it's harder to see women as inferiors after watching the dominating figures of Aeschylus's Clytemnestra, Sophocles's Antigone, and Euripides's Medea. At such moments, Greek audiences saw "the future in the present" and found their imaginations "enlarged by a sympathy with pains and passions so mighty, that they distend[ed] in their conception the capacity of that by which they are conceived."

For another instance of literature getting a jump on history, consider the example I mentioned in the introduction. Shakespeare's *Twelfth Night, or What You Will* (1601-02) is a remarkable exploration of gender identity, featuring a man experimenting with behavior typically regarded as female, two women experimenting with behavior typically regarded as male, and characters attracted to people of their own sex. We are only now, in the 21st century, beginning to affirm and to officially legitimate these multiple identities.

Since 17th century England had laws against such behavior, Shakespeare couldn't explore these identities directly. His "temporary dress" or "accidental vesture," therefore, was a familiar comedy of misunderstanding. Following the conventions of the genre, the author arranges an ending where Orsino, Olivia and Viola all return to their socially sanctioned gender identities and pair up accordingly: Viola sheds her male costume and marries Orsino while Olivia gets Viola's twin, who is indistinguishable from her other than being a man. If we look closely, however, we can see subtle signs that Shakespeare is not altogether satisfied with this ending: Orsino wants Viola to wear her male garb a little longer; Antonio, who clearly loves Sebastian, looks on heartbroken from the sidelines; and Olivia goes silent as she finds herself married to a stranger. In the epilogue we see the fool lamenting the end of childhood dreaming and the return to social reality, characterized by "the wind and the rain."

If Shakespeare's play outwardly concludes with a conventional "happily ever after" ending, perhaps it was because censorship demanded it or because his audiences weren't yet ready for a radical alternative. "Few poets of the highest class have chosen to exhibit the beauty of their conceptions in its naked truth and splendor," Shelley writes, before wondering "whether the alloy of costume, habit, etc., be not necessary to temper this planetary music for mortal ears."[10] Planetary music in this case would be a same sex couple allowed to express their love freely and openly, which Shakespeare has tempered into an acceptable comedy, with same sex relationships, sensitive men, and assertive women played for laughs. It's altogether possible that he himself couldn't grasp the beauty of his conception in all "its naked truth and splendor." After all, Shakespeare was a 17th century man. The work may have seen further than he himself could.

That's because, Shelley goes on to say, great works of literature are "infinite," with their "inmost naked beauty" hidden by countless veils, which can only be removed gradually. He also compares poetry to an acorn that contains a magnificent oak and a hidden water source that produces an overflowing fountain:

> All high poetry is infinite; it is as the first acorn, which contained all oaks potentially. Veil after veil may be undrawn, and the inmost naked beauty of the meaning never exposed. A great poem is a fountain forever overflowing with the waters of wisdom and delight; and after one person and one age has exhausted all its divine effluence which their peculiar relations enable them to share, another and yet another succeeds, and new relations are ever developed, the source of an unforeseen and an unconceived delight.[11]

Audiences, then, learn from a great work what they are capable of learning at that moment in time, even as much of its meaning eludes them. They cannot fully grasp the acorn's oak potential or all the "divine effluence" that the fountain will produce.

So what effect does great literature have on human behavior? It sets our creative Imagination in motion. Once poetry has gotten us to see new human possibilities and "new relations," the seed has been planted for us to make them a social reality. Indeed, we have been doing so throughout history, which is why, Shelley believes, history has progressed, albeit slowly and with occasional backsliding. Shelley agrees with Sidney that the end of poetry is "virtuous action," but he has expanded such action to include liberating the downtrodden by giving them equal rights. Poetry helps us imagine a world that will honor the full humanity of all.

The more literature we consume, the more we will demand of ourselves and of the world. Reading poetry, Shelley says, should be like regular gym workouts since it "strengthens the faculty which is the organ of the moral nature of man, in the same manner as exercise strengthens a limb." Both conservatives like Matthew Arnold and progressives like Bertolt Brecht will agree that poetry strengthens our moral natures.

While he himself is progressive in his vision of literature's liberatory potential, however, Shelley finds himself at odds with certain activists regarding art and social change. He says that authors who use their works to advance political ends, even if those ends are worthy, sell literature short. That's because they choose the local over the universal.

Artists' first obligation must be to truth, he declares. Only by making the universal value of truth their focus do they advance humanity's higher purpose. Therefore a poet does "ill" who embodies in his creations "his own conceptions of right and wrong, which are usually those of his place and time." To be truly great, Shelley contends, poets must necessarily give up their participation in causes—at least as far as their artistic creations are concerned—because to affect a "moral aim" diminishes the work. Shelley mentions Euripides, Lucan, Tasso and Spenser who, though great, he considers to be second tier because they "frequently affected a moral aim." The more they proselytized, he believes, the more their poetry suffered.[12]

Shelley even criticizes certain Enlightenment figures of his own period who forwarded political goals he agreed with. He denigrates Voltaire, who worked tirelessly for social justice, as a "mere reasoner." While such authors deserve our gratitude, Shelley says, they haven't changed history. If they had never lived, he opines, perhaps "[a] little more nonsense would have been talked for a century or two; and perhaps a few more men, women, and children burnt as heretics. We might not at this moment have been congratulating each other on the abolition of the Inquisition in Spain." Worthy achievements though these might be, that would be the extent of our "moral and intellectual improvement."[13]

By way of contrast, Shelley lists those who have changed "the moral condition of the world," a list that includes Dante, Petrarch, Boccaccio, Chaucer, Shakespeare, Calderon, Lord Bacon, Milton, the Hebrew Bible, and ancient Greek literature (Homer, Aeschylus, and Sophocles). Responding to Thomas Peacock's (perhaps joking) contention that "the progress of useful art and science" has made poetry outdated, Shelley responds that analytical reason alone could never have systematically addressed society's flaws. Voltaire, he says, would not have fought for justice if the "excitements" of these truly great poets who came before had not awakened the human mind.

In seeking to make his point in dramatic fashion, Shelley sounds rather callous. After all, if you're a non-Catholic under attack by the Spanish Inquisition, you might be grateful for *Candide's* satiric attack on religious intolerance. If, to use Sir Philip Sidney's formulation in praise of satire, Voltaire can shame villains into better behavior, how can Shelley dismiss this? At the very least, Voltaire supports those who fight villainy.

It's worth questioning Shelley's contention that "the moral condition of the world" would be far worse without the great authors he mentions. After all, Shakespeare and Milton did not themselves end slavery or liberate women. It took actual legislators, not unacknowledged legislators, to do that. Maybe Shakespeare's expansive vision of human beings would one day lead to liberté, égalité, and fraternité, but during the French Revolution legislators were more apt to quote Voltaire than the Bard. Shelley's need to rank authors, which we will see also in his admirer Harold Bloom, sometimes leads him to overlook tangible accomplishments.

He certainly does so when it comes to comedy. Shelley is a harsh critic, especially of the bawdy comedies of Great Britain's Restoration period. The plays of William Wycherley, George Farquhar, Aphra Behn, and William Congreve blaspheme (so he believes) "the divine beauty of life."

As he is with Voltaire, I think Shelley is being unfair. True, the Restoration-era playwrights don't focus on the true and the good. Their satire of social corruption, however, is also important. Mixing dazzling wit with sexual double-entendres, they challenge both the stifling conventions and the anarchic desires of their age, seeking balance.

Shelley here could take a page out of Sir Philip Sidney, who believes that a variety of genres can guide us to a life of virtue. (We'll see critic

Wayne Booth recommending that we sample a wide range of literature for best effect.) Sidney likes how comedy represents the "common errors of life" in "the most ridiculous and scornful sort that may be; so as it is impossible that any beholder can be content to be such a one." Sidney would also recognize the purpose of Voltaire's satire, which (according to his reasoning) deters us from misbehaving by shaming villainy and laughing at folly. By focusing so relentlessly on the ideal, Percy Shelley underrates these more earthy art forms. He would benefit from the ancient Greek comedy *The Clouds,* where Aristophanes satirizes airy Socrates, another man searching for the true and the good.

Whether or not we agree with all of Shelley's tastes, however, we must credit him for showing how literature can transform the world. The two major strains of thought that have resulted—progressives who see great literature advancing human freedom and conservatives who see it preserving traditional values—can both look back to Shelley as the thinker who asserted that literature has significant political and historical consequences.

KARL MARX AND FRIEDRICH ENGELS

LITERATURE AS A PORTRAYAL OF REAL CONDITIONS

I have learned more [from Balzac] than from all the
professional historians, economists, and statisticians
put together.

— **Friedrich Engels**, "Letter to Margaret Harkness"
(1888)[1]

NINETEENTH CENTURY POLITICAL THEORISTS Karl Marx and
Friedrich Engels, while very much interested in making our lives better, don't have a lot to say about how literature can help. Literature
played a role in shaping their ideas, however, and what little they did
say has proved influential. Marxist thought has helped many left-lean-
ing artists and thinkers discover ways that literature advances human
liberation.

Had things turned out differently, it's possible that Marx would
have written more about literature himself. At 17, he was a brilliant
student who wanted to study literature in college. Instead, his father

made him study law, which he finessed into law and philosophy. He did write some poetry and short fiction, along with a play, before shifting over to philosophy, where he focused on the work of Georg Wilhelm Friedrich Hegel. After leaving the university, he became a journalist and gave his life over to social causes.

Meeting fellow journalist Friedrich Engels was a major turning point in Marx's life. Engels, the son of a Lancashire textiles factory owner, had researched the abysmal living conditions of mill hands, producing the landmark study *The Condition of the Working Class in England* (1844). Marx by this time had become disenchanted with Hegel's idealism, which believes that ideas determine the course of history, and he turned his attention to economics and worker activism. When revolutions broke out all over Europe in 1848, Marx and Engels co-authored *The Communist Manifesto,* a polemical work designed to transform working class dissatisfaction into a mass movement.

As Marx and Engels saw it, society will gradually become more egalitarian, meaning that the proletariat (the working class) will one day replace the bourgeoisie (the middle class), just as the bourgeoisie had replaced the landed gentry and aristocracy. Marx and Engels desired a final communal state where each individual, free of worrying about physical needs, can develop his or her strengths to the fullest. Marx analyzed the workings of capitalism in his masterpiece, *Capital* (1867). Engels, meanwhile, authored several noteworthy works, most notably *The Origin of Family, Private Property, and the State* (1884).

According to his daughter Elaine, Marx admired Shelley, whom he considered as "one of the advanced guard of Socialism."[2] Indeed, there are moments when Marx sounds Shelleyan, such as when he writes in an 1843 letter, "[The] world has long dreamt of that of which it had only to have a clear idea to possess it."[3] If poets, as Shelley believes, have the clearest idea of the world's dreaming and do their best to communicate it to the rest of us, then they are indeed "unacknowledged legislators." They will become acknowledged legislators when the world finally sees what they see and moves to possess it.

Marx was to break with such idealism, however. When people say he stood Hegel "on his head," it's because he eventually came to see economic forces as influencing consciousness, not the other way around. Facts on the ground mean more than clear ideas. After all, how useful is such an idea when the people in charge won't give up their power?

Although Marx downplayed consciousness and literature, however, he still thought that they have a role to play in shaping history. To understand how, we must look at the relationship between what Marx and Engels call "the ideological superstructure" and "the economic base." The superstructure involves "ideas, concepts and consciousness"—the mental structures that influence how we see ourselves—while the base concerns "the material needs and realities of people." Perhaps think of it as the relationship of the mind to the body:

> The production of ideas, concepts and consciousness is first of all directly interwoven with the material intercourse of man, the language of real life. Conceiving, thinking, the spiritual intercourse of men, appear here as the direct efflux of men's material behavior...[4]

This Marx-Engels passage has led to many debates about which is more important, culture or material life ("literature or life" for our purposes). At first glance, it appears that Marx and Engels consider material life to be primary. "We do not proceed from what men say, imagine, conceive," they write, but rather "from the really active man." Seemingly breaking definitively with Hegel, they resoundingly conclude, "Life is not determined by consciousness but consciousness by life."[5]

But while this may seem to once and for all relegate consciousness (along with the literature that is bound up in it) to the second tier, Marx and Engels's views are actually more complicated. In pushing against Hegel's contention that consciousness determines history, they may overstate the case, going to the other extreme. Their use of the word "interwoven," I think, gives us a better sense of the actual relationship.

While literature can't act independently from the material conditions on the ground, it can influence how people see themselves. And since economic conditions must manifest themselves through people, this matters. Members of the entrepreneurial middle class, for instance, may not have fully grasped their potential until they read *Robinson Crusoe*. Defoe's 1719 novel cast them as heroic protagonists rebelling against a stagnant past to forge an exciting future.

That's how Marx and Engels regarded Defoe's novel. In it, a young man disobeys his father, who wants him to stay home and pursue a safe "middle way." Although Crusoe periodically feels guilty for his disobedience, something within him—he can't put his finger on exactly what—propels him to engage in risky ventures. Ultimately he creates a new economic and social world that far surpasses anything that his father could envision.[6] The story so engaged readers that *Robinson Crusoe* was the world's most popular novel for 200 years.

Marx could have pointed out that *Robinson Crusoe* was popular because it reflected the historical shift from the land-owning gentry to the mercantile and industrial middle class. The economic base, in other words, influenced people's reading habits (ideological superstructure). But Defoe did more than reflect material conditions. By giving entrepreneurs an identity, the novel actually helped propel historical forces forward. *Robinson Crusoe* put steel in their spines and confidence in their decision making.

Defoe was not the only novel changing history. In his seminal work *The Rise of the Novel*, scholar Ian Watt talks about how 18th century novels in general reinforced new notions of individualism that were part of the new economic order. Each time readers immersed themselves in the story of Crusoe or Jean-Jacques Rousseau's Julie or Goethe's Young Werther or Jane Austen's Elizabeth Bennet, they were invited to prioritize the thoughts, feelings, and actions of individuals over age-old traditions. Watt points out how the break is particularly striking in *Crusoe:*

Crusoe's island gives him the complete *laissez-faire* which economic man needs to realize his aims. At home market conditions, taxation and problems of the labor supply make it impossible for the individual to control every aspect of production, distribution and exchange. The conclusion is obvious. Follow the call of the wide-open places, discover an island that is desert only because it is barren of owners or competitors, and there build your personal Empire with the help of a Man Friday who needs no wages and makes it much easier to support the white man's burden.[7]

Such are the unrealistic but nevertheless galvanizing dreams of middle-class businessmen.

Marx was not entirely opposed to the middle class embracing this vision. In his dialectical view of history, the heroes of one era are the villains of the next. Although the capitalists who replaced the gentry would eventually become oppressors in their turn, they were initially heroes because they represented a new prosperity where, theoretically, the needs of all could be met. They were villains, however, because they ruthlessly exploited workers and refused to share the new wealth. Marx and Engels wanted workers to seize the factories and pay themselves directly.

So what are authors to do if their work serves progress at one point in history but oppression at another? Marx and Engels have a simple answer: it's not their concern. The artist's job is to tell the truth, not engage in politics. Authors are to be reality describers, not activists.

In this, Marx and Engels share with Aristotle, Samuel Johnson, and Shelley the belief that literature provides us access to larger human truths. Johnson, as we have seen, believed that "much instruction" can be gleaned from Shakespeare's deep understanding of human nature, while Shelley found evidence of humanity's yearning for freedom in literature's masterworks. For their part, Marx and Engels believe that novelists give us an even deeper understanding of the workings of society than economists, sociologists, and political scientists. "Scientific socialism"—which is to say, socialism based on social science, not on utopian dreaming—benefits from literature's insights.

A social and economic analysis of *Robinson Crusoe*, for instance, shows the dark side of capitalism as well as its revolutionary side. Even as the novel inspired entrepreneurs, for instance, it also dramatically shows us their self-absorption and their readiness to use other people as instruments of profit. Crusoe narcissistically thinks that God is using earthquakes to send him special messages, and he doesn't hesitate to sell a Muslim friend into slavery when it suits his purposes. His shipwreck, meanwhile, occurs when he is traveling to Africa to acquire slaves, and he steals the labor and the autonomy of the indigenous man he names "Friday."

If we reflect upon *Robinson Crusoe,* we recognize in it both the exciting energy of new capitalist entrepreneurs and the callous way that they sacrificed human beings. Because dynamic entrepreneurship still excites the imagination of many, progressive activists ignore it at their peril.

To cite another literary example, Marx and Engels praised the French novelist Honoré de Balzac, even though he had aristocratic and royalist sympathies. Engels even claimed to have learned more about French society and its history from him than from any historian or social scientist. Marx too admired Balzac and once planned to write a critical study of the author after his studies of economics were complete. Engels noted that, while Balzac was a royalist who lamented the decline of the aristocracy, he satirized aristocrats mercilessly. Balzac also spoke with "undisguised admiration" of the upcoming class of republicans, even though they were his "bitterest antagonists":

> That Balzac thus was compelled to go against his own class sympathies and political prejudices, that he saw the necessity of the downfall of his favorite nobles, and

described them as people deserving no better fate; and that he saw the real men of the future where, for the time being, they alone were to be found—that I consider one of the greatest triumphs of Realism, and one of the grandest features in old Balzac.[8]

If literary masterpieces like *Robinson Crusoe* and Balzac's *Comédie Humaine* novels are objective mirrors that provide political and economic theorists with invaluable information, then works that sacrifice truth to political agendas are unhelpful. Engels made this clear when he criticized the rough draft of an 1885 novel about salt miners. In his letter to the hopeful author, Engels began by pointing out that she appears chiefly interested in proclaiming her socialist convictions. While he is gentle—"You obviously felt a desire to take a public stand in your book, to testify to your convictions before the entire world"—he wants her to stop preaching: "This has now been done; it is a stage you have passed through and need not repeat in this form."[9]

Engels reassures the author he is not against taking a social stand per se. Some of the great authors have been partisan, a qualification that Shelley too should have made. "I am by no means opposed to partisan poetry as such," he qualifies, noting that "Aeschylus, the father of tragedy, and Aristophanes, the father of comedy, were highly partisan poets, Dante and Cervantes were so no less, and the best thing that can be said about Schiller's *Kabale und Liebe* [*Intrigue and Love*] is that it represents the first German political problem drama. The modern Russians and Norwegians, who produce excellent novels, all write with a purpose."[10]

The danger comes when partisanship clouds one's vision—when, in the words of D. H. Lawrence, "the novelist puts his thumb on the scale, to pull down the balance to his own predilection."[11] At that point, the author has surrendered literature's greatest strength, which is the ability to provide "a faithful portrayal of real conditions."

Engels would have endorsed 20th century novelist Iris Murdoch when she makes a similar point, distinguishing between the writer as citizen and the writer as artist. "A citizen has a duty to society, and a writer might sometimes feel he ought to write persuasive newspaper articles or pamphlets," she says, "but this would be a different activity. The artist's duty is to art, to truth-telling in his own medium, the writer's duty is to produce the best literary work of which he is capable, and he must find out how this can be done."[12]

If a socialist problem novel tells the truth, Engels says, then it will have done its job. Revealing to readers the grim facts about the world will undermine the optimism of the bourgeoisie and shake its aura of invincibility. The truth will make us free.

Given all that has happened since Marx and Engels wrote, the faith that a great novel will undermine middle class power sounds overly optimistic, if not downright naïve. Perhaps because Balzac opened Engels's eyes, the theorist assumed others would be similarly enlightened. By the end of his life, however, Engels had to acknowledge that there were countervailing forces that could cloud workers' minds. In a letter written two years before he died, Engels noted that he and Marx had underestimated the extent to which the working class would internalize the ideology of the ruling class, developing a "false consciousness."[13] Even though the workers' special relationship to the production of goods ought to give them a clear vision of what must happen for their needs to be honored, those in power can nevertheless manipulate the institutions of culture (the media, educational and religious institutions) to distract or otherwise mislead them. In the chapters on Bertolt Brecht and the Marx-influenced Frankfurt School, we will see how literature too can be used to mislead.

Italian Marxist Antonio Gramsci, a labor organizer, thought about these issues when locked up in Mussolini's prisons in the 1930s. As Gramsci sees it, if the middle class can use culture to get workers to consent to their own exploitation, then it doesn't need armies or the police to stay in power. All it need do is persuade the working class that the existing power relations are (to use Gramsci's words) "just the way things are" and "common sense."[14]

Romantic poet William Blake, a shrewd observer of the psychology of oppression, recognized this process. In his 1794 poem "London," for instance, he captures how the poor and oppressed forge mental shackles for themselves. Although the numbers are on their side, because they wear "mind-forg'd manacles" they do not rise up. The poet observes these "marks of weakness, marks of woe":

> I wander thro' each charter'd street,
> Near where the charter'd Thames does flow.
> And mark in every face I meet
> Marks of weakness, marks of woe.
>
> In every cry of every Man,
> In every Infant's cry of fear,
> In every voice: in every ban,
> The mind-forg'd manacles I hear.[15]

When the reigning power structure can convince people to shackle themselves, we see the successful results of what Harvard political scientist Joseph Nye calls "soft power."[16]

To counteract such soft yet still coercive power, Gramsci wanted economic workers and cultural workers (including poets) to work together to penetrate what he called "bourgeois cultural hegemony"—his name for false consciousness—and see where their *real* interests lie. Poets, philosophers, social scientists, and others can't do it alone because, without connection to the experience of actual working conditions, they are prone to airy abstractions. Likewise, without collaborating with intellectuals and artists, manual workers will fall prey to ruling class manipulation. Together, however, the two groups can challenge existing power relations. Gramsci is particularly hopeful about what he calls "organic intellectuals," who have their feet in both worlds. These would include novelists and poets from working class origins.[17]

While Gramsci himself is chiefly interested in how political philosophy can break the hold of "common sense" on worker minds, we will be examining various other activist intellectuals who explore how poetry, fiction and drama can expose and dismantle racism, classism, and sexism. If Sir Philip Sidney is right that literature effectively teaches virtue, then maybe literature also has the power to break the hold of oppressors over our minds.

Although Marx and Engels underestimated the power of bourgeois brainwashing ("cultural hegemony"), that doesn't mean their insistence on literary truth should be abandoned. To be sure, some on the left have advocated for working class propaganda to counteract ruling class propaganda. These people draw fire, however, from late 20th century Marxists like Britain's Terry Eagleton and America's Frederic Jameson, who deride as "vulgar Marxists" those who, like Engels's correspondent, want literature to function as a call to arms, as well as those who apply socialist litmus tests to authors.[18] Pointing out Marx and Engels's admiration for the monarchist Balzac, they reassert that there is more value in understanding the truth of our historical situation than in canceling reactionary writers.

To make the point, Eagleton even defends British novelist Joseph Conrad for the way he accurately depicts capitalism's late 19th crisis in such works as *Heart of Darkness* (1901). As we will see in the chapters on W.E.B. Du Bois and post-colonialism, *Heart of Darkness* has been attacked for its racist depictions of Africans, making Eagleton's defense of the novella surprising. But Eagleton points out that *Heart of Darkness* has value because it shows how capitalism has reached a dead end. Precisely because Conrad is a reactionary, Eagleton says, he sees the situation clearly.[19]

In other words, if you want to understand the crisis of capitalism, *Heart of Darkness* is a good book to study. Just don't read it to understand Africa. In it, Kurtz, the novella's monstrous anti-hero, represents Europe's failure to reconcile enlightened Christianity with unregulated capitalism. He has gone into the jungle with the dual purpose of civilizing the natives and making his fortune but, in the process, realizes he can't have both. As a result, he loses his idealism and descends into barbarism.

By the end, Kurtz is displaying the heads of his enemies on spikes while coupling up with a native queen. Greed and lust, as the narrator Marlow sees it, expose Christian civilization's values as hollow. Marlow himself, however, is at a loss when it comes to positive alternatives. He finds himself admiring Kurtz because at least Kurtz strives for big things—unlike Marlow, who doesn't believe in anything. In his grudging admiration, Marlow downplays the fact that Kurtz has become so corrupt that he wants to "exterminate the brutes." Marlow represents those who still want to believe in Western superiority but can't muster up any enthusiasm for it.

Conrad wasn't the only conservative writer of his era to critique capitalism. Rather than flagellate such writers for their politics, Eagleton says, activists who want a better world should build upon their insights:

> Whether those insights are in political terms "progressive" or "reactionary" (Conrad's are certainly the latter) is not the point—any more than it is to the point that most of the agreed major writers of the twentieth century—Yeats, Eliot, Pound, Lawrence—are political conservatives who each had truck with fascism. Marxist criticism, rather than apologizing for the fact, explains it—sees that, in the absence of genuinely revolutionary art, only a radical conservatism, hostile like Marxism to the withered values of liberal bourgeois society, could produce the most significant literature.[20]

Given Engels's own preference for truthful literature over politically correct literature, he would surely have criticized 20th century socialist realism, the party line art that arose in Stalin's Soviet Union and Mao's China. He and Marx would also have been appalled at the persecution of authors whose work didn't conform to orthodox dogma. When Stalin executed writers or imprisoned them in the Gulag, Marx and Engels would have pointed out that he was shutting himself off from the truths that artists could teach the Soviet Union about itself. Listen to literature or you will become stagnant.

Perhaps we have here another way to distinguish between great and lesser literature: one tells the truth, the other satisfies formulaic expectations. In either case, however, Marxists like Eagleton use literary analysis in the service of class struggle, figuring that studying literary works helps us understand the energies and tendencies of history. Just as (according to Samuel Johnson) "a system of social duty may be selected" from Shakespeare's plays, so scientific socialism can build upon literature's truth telling.

Marx and Engels, of course, would never say that knowing the truth is enough. Consciousness does not determine life. So while literature can expose the physical and mental chains that hold humanity back, it is up to the working class to usher in a new world—or to apply Gramsci's formulation, the world needs the working class to collaborate with cultural workers, including artists and philosophers.

In his essay "Contribution to the Critique of Hegel's *Philosophy of Right*," Marx provides us with a magnificent statement about how manual workers and cultural workers can collaborate. "Criticism has plucked the imaginary flowers on the chain," he writes, "not in order that man shall continue to bear that chain without fantasy or consolation, but so that he shall throw off the chain and pluck the living flower."[21] Literature helps us see the chain underneath the flowers and that revelation, while not enough in itself, is integral to throwing off the chain and ushering in a truly egalitarian society.

Although Marx and Engels saw artists as providing only the brain power for revolution, not the muscle power, not all activists have agreed. As we shall see, Bertolt Brecht especially breaks down the demarcation between poet and activist. He believed his own plays, which he labeled "epic theater," could function as revolution workshops, opening workers' minds to capitalist manipulation and inspiring them to throw off their chains.

Sigmund Freud and Carl Jung

Literature as a Road to Self-Mastery

Our actual enjoyment of an imaginative work proceeds
from a liberation of tensions in our minds.

— **Sigmund Freud,** "Creative Writers and
Daydreaming" (1908)[1]

KARL MARX AND SIGMUND Freud are sometimes paired in the history of thought because Marx sees invisible forces moving the course of history while Freud sees them moving the lives of individuals. If literature taps into these foundational currents, then surely it can change lives. But where literary Marxists see literature making lives better collectively in groups, literary Freudians and Jungians see it doing so one person at a time.

Freud (1856–1939), the founder of psychoanalysis, was an avid fan of literature, especially the plays of Shakespeare, Aeschylus, Sophocles, and Euripides. After receiving medical training at the University of Vienna and the Vienna General Hospital, Freud went into private practice, where he stumbled onto "the talking cure" when his severely neurotic patient Anna O discovered that recalling and recounting traumatic incidents from her past reduced her neurotic symptoms. Freud also examined and theorized about the impact of childhood trauma; the damage inflicted by repression; the dynamics of patient transference (from the love object to the analyst); and the significance of dreams. He attracted a set of noteworthy followers who spread the word about psychoanalysis, although some would evolve away from him and set up other schools. Freud spent his final years in London, having fled Vienna in the 1940s to escape the Nazis, who killed four of his five sisters.

Although psychologists acknowledge a founding debt to Freud, they often regard him as more of a poet than a scientist. They don't mean this as a compliment. Freud receives more respect from the literary community, and in truth he attributes many of his key discoveries to the literature he loved, *Hamlet* and *Oedipus* especially.

Psychoanalysis, in the words of Freudian psychologist Bruno Bettelheim, "was created to enable man to accept the problematic nature of life without being defeated by it, or giving in to escapism."[2] From a Freudian point of view, works of art help us to articulate our problems and to achieve (as sociologist and culture critic Philip Rieff puts it) "emotional stability" and "self-mastery."[3] Literature does this at two levels of engagement: First, simply immersing ourselves in stories takes us into and through debilitating inner conflicts. We experience those conflicts vicariously and, in so doing, get the satisfying sense that we can control them. This is what initially draws us to literature, Freud believes.

The second benefit occurs at the level of reflection. When we apply Freudian tools to a work of literature, we come away with a better understanding of inner conflicts and can apply the insights to make our lives freer and less neurotic. In addition, by reflecting upon our own personal responses *to* the works, we achieve even more self-knowledge: by using our reactions as case studies, as it were, we can diagnose what ails us.

To sum up: while simple immersion provides some solace, deliberate reflection and conscious application provides even more.

Freud most famous literary source is, of course, Sophocles's *Oedipus*, which provided him with the dynamics of his notorious "Oedipus complex." It's a good place to begin our discussion given Freud's keen interest in our forbidden and shameful desires. We can also see how Freud appropriates Aristotle's theory of audience catharsis for his own purposes.

Freud himself may well have identified with Oedipus, a hero who (like a psychologist) is determined to probe into society's dark secrets to solve the illness that is ravaging Thebes. Although Queen Jocasta begs for Oedipus to stop his search, he continues nonetheless, only for society to banish him upon his discovering the truth. While Freud wasn't banished from Vienna, his theory scandalized many throughout Europe and America, who regarded him as sex-obsessed.

We have already noted that Aristotle attributes the intense emotional responses generated by Sophocles's play to pity and fear. We speculated that, for Athenian audiences, the intense emotions arose from identifying with characters who (consistent with Athenian optimism) thought they could control their destinies, only to discover that certain aspects of existence were beyond them. *Oedipus* both captured their optimism and consoled them when they failed, assuring them they did not suffer alone.

Freud's take is slightly different. For him, the play articulates desires so socially taboo that we can't even acknowledge we have them. In his scenario, Oedipus represents the male child (Freud's initial focus) who harbors forbidden desires. First, he desires incestuous union with his mother—which is to say, he wants her all to himself. Second, he desires to kill the father, whom he sees as usurping his rightful place as the center of his mother's attention.[4]

Because the father is so powerful, however, the child imagines being punished for his transgressive wishes, perhaps by castration. For self-protection, therefore, the child represses the two desires, and what we repress, Freud contends, becomes toxic. Freud may or may not have said, when asked to describe the essence of his theories, "secrets make us sick," but the formulation functions as a useful summation. Taboos have such a hold on our minds that we feel nauseated at the mere mention of them, and when Oedipus discovers that he has killed his father and married his mother, he symbolically castrates himself, poking out his eyes with Jocasta's brooch to blot out the mental pain.[5]

Freud believes that when Greek audiences watched the play's protagonist slowly but inexorably realize that he has acted upon taboo desires, they would have been both horrified and relieved—horrified at the behavior and relieved at seeing these desires finally out in the open. Applying Aristotle's psychological explanation, they acknowledged the desires through identification (pity), even as they sought to distance themselves (fear). In sum, they felt cathartic relief at the realization that they could approach and survive that which they dared not name. While Plato doesn't specifically mention *Oedipus* in *The Republic,* one can see why he doesn't want the great tragedians in his rational utopia. Sophocles is playing with emotional dynamite that Plato's philosopher guardians would have difficulty containing.

Without literature, however, society cannot achieve psychic health, which is why Aristotle is a fan of literary catharsis. One of my favorite examples of literature's healing powers at work occurs in Christopher Marlowe's *The Tragical History of Doctor Faustus.* There we see the brilliant Faustus using Homer and the lyre musician Amphion (from Greek mythology) as anti-depressants and suicide prevention treatment. Finding himself torn between his illicit desire for God-like power and his fear of damnation, Faustus considers multiple ways of killing himself before finding relief in poetry:

> My heart's so harden'd, I cannot repent:
> Scarce can I name salvation, faith, or heaven,
> But fearful echoes thunder in mine ears,
> "Faustus, thou art damn'd!" then swords, and knives,
> Poison, guns, halters, and envenom'd steel
> Are laid before me to dispatch myself;

And long ere this I should have slain myself,
Had not sweet pleasure conquer'd deep despair.
Have not I made blind Homer sing to me
Of Alexander's love and Oenon's death?
And hath not he [Antiphon],
that built the walls of Thebes
With ravishing sound of his melodious harp,
Made music with my Mephistophilis?
Why should I die, then, or basely despair?[6]

This turning to art when we are hammered by our socially forbidden desires Freud calls "sublimation," which is the process of making sublime or elevated that which is base.[7] To cite another famous literary example, Thomas Mann's novella *Death in Venice* transmutes an old man's unacceptable desire for an adolescent boy into sublime poetry. When we read such works, rather than allowing ourselves to be pulled down by our guilt, we feel ennobled by our suffering.

Our dreams also come to our rescue, which is significant for our purposes given literature's special relationship with dreaming. While our forbidden desires do damage when we push them into our unconscious, our dreams provide an outlet, transforming our mental distress into fictional stories, poetic images, and dramatic enactments. That's not the end of the process, however, because, even when asleep, we still regard our desires as dangerous and unacceptable. Our dreams, therefore, disguise these concerns yet again, transforming them into weird and wild phantasmagoria.

If we are to identify what troubles us, then, we must interpret our dreams, and in his *Interpretation of Dreams* (1899) Freud shows us how to do so. First, he contrasts the actual or "latent" content of our dreams with their mere surface or "manifest" content.[8] We must figure out what the dreams are really about, which we can do if we understand the dreamwork process. Dreams, according to Freud, change our repressed feelings into safe images and stories. Freud's disciple Jung says that Freud had a remarkable ability to help patients interpret their dreams, unearthing the underlying feelings and thereby lessening their toxic effects.

Oedipus's mother/wife Jocasta is partially right, partially wrong when, in response to his fears, she tells him,

> As to your mother's marriage bed,—don't fear it.
> Before this, in dreams too, as well as oracles,
> many a man has lain with his own mother.
> But he to whom such things are nothing bears
> his life most easily.[9]

Jocasta is right that the incest wish is the stuff of dreams (although Freud would say that even in dreams it gets disguised) but wrong that such desires can be ignored. When repressed, they return as neurosis, which in the play is symbolized by the plague that has broken out in Thebes.

By facing up to these dark desires, however, we can keep them from tearing us apart. Sophocles captures this in the sequel to *Oedipus* that he wrote when he was 90, *Oedipus at Colonus*. Oedipus may be overwhelmed by self-horror at the conclusion of the first play, but by the conclusion of the sequel, Sophocles has managed to transform his suffering into spiritual transcendence. Because he has faced up to his forbidden desires, they no longer have power over him.

Contemporary cultural critic Rieff spells out art's relationship with dreams. Like a dream, he says, art functions as "a safety valve, a form of exhibitionism, in which the tension accumulated by private motives is drained off in public display."[10] That being noted, literature is also different from a dream in ways that Freud lays out in his essay "Creative Writers and Day Dreaming."

As the title indicates, Freud describes imaginative writing as a form of conscious dreaming. Creative authors, he believes, tap into the same repressed desires that lead to dreams, only in this case they can consciously shape the dream material.[11] Normally, as he observes in another essay ("The Uncanny"), we respond passively to real experience. The storyteller, by contrast, guides "the current of our emotions, to dam it up in one direction and make it flow in another."[12]

In short, the author achieves a certain mastery over emotional turbulence by composing the work. Audiences, meanwhile, achieve that mastery by reading it.

Freud spells out some of this turbulence in his daydreaming essay. Look carefully at stories, he says, and you will see them dealing with sides of ourselves that shame us: ambition fantasies for men, love fantasies for women. (Freud's gender typing was a product of his time.) Repression has entered in because, he asserts, "the well-brought up young woman is only allowed a minimum of erotic desire, and the young man has to learn to suppress the excess of self-regard which he brings with him from the spoilt days of his childhood, so he may find his place in a society which is full of other individuals making equally strong demands."[13] While reading such books, Freud believes, women can indulge their sexual fantasies and men their domination fantasies without feeling ashamed.

Although such fantasies are to be found in all literature, Freud says they are particularly evident in popular works by what he charitably calls "less pretentious authors." Today some refer to these genres as "chick lit" and "dick lit." Sounding like Plato, who regards poets as "deceivers" that trick us through beauty, Freud says the writers "bribe" us with formal technique: they soften "the character of [our] egoistic daydreams by altering and disguising it." As a result, they make us feel less guilty for having these shameful daydreams, thereby releasing the "tensions in our minds." This release, as Freud sees it, is a big reason why we read novels.[14]

To argue that great and popular lit differ only because great writers bribe us better, however, does not do justice to literature's therapeutic powers. As I will argue in the upcoming feminism and Jane Austen chapters, great literature serves us better psychologically than "less pretentious" potboilers simply because the treatment is of a higher quality. We might get momentary tension relief from reading about the girl getting the guy or the guy killing the bad guy, but that's it. By contrast, the mental work you put into a great work returns dividends: it moves us at deeper levels, better helping us to wrestle with our demons and understand our state of mind. Which is to say, we get the therapy we pay for.

I conclude this examination of Freud with a quick glance at the therapy provided by two genres that lend themselves particularly well to his approach. People generally read fairy tales and horror fiction without looking for deeper meaning, which gives us the opportunity to examine their benefits at both the immersive and reflective levels.

In *The Uses of Enchantment: The Meaning and Importance of Fairy Tales* (1976), Bruno Bettelheim talks about how children need folk fairy tales to find meaning in their confusing lives. Because children are bewildered by the world, Bettelheim says they require some way of making "coherent sense" of things. Fairy tales provide them with the ideas they need to bring their "inner house into order." Once having done that, they can build outer order. Or as Bettelheim puts it, the child needs "a moral education which subtly, and by implication only, conveys to him the advantages of moral behavior, not through abstract ethical concepts but through that which seems tangibly right and therefore meaningful to him."[15]

Folk fairy tales, Bettelheim continues, confront children with basic human predicaments—maturation, conflict, aging, death, the limits of our existence—without talking down to them. Rather, the stories respect young people for their anxieties and reassure them that they can achieve satisfactory resolutions. Different fairy tales specialize in different anxieties, as a quick glance indicates. In "Hansel and Gretel," for instance, children replay (among other things) abandonment fears; in "Snow White," conflict with the mother; in "Jack and the Beanstalk," conflict with the father; in "Cinderella," sibling rivalry; in "Little Red Cap" (or "Little Red Riding Hood"), anxieties about growing up; and in "Sleeping Beauty," turbulent adolescence. The child instinctively recognizes that these stories speak to primal concerns, providing images and a language for what otherwise would feel like murky chaos.

"Hansel and Gretel," for instance, sees the panicked children, when confronted with adult problems, reverting to an infantile state, so that they gorge themselves on the gingerbread house. In the witch's cannibalism, however, Bettelheim says that they come to recognize "the danger of unrestrained oral greed and dependence." To survive, therefore, they "must develop initiative and realize that their only resource lies in intelligent planning and acting." Having previously been at the mercy of their primal drives—what Freud calls the id—they now "act in accordance with the ego," which is the Self that mediates between our untamed energies and society's rules. A strong and healthy ego or Self, Bettelheim says, balances between our drives and the norms of society.[16]

By the end of the story, the two child protagonists have acquired new treasures: "new-won independence in thought and action, a new self-reliance which is opposite of the passive dependence which characterized them when they were deserted in the woods."[17] Bettelheim conducts similar analysis of the other fairy tales he mentions.

Children, of course, do not reflect upon the stories. For them, the comfort comes all from their immersion. But their parents and teachers can use their knowledge about how the stories are working to identify anxieties and talk with their children about them.

Freud's essay on the uncanny or the spooky, meanwhile, is particularly useful for understanding why we often find ourselves attracted to writers that repulse us, such as E.T.A. Hoffman, Mary Shelley, Edgar Allan Poe, H.P. Lovecraft, Stephen King, Anne Rice, and other masters of gothic horror. Simply put, horror fascinates us because we sense something recognizable in the monsters. "We have met the enemy and he is us," *Pogo* cartoonist Walt Kelly famously wrote,[18] while the narrator Marlow in Joseph Conrad's *Heart of Darkness* talks of "the fascination of the abomination."[19] The energy we put into denying our dark desires comes back to us in feelings of dread, a phenomenon often referred to as "the return of the repressed." The more we deny, the greater the horror.

We see this dynamic played out in Robert Louis Stevenson's Victorian novel *Dr. Jekyll and Mr. Hyde* (1886) where Jekyll does all he can to deny his repressed dark self, which is at odds with his sense of himself as a civilized gentleman. Jekyll uses strong drugs to suppress the self he "hides," but as a result Hyde only grows in power, trampling on children and clubbing people to death. Reading such fiction allows us to approach, acknowledge, and thereby defuse our guilt and shame over our hidden, unsavory side.

All this occurs at the immersive level. Once we reflect, however, new windows open into both our own psyches and those of others. By analyzing why certain literary monsters frighten us, we can better understand our inner turmoil—and by so doing, we achieve at least a modicum of self-mastery. Freud reports telling a patient that "much will be gained if we succeed in transforming your hysterical misery into common unhappiness. With a mental life that has been restored to health, you will be better armed against that unhappiness."[20]

In other words, while literary therapy may not bring an end to all our psychic problems, Freud assures us that it will make the chaos within more manageable.

While Freud contended that literature helps relieve the tensions that lead to neurosis—making the best of a bad situation, as it were—his innovative disciple Carl Jung was more ambitious. Literature, Jung believes, points the way towards a growth-oriented process that he calls individuation and that others have called self-actualization. By interpreting the texts that we are drawn to, we find a blueprint on how to actualize our individual potential.

Born in German-speaking Switzerland, Carl Jung (1875-1961) at one time aspired to be a minister like his father but was drawn to medicine and psychiatry at the University of Basel, with psychiatry's focus on mental and emotional states balancing out medicine's biological emphasis. His first job was at Zurich's Burghölzi psychiatric hospital, where in short order he became a senior doctor before leaving to set up his own private clinic. His publications caught the attention of Freud, and the two developed a six-year relationship, with Freud at one point designating him as his intellectual and scientific heir. They split eventually, however, in part because Jung disagreed with what he saw as Freud's overemphasis on childhood sexual development. They also had different aspirations for psychoanalysis. Whereas Freud thought that humans could hope for little more that *managing* their internal conflicts, Jung believed the conflicts could be *resolved*.

The hero in Jung's interior drama is the Self, which is like Freud's ego but slightly expanded. For Freud, the ego mediates between our drives (the id) and our internalization of society's rules (the superego). For Jung, the Self is our inner essence that seeks fulfillment. The Self can do so, however, only if our conscious mind (Freud's ego) listens to the Unconscious, which knows more about us than does the conscious mind, including the sides of ourselves of which we are ashamed.[21]

Jung agrees with Freud that repressing our animal side (Jung calls this our Shadow) will result in devouring monsters, which show up in our nightmares, our neuroses, and our literature. He also believes, however, that we can integrate our Shadow side into the Self, thereby achieving a well-rounded fullness.[22] This seems to imply that if Dr. Jekyll would frankly acknowledge he has an animalistic side rather than turning away in shame and horror, he and Hyde could live happily together in the same body and mind. This is easier said than done, given how we are set in our ways, but Jung is more optimistic than Freud that a full reconciliation is possible.

Jung's theories tackle gender differently from Freud as well, tying it to the Shadow side we want to repress. For example, Jung believes that when men who are ashamed of being effeminate deny their female side, they become haunted by fears of emasculating female monsters. Similarly, women who fear being too manly—say, too loud and assertive—dream of dark beasts or Bluebeard killers that will carry them away. (Jung called men's female side the Anima, women's male side the Animus.) Overcoming one's revulsion can be difficult given social messaging, and the individual who is stuck in a narrow gender identity cannot become fully individuated. The trapped Self, longing to fulfill its potential, will communicate its distress through nightmares and neurosis, which operate as warning signals and cries for help.[23] Jung owes this insight to Freud.

To communicate with us, our dreams draw on a rich series of images that are housed in what Jung calls "the collective unconscious." This storehouse of archetypes has been around for millennia, providing creative writers and storytellers with their raw material. Artists for Jung function as society's dreamers or shamans, showing the Self how to achieve fulfillment in a hostile world.

While archetypes show up particularly clearly in myths and folk tales, Jungian scholars find mythic archetypes in pretty much all of literature, realist as well as fantasy. To cite a random example, the Garden of Eden archetype plays a major role in the social realism of novelist John Steinbeck, from his *Grapes of Wrath* to (as the title indicates) *East of Eden.*

Joseph Campbell, an American literature professor who drew heavily on Jung's theories, found evidence for the individuation process in myths from all over the world. In *The Hero with a Thousand Faces* (1949), Campbell identified a universal set of stages that comprise what he calls "the journey of the hero." In this journey, the Self, symbolized by the hero, must respond to "the Call" if it is to begin realizing its potential. Because stepping out of one's comfort zone is difficult, the hero may initially engage in "resistance" (for instance Frodo is reluctant to leave the Shire when "called" by Gandalf), but the Self can only grow and mature if the Call is accepted. Otherwise, one remains stuck in childhood.[24]

In the subsequent journey, there will be moments of self-doubt (heroes may find themselves in "the belly of the whale"), and sometimes the hero will be seduced or led astray (say, by temptresses). But the hero also encounters guides, mentors, and goddesses that provide advice and necessary resources. In the end, the hero attains the object of his or her quest, which is symbolic of the newly actualized Self. Doing so involves coming to terms with an antagonist who represents one's shadow side. Returning to the world with his or her newly acquired powers, the hero can now benefit society at large.[25]

The journey of the hero inspires us to grow and move forward in our lives. It also provides us a way to assess our progress (or lack thereof) and our life choices. Take, for instance, the protagonist Gawain in the medieval romance *Sir Gawain and the Green Knight.* As the premier knight in Camelot, Gawain thinks he has life figured out, only to be challenged by a green giant from the wilderness. This shadow figure is Gawain's nature side, which as a Christian knight Gawain undervalues. (He thinks he shouldn't care about his body because honor and Heaven await.) His quest, therefore, involves grappling with the meaning of life and of sexuality in the face of mortality. Ultimately, his view of the world becomes richer and more complex as he learns that he values his life far more than he realized. The romance tale ends ambiguously since it's not clear that Gawain has learned everything the "Green Knight" part of himself wants to teach him, but he appears to carry something of value back to Camelot. The greatest stories yield the most profound insights.

Just as, in our discussion of Freud, we saw cheap wish fulfillment stories about heroines who just get married and heroes who just kick butt, so there are also cheap hero stories. If a work grapples with only superficial aspects of the journey, as do many of the "sword and sorcery" novels that flood the market every year, then the reader experiences the literary equivalent of a sugar high rather than substantive nutrition. This is true even of a work that Jung himself quotes frequently, Rider Haggard's pulp novel *She* (1886-87). While Jung appreciates the work for how it dramatizes several of his archetypes, this facile story of men losing their minds over a beautiful, cruel, and immortal woman residing in the heart of Africa does not delve deeply into the human heart. Shallow hero stories can appeal to an inflated sense of self-importance without spurring us to do the hard work required to mature. They give us what we already expect without deepening our appetites.

We needn't altogether avoid such stories, just as it's okay to eat occasional junk food. But the greatest benefits in using Freud's and Jung's approaches come from diving into the best literature, which first provides therapeutic relief through immersion and then further relief once we reflect upon the work and our response to the work. Through this practice we can gain self-understanding, self-mastery, and self-actualization. In my final chapter I lay out an exercise on how, by examining the books in your life that have touched you deeply, you can extract vital advice.

Matthew Arnold

Poetry as Civilization's Savior

More and more mankind will discover that we have to
turn to poetry to interpret life for us, to console us,
to sustain us. Without poetry, our science will appear
incomplete; and most of what now passes with us for
religion and philosophy will be replaced by poetry.

— **Matthew Arnold,** "The Study of Poetry" (1880)[1]

As you have may have gathered by now, the 19th century was a time
when people thought about literature in sweeping terms, with William
Wordsworth, John Stuart Mill, Percy Shelley, Karl Marx, and Friedrich
Engels seeing authors playing an important role in humankind's long
struggle for freedom. Matthew Arnold too thought poetry could con-
tribute to humanity's higher destiny although, in his view, this destiny
was the ascendency of the middle class, where it was then to stop.
The bourgeoisie, in his view, were to inherit the mantle of Western
civilization, and he believed literature would help them get there.

Arnold (1822-88) was solidly middle class himself. Raised on the campus of Rugby School, where his father was headmaster, he attended first Rugby and then Oxford, where he won a scholarship. Needing a higher income to marry, he took on a position of inspector of schools and traveled all over England inspecting. He was also publishing his poetry and, at 35, became Oxford's Professor of Poetry. He is best known for his poems "Dover Beach" and "The Scholar Gypsy" and for his essays of social criticism, especially *Culture and Anarchy.*

Arnold worried that the middle class, because they were focused on making money, weren't prepared to assume leadership. What they needed was "Culture," which for Arnold includes the arts and humanities generally, with poetry his particular passion and the example he most often uses. In his view, poetry isn't just a side activity but the chief means for interpreting life and for consoling and sustaining us. While religion has served this purpose in the past, he writes, its power is waning. Science can't take its place, however, because "without poetry, our science will appear incomplete." Therefore, it is poetry's time to step up to the plate. Poetry is to be the new religion. Or as he puts it, "We should conceive of poetry worthily, and more highly than it has been the custom to conceive of it. We should conceive of it as capable of higher uses, and called to higher destinies, than those which in general men have assigned to it hitherto."[2]

Elsewhere Arnold says that the dominant idea of poetry is "the idea of beauty and of a human nature perfect on all its sides." He believes it to be central in pursuing moral perfection and conquering "the obvious faults of our animality."[3]

Borrowing from Horace's and Swift's dualities (delight and instruction for Horace, honey and wax for Swift), Arnold says that Culture's "pursuit of our total perfection" is "a pursuit of sweetness and light." Sweetness is the sensual delight we get from literature (say, musical wordplay, arresting images, engrossing stories), light its rational and moral wisdom. He parrots Horace ("he who joins the instructive with the agreeable, carries off every vote") when he writes, "He who works for sweetness works in the end for light also; he who works for light works in the end for sweetness also. But he who works for sweetness and light united, works to make reason and the will of God prevail."[4]

Again like Horace and like Sir Philip Sidney as well (poetry as "medicine of cherries"), Arnold says that literature employs delight to instruct us in higher principles. Poetry both shows us how to become more perfect people and pumps us up so we will *want to be* more perfect people. It enflames our inner passions so that we will work hard to create a society where sweetness and light prevail:

> Culture looks beyond machinery, culture hates hatred; culture has but one great passion, the passion for sweetness and light. It has one even yet greater!—the passion for making them prevail. It is not satisfied till we all come to a perfect man; it knows that the sweetness and light of the few must be imperfect until the raw and unkindled masses of humanity are touched with sweetness and light.[5]

Suddenly poets and poetry lovers have been elevated to evangelists, responsible for spreading the good news of literature to everyone, even "the raw and unkindled masses of humanity." Arnold's job as school inspector becomes significant here: Because Victorians were beginning to embrace the idea of universal education, suddenly he saw a concrete means of enacting his vision. If everyone were to start reading poetry, we could have another Renaissance. Arnold becomes positively euphoric at the prospect:

> If I have not shrunk from saying that we must work for sweetness and light, so neither have I shrunk from saying that we must have a broad basis, must have sweetness and light for as many as possible. Again and again I have insisted how those are the happy moments of humanity,

> how those are the marking epochs of a people's life, how
> those are the flowering times for literature and art and
> all the creative power of genius, when there is a national
> glow of life and thought, when the whole of society is
> in the fullest measure permeated by thought, sensible
> to beauty, intelligent and alive. Only it must be real
> thought and real beauty; real sweetness and real light.[6]

Arnold sounds here like an early advocate of a liberal arts education. Thanks to thinkers such as Arnold, many college core curricula require students to take arts and humanities courses, and we will see philosopher Martha Nussbaum advocating literature instruction as essential in the formation of good citizens and competent voters.

Arnold has a less benign side as well, however, which Marxist Terry Eagleton has pointed out. For all his talk of a new Renaissance, Arnold saw literary instruction also as a means to keep the working classes from grumbling about their lower status. As Eagleton bitingly depicts Arnold's view, "If the masses are not thrown a few novels, they may react by throwing up a few barricades."[7]

We can draw here a useful contrast between Shelley and Arnold. Shelley is a radical who sees literature inspiring men and women to fight against the forces that prevent them from fulfilling their potential. Arnold, on the other hand, takes the conservative line that, if we all read literature, we will stop focusing on structural inequality and simply work at getting along.

In *Culture and Anarchy* Arnold sees real danger in class conflict. The contending parties are the aristocracy, the middle class, and the working class, each of whom is "selfishly" focused on its own special concerns. Without culture, as Arnold sees it, we have anarchy, a world where, as the 17th century philosopher Thomas Hobbes put it, we are in perpetual warfare "where every man is enemy to every man." Arnold writes,

People of the aristocratic class want to affirm their ordinary selves, their likings and dislikings; people of the
middle-class the same, people of the working-class the
same. By our everyday selves, however, we are separate,
personal, at war; we are only safe from one another's
tyranny when no one has any power; and this safety,
in its turn, cannot save us from anarchy. And when,
therefore, anarchy presents itself as a danger to us, we
know not where to turn.[8]

To borrow from Arnold's best-known poem "Dover Beach," in the
present era the sea of faith has receded

And we are here as on a darkling plain
Swept with confused alarms of struggle and flight,
Where ignorant armies clash by night.[9]

On the other hand, if each class would only turn its attention to
something higher than itself, then we could live in harmony. We have
but to get in touch with "our best self," by which "we are united,
impersonal, at harmony." This best self is our "truest friend," Arnold
says, offering protection "when anarchy is a danger to us."[10]

Nothing gets us more in touch with our best self, Arnold says, than
poetry. Each class will behave properly, he believes, if culture is the
basis of the state. The aristocracy will act responsibly, giving up its
ancient but now out-of-date privileges, while a cultured middle class
will command the moral sway once held by the aristocracy. A cultured
populace, finally, will refrain from "rowdy" behavior. In other words,
all classes will read poetry, embracing its sensuous images (sweetness)
and lofty sentiments (light) to create a more peaceful society.

Notice who comes out ahead in this formulation: the upper class
gives up power, the lower class ceases to strive for power, and the

middle class takes power. Literature's role is to make everyone happy with this situation.

To think that a particular view of the world is natural or common sensical is an instance of Engels's false consciousness, Marxist theorist Antonio Gramsci's "hegemony," and political scientist Joseph Nye's "soft power." It's easier to maintain existing class hierarchy if most people see it as just the way things are. Arnold essentially says that the middle class had better learn how to use culture to bolster its position if it wants to prevent the lower classes from taking over—which is to say, from anarchy:

> With their narrow, harsh, unintelligent, and unattractive spirit and culture, [the middle classes] will almost certainly fail to mold or assimilate the masses below them, whose sympathies are at the present moment actually wider and more liberal than theirs. They arrive, these masses, eager to enter into possession of the world, to gain a more vivid sense of their own life and activity. In this their irrepressible development, their natural educators and initiators are those immediately above them, the middle classes. If these classes cannot win their sympathy or give them their direction, society is in danger of falling into anarchy.[11]

We will see in the upcoming chapters how figures like W.E.B. Du Bois, Bertolt Brecht, and Rachel Blau DuPlessis believe that certain literature works exactly as Arnold wants it to: it perpetuates existing power relations. Arnold's elevated ideals seem a little less benign when he reveals his readiness to resort to hard power if his soft power approach doesn't work. We see this when he quotes and then endorses his father's harsh views.

Upset with the "gloomy and troubled" state of affairs, which included labor riots, Arnold Sr. wrote in an 1830s letter, "As for rioting, the old Roman way of dealing with that is always the right one; flog the rank and file, and fling the ringleaders from the Tarpeian Rock!" To which endorsement of state violence the Rugby headmaster adds, "And this opinion we can never forsake... that monster processions in the streets and forcible irruptions into the parks... ought to be unflinchingly forbidden and repressed; and that far more is lost than is gained by permitting them."[12]

Sweetness and light seem less inspirational if they are yoked to a repressive political agenda. One imagines Arnold striking the stance of his father and addressing striking workers: "Men, you have a choice: either read poetry and be nice or it's *The Rock*!" His class bias is clearly seen in the way he characterizes the working class as faceless masses and rioters.

In other words, the conversation about literary impact needs more diversity, which the next century served up in spades. One thinker critical to the emerging perspective was W. E. B. Du Bois, one of the towering activist intellectuals in American history.

VOICE FOR THE OPPRESSED

W. E. B. Du Bois

EXTENDING LITERATURE'S REACH

We can afford the Truth. White folk today cannot.

— **W. E. B. Du Bois**, "Criteria of Negro Art" (1926)[1]

ALL THE THINKERS WE have surveyed so far—at least going back to Sir Philip Sidney but also including Aristotle—see a clear division of labor between the poet and the citizen. The poet simply tells the truth about life, giving us a valuable store of knowledge that we can draw on to become virtuous or enlightened. Indeed, we have Engels, a dedicated revolutionary, criticizing a writer for being political rather than truthful. Authors, Engels says, should simply describe while leaving it up to others to act upon what they see.

But what if describing is itself a political act? What if one person's truth appears as propaganda to someone else? The very way that a poem or story is framed can have a self-serving agenda behind it. It took an American Black intellectual to add this perspective to the conversation.

William Edward Burghardt Du Bois (1868–1963) was an extraordinary figure. The first African American to earn a doctorate from Harvard, he was actively engaged in the fight against racism, segregation and lynching his entire life. As editor of the NAACP's *Crisis*, he had a prominent voice in American politics. His *Souls of Black Folk* is one of America's great political documents, pointing out (among other things) that Blacks are constantly negotiating between two identities: how they see themselves and how Whites see them. His *Black Reconstruction in America*, meanwhile, makes a compelling case that White violence, not Black incompetence, brought an end to the project of Reconstruction. (Few historians disagree with this now.) Du Bois, who described himself as a socialist, was viciously attacked by Senator Joe McCarthy and the House on Un-American Activities in the 1950s but kept going. Among his many publications are five novels.

In "Criteria of Negro Art" (1926), Du Bois makes a point about unacknowledged racism in a provocative way that people cannot choose but hear: he declares that "all Art is propaganda" and that "I do not care a damn for any art that is not used for propaganda."[2] Du Bois knows this view flies in the face of those who worry about art being reduced to a specific agenda (such as Shelley and Engels). He understands, however, that what passes for objective truth often carries within it a hidden set of value assumptions. Du Bois makes the point by contrasting two plays of the time, *White Congo* and *Congo*. In the first, the fallen women is Black while in the second she is White. You can guess what comes next: "In *White Congo* the black woman goes down further and further and in *Congo* the white woman begins with degradation but in the end is one of the angels of the Lord."[3]

In pointing out the double standard and crude racialized tropes in popular art, Du Bois blazed the trail for such criticism. Since the 1960s we have become much more attuned to racial stereotyping, which can show up in even literary masterpieces.

For instance, in his 1975 essay "An Image of Africa: Racism in Conrad's *Heart of Darkness* (1975)," Nigerian author Chinua Achebe notes how the Congolese in Conrad's novella, regarded at the time as a British masterwork, are nothing more than a foil for the narrator's existential despair. Achebe points out that Conrad's Marlow, upon looking at Africans, sees nothing but abstracted and objectified yells and bodies, as in the following passage:

> But suddenly, as we struggled round a bend, there would be a glimpse of rush walls, of peaked grass roofs, a burst of yells, a whirl of black limbs, a mass of hands clapping, of feet stamping, of bodies swaying, of eyes rolling, under the droop of heavy and motionless foliage.[4]

One need only read the opening paragraphs of Achebe's own masterpiece, *Things Fall Apart* (1958), to realize how reality changes when one gives individual names, personalities, and stories to this "whirl of black limbs":

> Okonkwo was well known throughout the nine villages and even beyond. His fame rested on solid personal achievements. As a young man of eighteen he had brought honor to his village by throwing Amalinze the Cat. Amalinze was the great wrestler who for seven years was unbeaten, from Umuofia to Mbaino. He was called the Cat because his back would never touch the earth. It was this man that Okonkwo threw in a fight which the old men agreed was one of the fiercest since the founder of their town engaged a spirit of the wild for seven days and seven nights.[5]

After appearing to reject the "art is truth" tradition, however, Du Bois then reasserts it. It turns out he does not actually believe that "Negro Art" should advocate for, say, civil rights legislation the way a political activist would. He doesn't, in other words, believe his own statement that "all art is propaganda." Instead, he uses the claim to catch our attention and alert us to our hidden beliefs. Above all, he wants authors to become more aware of their biases in how they describe the world.

In other words, he wants them to become truth tellers, not propagandists.

So no less than Johnson, Shelley or Engels, Du Bois says that an artist's "bounden duty" is to beauty and truth—and that to achieve beauty, he or she must commit to Truth. If artists do their job, Du Bois contends, they will honor "goodness in all its aspects of justice, honor and right," thereby gaining "sympathy and human interest":

> Thus it is the bounden duty of black America to begin this great work of the creation of Beauty, of the preservation of Beauty, of the realization of Beauty, and we must use in this work all the methods that men have used before. And what have been the tools of the artist in times gone by? First of all, he has used the Truth—not for the sake of truth, not as a scientist seeking truth, but as one upon whom Truth eternally thrusts itself as the highest handmaid of imagination, as the one great vehicle of universal understanding. Again artists have used Goodness—goodness in all its aspects of justice, honor and right—not for sake of an ethical sanction but as the one true method of gaining sympathy and human interest.[6]

Like Arnold, then, Du Bois sees the artist as an evangelist, or as he puts it, an "apostle of Truth and Right." Artists are only free when they commit themselves to truth and justice. "Slavery only dogs him," Du Bois writes, "when he is denied the right to tell the Truth or recognize an ideal of justice."[7]

A true artist avoids not only White stereotypes of African Americans but also idealized versions that African Americans have of themselves. To do so requires courage and integrity because Black readers "are bound by all sorts of customs that have come down as second-hand soul clothes of white patrons." For example, "We are ashamed of sex and we lower our eyes when people will talk of it. Our religion holds us in superstition. Our worst side has been so shamelessly emphasized that we are denying we have or ever had a worst side. In all sorts of ways we are hemmed in and our new young artists have got to fight their way to freedom."[8]

Langston Hughes says something similar in "The Negro Artist and the Racial Mountain," which also appeared in 1926. The Harlem poet talks about the pressures that Black and White readers alike apply to Black writers. In Jean Toomer's modernist novel *Cane*, for instance, the author neither idealizes nor demonizes rural Blacks and Whites but unflinchingly depicts them in their full and flawed humanity. Hughes points out that middle class Blacks didn't appreciate this portrait, fearing it reinforced White stereotypes of them as uncultured and ignorant. Hughes writes that "the Negro artist" works against "sharp criticism and misunderstanding" from fellow Blacks and "unintentional bribes" from Whites:

> "Oh, be respectable, write about nice people, show how good we are," say the Negroes. "Be stereotyped, don't go too far, don't shatter our illusions about you, don't amuse us too seriously. We will pay you," say the whites. Both would have told Jean Toomer not to write *Cane*. The colored people did not praise it. The white people did not buy it. Most of the colored people who did read *Cane* hate it. They are afraid of it. Although the critics gave it good reviews the public remained indifferent.

> Yet (excepting the work of Du Bois) *Cane* contains the finest prose written by a Negro in America. And like the singing of Robeson, it is truly racial.[9]

For his part, Du Bois sounds like Shelley when he asserts that art is ultimately about freedom, not constraint. Readers that encounter truth have the potential to become "free of mind, proud of body and just of soul." If authors do their jobs, then readers can do theirs. "The ultimate judge," he tells his readers, "has got to be you and you have got to build yourselves up into that wide judgment, that catholicity of temper which is going to enable the artist to have his widest chance for freedom. We can afford the Truth. White folk today cannot..."[10]

The literary culture wars of the early 1990s were heated in part because certain readers—often readers of color—found themselves deeply moved by powerful works that (mostly White) traditionalists claimed were inferior. At the same time these readers, like Du Bois, detected certain blind spots in even revered classics and insisted upon talking about them. The culture wars of that decade became a proxy battle for those who wanted to hold on to their traditional power and those formerly disenfranchised groups that wanted a seat at the table.

The battle wasn't always symmetrical since many Black readers were willing to acknowledge the greatness of past White authors. In fact, Du Bois himself saw an acquaintance with the traditional classics as essential, writing,

> I sit with Shakespeare, and he winces not. Across the color line I move arm and arm with Balzac and Dumas, where smiling men and welcoming women glide in gilded halls. From out of the caves of evening that swing between the strong-limbed Earth and the tracery of stars, I summon Aristotle and Aurelius and what soul I will, and they come all graciously with no scorn nor

condescension. So, wed with Truth, I dwell above the veil.[11]

We see a similar point made in a fascinating interchange between two powerful African American women, poet Maya Angelou and critic and essayist bell hooks, as they similarly express a debt to White authors. When there was a horrific lynching of a Black man during her childhood, Angelou says she used Dickens to assure herself that not all Whites were like the mob:

> In the meantime, I was reading Charles Dickens, and Dickens liberated me from hating all whites all the time. I knew that I liked some of these people, because I felt for Oliver, and I felt for Tim. I read the Bronte sisters and I felt for those people. I decided that the people in my town were a different race than the whites on the moors and in the poor people's homes and in orphanages and prisons. So I was saved from hating all whites, you see.[12]

Hooks, meanwhile, remembers using Emily Bronte to negotiate her own way through American racism:

> When I read *Wuthering Heights* as a workingclass girl struggling to find herself, an outsider, I felt that Heathcliff was me, you know? He was symbolic to me of a kind of black race: he was outcast, he was not allowed into the center of things. I transposed my own drama of living in the apartheid south onto this world of *Wuthering Heights* and felt myself in harmony with those characters.[13]

These anecdotes by eminent Black artists and intellectuals suggest that when one closes oneself off from literature's rich variety, whether for rightwing or leftwing reasons, one diminishes one's humanity. Conservatives demeaning significant Black authors in the early 1990's denied themselves vibrant voices, and the Black liberals that Langston Hughes mentions, fearful of offending Whites with jarring but truthful depictions of African Americans, did the same. During the militant 1960s, the pendulum had swung so far the other way that Black activists sometimes castigated writers if they were *too* open to White writers, so that even the major African American poet Robert Hayden found himself labeled an Uncle Tom and a "white n----" for refusing to be more "political" in his poetic topics.[14] For their part, hooks and Angelou express some of these same concerns about their own students of color, with hooks at one point observing, "I'm so disturbed when my women students behave as though they can only read women, or Black students behave as though they can only read Blacks, or White students behave as though they can only identify with a White writer. I think the worst thing that can happen to us is to lose sight of the power of empathy and compassion."[15]

Angelou agrees, observing that, when we close ourselves off from people who are different, "we risk being consumed by brutism":

> I will not have my life narrowed down. I will not bow down to somebody else's whim or to someone else's ignorance. When I finish lecturing, I find that the whole audience, Black and White, is a little bit changed, because I will have recited Sonya Sanchez, Anne Marie Evans, and probably Eugene Redmond, and Amiri

Baraka, and Shakespeare and Emerson, and maybe talk about Norman Mailer a little bit, because he writes English, and Joan Didion, who writes this language. People see something. I don't know how long the change maintains, but if you have changed at all, you've changed all, at least for a little while.[16]

Angelou and Du Bois's faith that literature can change people contrasts dramatically with the beliefs of another major African American thinker, Booker T. Washington, and that clash is worth revisiting since it is replicated in today's debates over the respective values of a liberal arts and a vocational education. Washington, a contemporary of Du Bois, believed that Blacks would earn the respect of Whites if they mastered practical skills in such fields as mechanics and agriculture, and he established the Tuskegee Institute to provide vocational training to that end. Du Bois, on the other hand, feared that such a system would create a permanent caste system in the United States. He advocated instead for a classical liberal arts education, which he saw preparing Black students to become members of "the talented tenth," future leaders in the fight for social justice and equality.[17]

While Du Bois's easy embrace of Shakespeare, Balzac, Dumas, and Dante might not sit well with certain activists, his pointing out White bias in literary works has become one of the major tools in the modern activist arsenal. At the same time, his advocacy of a classical education would probably win him fans nowadays amongst cultural conservatives. Finally, his insistence that authors render their greatest service when they unflinchingly tell the truth places him in the tradition of Aristotle, Shelley and Johnson. Unlike these predecessors, however, he realizes that truth is harder to see if one is blinkered by race, class, gender, and other biases. By reading works by a diverse set of authors, one is alerted to one's blindnesses, at which point one's perspective widens. The cause of truth is served.

Bertolt Brecht

Art as a Hammer to Shape Reality

It is not enough to demand insight and informative images of reality from the theater. Our theater must stimulate a desire for understanding, a delight in changing reality. Our audience must experience not only the ways to free Prometheus, but be schooled in the very desire to free him. Theater must teach all the pleasures and joys of discovery, all the feelings of triumph associated with liberation.

— **Bertolt Brecht**[1]

PLAYWRIGHT AND POET BERTOLT Brecht firmly allies himself with the liberation struggle. While he probably didn't write a maxim commonly attributed to him—"Art is not a mirror to reflect reality but a hammer with which to shape it"—it does a good job of capturing his project. The saying resembles one of Marx's observations that Brecht frequently quotes and that sets up a possible activist agenda for literature: "The philosophers have only *interpreted* the world in various ways; the point, however, is to *change* it."[2]

Brecht (1898–1956) was one of the 20th century's greatest playwrights, pushing drama in exciting new directions while articulating theories of art that inspired artists in multiple fields. As a young German during World War I, Brecht took a pre-med course to put off being drafted, and while at the University of Munich he studied theater on the side. After 1918 he linked up with various theatrical companies and began producing his own plays, including the very successful and influential *Threepenny Opera*. He was also an accomplished poet.

Brecht fled Germany with the ascension of Adolf Hitler, ultimately ending up in the United States, where he wrote some of his greatest plays, including *Life of Galileo, Mother Courage and Her Children, The Good Person of Szechwan,* and *The Caucasian Chalk Circle.* Although never an official member of the Communist Party, Brecht was so hounded by the American House on Un-American Activities Committee after the war that he left for East Germany. While he remained there the rest of his life, he had a mixed relationship with that government as well.

Brecht shares with Shelley and Marx the belief that the arc of history bends towards liberation. As he sees it, the working class has the power to seize the means of production and establish a true communist state. "From each according to his ability, to each according to his need" is an ideal that Brecht endorses and that shows up in his collaborative theater projects.

If the working class does not take power into its own hands, Brecht believes, it is not only because the ruling class possesses the police and the armed forces. Their use of soft power, as we noted in the Marx-Engels chapter, can be just as effective: better an army in your head than an army at your doorstep, with this internal army insisting that existing power relations are just the way that life is and always will be. (Antonio Gramsci, with intentional irony, calls this "common sense.") If people fatalistically accept their situation in life as a given, they are less likely to rebel.

As Brecht saw it, art operates as a hammer if it convinces the oppressed that reality can be different. Brecht scholar Anthony Squiers writes, "For Brecht, the dominant *Weltanschauung* [world view] has to be disrupted, ruptured before a new worldview can come into existence and emancipation becomes possible." Brecht believed (Squiers reports) that one must "doubt the viability" on one worldview for it to be replaced with another.[3]

Brecht distinguishes between complicit drama that upholds the dominant world view and revolutionary drama that challenges it. The first he calls "conventional dramatic theater," which he describes as Aristotelian because it offers audiences a cathartic experience. Brecht is concerned that such theater, even if it presents, say, tear-jerking images of poverty, does not bring about social change. Audiences may cry over an abused orphan or an evicted family, but they cry over the way the world *is* rather than imagining the way the world *could be*. Indeed, their emotional release might work as a safety valve so that, although they mourn cruelty and poverty, they emerge from the theater prepared to behave no differently than they've been behaving.[4]

Brecht, therefore, sees it necessary to replace such theater with what he calls epic theater, which disrupts what passes for reality and shows audiences a revolutionary way forward. He sets up the contrast as follows:

> The theatergoer in conventional dramatic theater says: Yes, I've felt that way, too. That's the way I am. That's life. That's the way it will always be. The suffering of this or that person grips me because there is no escape for him ... But the theatergoer in the epic theater says: I would never have thought that. You can't do that. That's very strange, practically unbelievable. That has to stop. The suffering of this or that person grips me because there is an escape for him."[5]

Rather than settle for a theater that "only releases the feelings, insights and impulses" that arise within a certain reality, Brecht employs and encourages "those thoughts and feelings which help transform the field itself."[6] Brecht invokes the mythic figure of Prometheus, the Titan who stole fire from the gods to benefit humankind and who was frequently used by 18th and 19th century radicals as the archetype of the Enlightenment rebel, to make his point:

> It is not enough to demand insight and informative images of reality from the theater. Our theater must stimulate a desire for understanding, a delight in changing reality. Our audience must experience not only the ways to free Prometheus, but be schooled in the very desire to free him. Theater must teach all the pleasures and joys of discovery, all the feelings of triumph associated with liberation.[7]

It was with such liberation in mind that Brecht has memorably written, "Every art contributes to the greatest art of all, the art of living."[8]

In certain ways, Brecht is replaying the old Plato-Aristotle debate. Plato distrusts art because it is emotional and clouds judgment whereas Aristotle embraces the emotional response. Suspicious of Aristotle, Brecht is closer to Plato, desiring audiences to move into a rational space to see the true state of the world.

But Brecht doesn't dispense with emotion altogether and his differences with Aristotle can be overstated. After all, Aristotle too thinks we should turn to philosophy. He just wants us to do so *after* emotional immersion. For his part, Brecht creates emotionally engaging characters to "stimulate a desire for understanding, a delight in changing reality." Epic theater uses the emotions to move past a purely emotional response and begin a constructive dialogue with the world.

For all the talk of conventional vs. epic art, Brecht's distinction isn't much different from Samuel Johnson distinguishing between literature that appeals to the baser instincts and literature that leads to deeper understanding. As we will see, certain feminists distinguish between sensationalist romances that bolster traditional marriage and tough minded literature that questions it. Recall that Shelley finds all great literature to be socially liberating, and we have seen several thinkers who associate great literature with freedom and bad literature with repression. Indeed, we can argue that a deep commitment to honoring humanity in all our complexity is what makes great literature great.

In Brecht's own plays, we see him attacking false consciousness by prodding his audiences to distance or alienate themselves from sympathetic characters in whom they have become invested. Through this two-step process, he hopes audiences will realize they have been interpreting the world through ruling class eyes and shift to imagining new ways that society could be structured. In *Galileo*, for instance, Brecht shows the effort required to challenge an accepted view of the universe and notes that we shouldn't have to rely on a single great man for change. We want Galileo to be a gallant rebel (sympathetic identification) and are disillusioned when he capitulates to the pope (alienation effect). Galileo then gets us to think in broader terms with the memorable line, "Unhappy is the land that needs a hero."[9]

In other words, if we require a hero, we are in dire straits indeed. Only collective action can save us.

Likewise, Brecht shows how sympathetic people, like Mother Courage and the Good Woman of Szechwan, must engage in unsavory tactics to survive. By getting audiences to first root for the characters and then recoil in distaste, he seeks to shift our attention from individuals to the system that pressures them. Our mixed responses, he hopes, will persuade us that capitalism cannot provide satisfactory endings for good people. We look elsewhere for solutions.

A 1929 play that Brecht wrote to politicize workers clearly illustrates his approach. *The Exception and the Rule* is about a merchant who must cross a desert to make a fortune. We watch the mixed relations he has with his guide and his porter, especially when he kills this porter guide after mistaking a helpful gesture as a hostile move. Although the porter has offered him some of their dwindling water supplies, he thinks he is being attacked and shoots.

Despite the killing, the judge in the subsequent trial exonerates him, ruling, "In the circumstances as established it was inevitable that he should believe himself threatened."[10] Existing class tensions, in other words, lead to paranoia, even though the merchant's paranoia in this case is baseless.

Americans may see here a resemblance to their "stand your ground" laws where citizens (White) may shoot others (people of color) if they feel threatened, whether or not there is an actual threat. Note that Stand Your Ground laws don't work in reverse because many judges see Whites, by definition, as non-threatening.

The judge's "circumstances as established" is another way of saying "reality as those in power define it." *The Exception and the Rule* reads like a parable about this dynamic. While the audience initially hopes that the characters will find a way to work through their differences, ultimately they conclude that things will improve only if the system itself changes. The boss will inevitably be at odds with his employees and the courts will invariably side with him. The rule of systemic classism will override any individual exceptions.

Brecht hopes his audiences will apply this new political awareness to their own situations. It doesn't matter whether bosses are good or bad or whether they have good or bad intentions. Systemic pressures on them are such that they will always sacrifice the workers, who therefore must refuse to be coopted and keep their eyes fixed on the prize. Only collective resistance, Brecht wants his audiences to conclude, will bring about meaningful change.

In certain ways, Brecht's desire for art is like Matthew Arnold's in that he wants art, not only to help us see better, but to move us to action. Unlike Arnold but like Shelley and Du Bois, Brecht believes the oppressed will determine whether a better world emerges. In Samuel

Johnson we saw distinctions made between literature that corrupts and literature than enlightens. For Du Bois and now Brecht, there is literature that collaborates with existing oppression and literature that liberates us from it. The revolutionary Frantz Fanon, our next thinker, sees "literature of combat" as an important political ally.

Frantz Fanon

Post-Colonial Literature, a Form of Combat

This may be properly called a literature of combat, in the sense that it calls on the whole people to fight for their existence as a nation. It is a literature of combat, because it molds the national consciousness, giving it form and contours and flinging open before it new and boundless horizons; it is a literature of combat because it assumes responsibility, and because it is the will to liberty expressed in terms of time and space.

— **Frantz Fanon,** *The Wretched of the Earth* (1961)[1]

REGARDING THE ROLE OF culture in relation to politics, Frantz Fanon is to post-colonial literature studies what W.E.B. Du Bois is to African American Studies. The legendary author of *The Wretched of the Earth* (1961) has much to say about how literature can be used both to oppress and to liberate.

Fanon is a fascinating figure. Hailing from the French territory of Martinique and a descendant of African slaves, he became acquainted with the great Martinique poet and writer Aimé Césaire at his high school. He also saw fascism firsthand when French sailors, unleashed by the collaborationist Vichy government during World War II, established an oppressive regime on the island, harassing the inhabitants. Fanon enlisted in the Free French Army and was wounded in action when the allied forces invaded Germany. After the war he gained a doctorate in psychiatry at the University of Lyon in France, writing his dissertation on the negative psychological effects of colonialism on people of color. When the dissertation was rejected (he had to write a second one on a narrower topic), he published it as the book *Black Skin, White Masks* (1952), a groundbreaking work about how people of color must adapt their behavior to negotiate White society.

Fanon went on to practice psychology in Algeria, where he found himself treating both French torturers and Algerian torture victims during Algeria's fight for independence. Eventually he resigned and then was expelled from the country, moving to Tunis, where he openly supported Algeria's independence movement. Eventually he developed leukemia but, before dying, dictated the highly influential *Wretched of the Earth*, which examines the impact of colonialism on the colonized and what the colonized must do to fight back.

Just as we saw Du Bois and Langston Hughes complaining about middle class African American authors who cater to white audiences, so Fanon describes native authors who are ashamed of their own culture. Soft power backed by hard power corrupts these authors, turning them against their own people. "Every effort is made to bring the colonized person to admit the inferiority of his culture," Fanon writes, adding that this campaign extends to the nation, which is made to seem unreal, and even to the individual's own "biological structure," which appears confused and imperfect.[2]

Fanon notes that the colonialists' efforts prove effective. Imported culture overwhelms native culture, which becomes "more and more shriveled up, inert, and empty."[3] Fanon's diagnosis also applies to literature. As African children are brought up reading, say, the French tragedies of Corneille and Racine, little is left of indigenous culture other than "a set of automatic habits, some traditions of dress, and a few broken-down institutions." In these "remnants of culture," Fanon says, "there is no real creativity and no overflowing life."[4] For instance, old folktales that grandparents tell their children, while they may survive, cannot address the issues of the day.

Fanon appears to say that literature can't do much so long as the colonial powers are firmly in place. By itself, it cannot overthrow them. Once the anti-colonial struggle heats up, however, literature becomes an important ally.

Fanon even suggests that different genres will predominate at different stages of the revolt. When resistance to colonial rule is in its early stages, for instance, literature may "confine itself to the tragic and poetic style."[5] As such times, we are most likely to see locally written tragedies and melodramatic poetry.

Fanon is critical of these genres, regarding them as mainly reactive. He characterizes them as "bitter, hopeless recrimination" and "violent, resounding, florid writing."[6] The occupying power may even promote them, believing that they provide a safe cathartic release for grievance. Fanon points out, "Stinging denunciations, the exposing of distressing conditions and passions which find their outlet in expression, are in fact assimilated by the occupying power in a cathartic process." Through venting, grievance literature appears to "clear the atmosphere."[7]

Fanon here appears to be channeling Brecht, who as we have seen accused bourgeois theater of encouraging audiences to weep for—but not to change—existing injustice. All is not lost, however, as such writing sets the stage for the later conversations about the emerging nation. At the very least, melodramatic lament allows the intellectual to see that there is a cohesion to the people. Following this, we see indigenous literature making indictments, then appeals. Finally, "in the period that follows, the words of command are heard."[8] In other words, first indigenous literature accuses oppression, then it asks for something better, and finally it demands a free and independent nation ("the crystallization of the national consciousness").[9]

Older literary styles and themes having been disrupted, emerging writers speak with a new voice as they begin addressing a new audience. "While at the beginning the native intellectual used to produce his work to be read exclusively by the oppressor," writes Fanon, "now the native writer progressively takes on the habit of addressing his own people."[10] "It is only from that moment," he contends, "that we can speak of a national literature." He labels literature that takes up and clarifies nationalist themes "a literature of combat."[11]

Combative literature "calls on the whole people to fight for their existence as a nation," Fanon writes. As such, it "molds the national consciousness, giving it form and contours," thereby opening "new and boundless horizons." Such literature Fanon characterizes as "the will to liberty expressed in terms of time and space."[12]

While Fanon is not precise in his literary theorizing—despite having studied literature in college and having written three plays, his major concerns are elsewhere—he appears to see an evolution from poetry to fiction and creative non-fiction as the struggle's outlines become clearer. "It is as if a kind of internal organization or law of expression existed," he writes, "which wills that poetic expression become less frequent in proportion as the objectives and the methods of the struggle for liberation become more precise."[13] The novels Fanon has in mind may include such works as Nigerian author Chinua Achebe's *Things Fall Apart* and *No Longer at Ease,* which spell out clearly the key conflicts. In the first, Achebe describes colonialism's disruptive impact upon an Igbo tribal village, in the second the internal conflicts experienced by an Igbo man who studies in Britain and then returns to Nigeria.

Fanon sees a similar evolution underway in oral literature. What were once "set pieces" and "inert episodes" come alive as storytellers turn their attention to contemporary conflicts. "The formula 'This all happened long ago,'" Fanon writes, "is substituted with that of 'What we are going to speak of happened somewhere else, but it might well have happened here today, and it might happen tomorrow.'" In Fanon's telling, storytellers who in the past were "stereotyped and tedious to listen to" now overturn their traditional storytelling methods and contents. In response, their public, "which was formerly scattered, became compact. The epic, with its typified categories, reappeared; it became an authentic form of entertainment which took on once more a cultural value."[14]

Proof of storytelling's effectiveness, Fanon adds, is that the colonialists, from 1955 on, proceeded to systematically arrest these storytellers. The authorities felt threatened by the way that evolving oral literature "gives rise to a new rhythm of life and to forgotten muscular tensions, and develops the imagination." The end result is that "the existence of a new type of man is revealed to the public":

> The present is no longer turned in upon itself but spread out for all to see. The storyteller once more gives free rein to his imagination; he makes innovations and he creates a work of art. It even happens that the characters, which are barely ready for such a transformation—highway robbers or more or less anti-social vagabonds—are taken up and remodeled. The emergence of the imagination and of the creative urge in the songs and epic stories of a colonized country is worth following.[15]

Fanon is careful to say that the storyteller does not operate in a vacuum. Rather, he is buoyed by the public to seek out "new patterns, that is to say national patterns." The result is a reordering of genres. Comedy and farce disappear or "lose their attraction," as do the tormented dramas of troubled intellectuals. In their place arises a new kind of drama, which becomes part of the common lot of the people and forms part of an action in preparation or already in progress.[16]

Literature then (and culture in general) helps people transition from their identities as "colonized man" to "a new humanism." While it may appear that armed struggle is the major game in town, literature should not be suspended or "put into cold storage."[17] Rather, writers should keep writing during an active revolution because their work is an integral part of the struggle.

Some cautions are in order about Fanon's preferred genres. He wrote *Wretched of the Earth* at a time of revolutionary upheaval (1961) as independence movements cast off colonial powers around the world. It's not surprising, then, that he applauds the epic, which specializes in national themes and nation building (think of *Gilgamesh, The Iliad, The Aeneid*) and downplays other forms.

Since not all times are revolutionary, however, one can come to the defense of the rejected genres. Fanon mentions the disappearance or irrelevance of comedy and farce and talks about how "the tragic and poetic" style must be superseded. Comedy and farce, however, can provide important emotional outlets to the oppressed in down times, a form of quiet resistance, while tragedy and melodrama provide ways of holding on to one's integrity in the face of hostile forces. Fanon talks about the latter as colonialist safety valves, but sometimes one must do whatever it takes to keep the flame of hope and human dignity alive.

Another problem with Fanon's framing of the issues is that all the literature of the colonizer is painted with the same brush. It's worth noting, however, that, as indigenous literature develops its own legs, its relationship to the literature of the colonizers also changes, and it learns to distinguish between the helpful and the harmful. Likewise, when there is already a long-established literary tradition in a colonized nation, there can be an evolution in how authors of the colonial power are regarded. Therefore (to cite one example), while certain Indian nationalists, fighting to break free of British rule and influence, once rejected Shakespeare in favor of the classic Sanskrit author Kalidasa, now many Indians find room for both artists.

Fanon died in 1961 and so did not live to see both the successes and the failures of post-colonial Africa. All the literary forms he mentions continue to play roles in the life of the former colonies.

The Frankfurt School

Great Literature vs. One-Dimensional Society

Fiction calls the facts by their name and their reign collapses; fiction subverts everyday experience and shows it to be mutilated and false.

— **Herbert Marcuse**, *One-Dimensional Man* (1964)[1]

THE INFLUENTIAL FRANKFURT SCHOOL comprised a group of German Marxist intellectuals who, like Shelley, believed that high culture captures humankind's deep longing for liberation. While not as optimistic as Marx and Engels about literature's direct power to develop a revolutionary consciousness, they thought it could at least chip away at the false consciousness that keeps workers from seeing where their true interests lie. If they thought that great literature could open worker eyes, however, they were even more focused on how pop lit could close them.

The member who gained the most political prominence was Herbert Marcuse (1898–1979). Drafted into the German army in 1916 but seeing no action, Marcuse would participate in the ill-fated

Spartacist uprising following the war. He went on to study at the University of Freiburg but, blocked because of politics from university posts, in 1932 he joined the Institute for Social Research, popularly known as the Frankfurt School. Almost immediately afterwards, however, he and the others had to flee.

He ended up in America, where for a while he worked for the CIA on anti-Nazi propaganda projects. Later he taught at several American universities, ending up at the University of California at San Diego, where he was heralded by the anti-Vietnam War movement as "the father of the New Left." His ambitious project to reconcile Marx and Freud led to his book *Eros and Civilization,* while his indictment of capitalist materialism found expression in *One-Dimensional Man.* This challenging book became an unlikely bestseller amongst leftist activists.

Marcuse and the other members of the Frankfurt School were among the first scholars to take popular culture seriously. To be sure, they had a negative view of it. In their minds, those in power use "low culture" to distract the working class, preventing them from imagining revolutionary alternatives. Echoing Marx's contention about religion, the Frankfurt School saw pop culture as an "opiate of the masses."

Two other Frankfurt members, Theodor Adorno and Max Horkheimer, were the first theorists to use the phrase "culture industry," which they regarded as capitalism's way of dominating and manipulating mass consciousness.[2] Popular fiction, popular music, and the media, Adorno, Horkheimer and Marcuse argue, distract us from what we should really want. If, for instance, women retreat into cheap romances that assure them the right man will save them, they won't develop a strong sense of self.

I use this as an example because it fits well with Marcuse's discussion of Gustave Flaubert's *Emma Bovary.* Although the novel itself is not a problem, it describes the problem. Marcuse writes that Emma, who is locked in a sterile marriage in a provincial town, doesn't know what she really wants. Capitalism can't satisfy her inchoate longings and she herself lacks the language for them.[3] She therefore turns to sentimental novels like Jacques-Henri Bernardin's de Saint-Pierre's *Paul and Virginia* (1788), about lovers who find love and social harmony in an idealized new world free of class conflict. This shallow novel comes to define love and happiness for Emma. As Flaubert describes it,

> Before marriage she thought herself in love; but the happiness that should have followed this love not having come, she must, she thought, have been mistaken. And Emma tried to find out what one meant exactly in life by the words felicity, passion, rapture, that had seemed to her so beautiful in books.[4]

When reading *Paul and Virginia*, for instance, Flaubert mentions Emma dreaming of "the little bamboo-house, the Black slave Domingo, the dog Fidele, but above all of the sweet friendship of some dear little brother, who seeks red fruit for you on trees taller than steeples, or who runs barefoot over the sand, bringing you a bird's nest."[5]

Unlike *Paul and Virginia*, *Madame Bovary* is a great novel, and such works, Marcuse says, have always stood in opposition to the world. Marcuse calls this Art's "Great Refusal" and says that the world's masterpieces should be seen as a protest "against that which is."[6] In this vision, which supplements Shelley's ideas, great literature indirectly negates or opposes power relations as they currently exist.

The negation, Marcuse believes, is conveyed through Emma Bovary's tragedy. Identifying with her longings, we feel the full tragedy of her life as she experiences it in existing society. The novel gives shape and solidity to our feelings of dissatisfaction and alerts us to our desire for something more. As Marcuse puts it, Flaubert "subverts everyday experience" by showing it to be "mutilated and false." Marcuse cautions, however, that art has only "the power of negation." It can "speak its own language only as long as the images are alive which refuse and refute the established order."[7]

Marcuse's view of art as negation invites the question why it is not simply enough to "call facts by their name" to expose capitalist oppression. Why must art operate only indirectly? Shelley, after all, talks of poetry enlarging "the circumference of the imagination by replenishing it with thoughts of ever new delight." Shelley, however, lived in different times and so had a different vision of what was historically possible. Because it was clear to him what it meant to be liberated and what it meant to be enslaved, indirection was unnecessary. One could distinguish the good guys from the bad, with great poetry clearly making common cause with the former.

Marcuse, by contrast, wrote at a time when state power seemed capable of co-opting any rebellion. As Marcuse sees it, the ruling class uses pop culture to turn people into "one-dimensional" men and women who settle for shallow gratification. He fears that even serious art loses its power in a society where, although all works are tolerated, none are taken seriously.

As a result, masterpieces are "deprived of their antagonistic force, of the estrangement which was the very dimension of their truth." Although they may have once "stood in contradiction to the status quo," that contradiction is now "flattened out."[8] Marcuse's view makes him skeptical of new works of art, which he believes are far too easily accepted, even when they contain controversial material. Marcuse therefore believes that playwrights Eugene O'Neill and Tennessee Williams and novelists William Faulkner and Vladimir Nabokov do not seriously challenge our one-dimensional society. Instead, they perpetuate it:

> [Non-repressed and guilt free] sexuality is rampant in O'Neill's alcoholics and Faulkner's savages, in the *Streetcar Named Desire* and under the *Hot Tin Roof*, in *Lolita*, in all the stories of Hollywood and New York orgies, and the adventures of suburban housewives. This is infinitely more realistic, daring, uninhibited. It is part and parcel of the society in which it happens, but

nowhere its negation. What happens is surely wild and obscene, virile and tasty, quite immoral—and, precisely because of that, perfectly harmless.[9]

Marcuse almost sounds like Shelley's adversary Thomas Peacock here, wondering if scientific and technological advancements have made poetry irrelevant. Indeed, it appeared in Marcuse's day that capitalism could have its cake and eat it too, make money for the wealthy while providing a decent living for everyone else. America at the time was experiencing what has been characterized as "the Great Prosperity," a moment when the American gross national product was steadily rising, when workers could be placated with ever higher wages, when women were declaring independence, and when newly enfranchised groups were gaining more rights. He did not anticipate the 1980s, when living standards would fall and those with wealth and power would attack unions and attempt to hold back newly liberated women and people of color.

It so happens that, when that decade rolled around, the American right did not share Marcuse's view of contemporary art's ineffectiveness. Why else would they attack university literature departments, not only in the late 1980s and early 1990s but again in the 2020s? Reactionary forces might no longer put novels like *Madame Bovary* on trial, but they accused (and still accuse) English teachers of shifting the values of young people, making them more open to the rights of women, the working class, people of color, members of the LBGTQ+ community, citizens of underdeveloped nations, and the like. This helps explain why, in the years since Marcuse, there have been battles over "political correctness," "cancel culture," "critical race theory," and "wokeness," with the promise of more to come.

Marcuse might not be quite so dismissive of Faulkner, O'Neill, Williams, and Nabokov if he saw America and Europe today. These authors, no less than great authors of the past, can be seen as struggling with the spiritual emptiness of capitalism, striving through their tragic outcomes to hold on to a vision of human fulfillment. One could argue that modern society has warped Humbert Humbert, who thinks that salvation lies in a 12-year-old nymphette, and Blanche DuBois, who thrashes around in sterile promiscuity. Both, like Emma Bovary, have precious dreams, which we see all the more vividly as they are crushed. A similar dynamic is at work in Faulkner and O'Neill. Marcuse's discomfort with these works may say more about his distaste for changing sexual mores than with their vision of the world.

Marcuse's heirs have also been modifying his theories of popular literature. This has been especially true of Fredric Jameson, widely regarded as America's leading Marxist literary theorist and the one who brought the Frankfurt School to the attention of many scholars with his book *Marxism and Form: Twentieth-Century Dialectical Theories of Literature* (1971). Jameson agrees with Marcuse that, if we have difficulty imagining a better world, it is "not owing to any individual failure of imagination but as the result of the systemic, cultural, and ideological closure of which we are all in one way or another prisoners."[10] In other words, those in power limit our very ability to imagine. Where he differs from Marcuse is in seeing pop lit as not altogether bad.

Jameson grants that pop lit can distract us from our real problems. Here the two are in agreement. But Jameson adds that such fiction can also reawaken stultified imaginations. Pop lit, in fact, can help us rediscover revolutionary hope.

For an example, Jameson turns to utopian science fiction. Looking at such novels as Ursula K. Le Guin's *Dispossessed*, Joanna Russ's *Female Man*, Marge Piercy's *Woman on the Edge of Time*, and Samuel Delany's *Triton*, Jameson writes that their "deepest vocation is to bring home, in local and determinate ways, and with a fullness of concrete detail, our constitutional ability to imagine Utopia itself."[11]

Jameson is less interested in the utopian visions of this or that writer—indeed, he critiques what he sees as Le Guin's conventional liberal thinking[12]—than in the imagining process itself. By immersing ourselves in literary sci-fi, we begin chipping away at the impediments to imagining, thereby creating a space for radical aspiration.

To be sure, like other Marxists Jameson acknowledges that literature can't do the work alone. It must ally itself with revolutionary forces. Once readers have immersed themselves in utopian science fiction, however, they will be better prepared to recognize and accept the revolutionary moment when it comes.

It must be said that Marxist hopes for literature have dwindled considerably since the days of Marx and Engels, who saw *Robinson Crusoe* galvanizing middle class entrepreneurs in their struggle with the landed classes. Recall that Engels once imagined future literature undermining the confidence of the bourgeoisie. Now it appears that, at least in the eyes of current Marxists, literature can do no more than help us to see capitalism's sterility (Terry Eagleton) or keep our hope muscles from atrophying (Jameson). So much for it having a direct impact.

It's worth mentioning one other Frankfurt member who helps us understand how art can set us free. While Walter Benjamin doesn't mention literature in his "Theses on the Philosophy of History" (1940), what he says of history can also be applied to works of culture. Benjamin says history should not be seen as a mere timeline of events, like "beads on a rosary,"[13] but rather as a vibrant force where powerful moments of the past flash up when needed. If the French Revolution sometimes depicted its heroes in Roman togas (as did the American Revolution), it was because it "viewed itself as Rome incarnate." The past was "charged with the time of the now" and "blasted out of the continuum of history."[14] Historical actors, Benjamin says, will "seize hold of a memory as it flashes up at a moment of danger."[15]

Literature too can work this way. Works that have been relegated to dusty museums can, in revolutionary times, suddenly speak with a modern voice. This has been especially true of past women writers during the feminist revolution. In the 1970s and 1980s, feminist scholars resurrected forgotten texts and reinterpreted familiar ones in ways that directly addressed present day concerns. The works were there when history needed them, charged with the time of the now.

Twentieth Century Feminists

The Marriage Plot

> Once upon a time, the end, the rightful end, of
> women in novels was social—successful courtship,
> marriage—or judgmental of her sexual and
> social failure—death.

— Rachel Blau DuPlessis, *Writing Beyond the*
Ending (1985)[1]

IT'S DIFFICULT TO SINGLE out a representative issue for feminism's
contribution to literary impact given the many different avenues one
could take. I focus on "the marriage plot" since many of the greatest female authors—Fanny Burney, Jane Austen, the Bronte sisters,
George Eliot—employ it. Furthermore, as Tania Modleski points out
in *Loving with a Vengeance: Mass Produced Fantasies with Women*
(1982), the marriage plot continues to dominate the women's publishing, film, and television markets. The debate is whether (as Marcuse and Adorno would contend) these works necessarily reenforce a

patriarchal agenda or whether they subtly undermine it, delivering a blow for female self-determination.

A key figure in the discussion has been poet, editor, and scholar Rachel Blau DuPlessis (b. 1941). DuPlessis received her PhD in literature from Columbia University, examining "the endless poem," as practiced by William Carlos Williams and Ezra Pound, while also producing long poems of her own. In *Writing beyond the Ending: Narrative Strategies of Twentieth-Century Women Writers* (1985), she writes about the damaging effect of the marriage plot on women readers.

For the longest time, DuPlessis observes, there were only two possible plot endings for women: marriage or death. As the title of her work indicates, she is interested in how 20th century women writers such as Woolf, H.D., Denise Levertov, Adrienne Rich, and others sought to break free of the marriage plot. Or if not break free, then at least reconcile the marriage plot with the *Bildungsroman* or growth story.

DuPlessis says that no reconciliation has seemed possible for much of the novel's history. While many of the great male novels are growth stories—Henry Fielding's *Tom Jones,* Charles Dickens's *David Copperfield,* Goethe's *Apprenticeship of Wilhelm Meister,* Mark Twain's *Huckleberry Finn,* James Joyce's *Portrait of the Artist as a Young Man*—such stories were not seen as possible for women. Although stories featuring female protagonists might have growth elements in "the narrative middle," DuPlessis contends that, by the end, the woman's "quest or *Bildung* is set aside or repressed."[2]

While it's easy to say that women should insist on growth stories for themselves, DuPlessis points out that the "yearning, pleasing, choosing, slipping, falling, and failing" that are at the heart of romance novels are "some of the deep, shared structures of our culture."[3] That's why these works prove so effective at socializing women into the marriage plot. Immersed in such stories from an early age, it's difficult for women readers to think their own lives could be different.

While DuPlessis doesn't say so explicitly, it appears that she regards authors like Austen, the Brontes, and Elizabeth Barrett Browning as complicitous with patriarchy, which means they are guilty of doing some harm. Even when these unquestionably great authors push against the marriage plot, as they do in the middles of their narratives, ultimately they surrender. While one might regard their female protagonists as "heroes" in the earlier chapters, according to DuPlessis's framing they have dwindled into married heroines by the end.

Jane Austen's "handsome, clever, and rich" Emma Woodhouse, for instance, may initially think she can resist the marriage plot, but eventually she succumbs. For much of the novel she proclaims that marriage is not for her, even as she attempts to arrange marriages for other people. She receives a shock, however, when she discovers that her young protégé loves George Knightley, the man Emma herself desires. DuPlessis notes that Emma is shocked at how "her impetuous scheming may have hurt her own best interests. At the point when she is sincerely repentant for her assumed powers, she is marriageable, and is therefore proposed to. Her proper negotiation with class and gender makes the heroine from an improper hero."[4]

Something similar occurs in *Pride and Prejudice*. DuPlessis writes that, because of the novel's concentration on Elizabeth Bennet's "force and her growing capacity for insight," it appears for a while that she has hero potential. Unfortunately, this means that, when Elizabeth does choose to marry a man with ten thousand pounds a year, she validates the institution even more. After all, who will argue with one of literature's most popular female protagonists?

Not all feminists agree with DuPlessis that the great 19th century women novelists capitulated to the marriage plot, however. Sandra Gilbert (b. 1936) and Susan Gubar (b. 1944), two scholars famous for working in tandem (itself an assertion of female solidarity), believe that the great Victorian female novels empowered rather than handicapped women. They did so by helping women articulate rebellious longings.

Writing about *Jane Eyre* in *The Madwoman in the Attic: The Woman Writer and the Nineteenth-Century Literary Imagination*, Gilbert and Gubar argue that Bertha Mason, the mad wife locked away in the attic, is Jane Eyre's alter ego. Given social expectations, Jane may not be able to strike out against the imperious Rochester but Bertha Mason can. In other words, instead of revolving around Jane's marriage to Rochester, Bronte's novel is grounded in repressed anger.[5]

The disagreement between DuPlessis and Gilbert and Gubar is ultimately about whether readers pay more attention to a novel's end or to its energy points. The feminist scholars all agree, however, on the corrosive power of the patriarchal narrative. Therefore, it's important to pay attention to those writers who have overtly—not just secretly—attempted to break with it, as DuPlessis does with 20th century women authors.

To capture the challenges facing women, DuPlessis draws on Raymond Williams, author of *Marxism and Literature* (1977). Williams says that imagining a new kind of consciousness "can be the long and difficult remaking of an inherited (determined) practical consciousness." This remaking requires "confronting a hegemony in the fibers of the self and in the hard practical substance of effective and continuing relationships."[6] Put in terms of the marriage drama, the lives that women have been culturally taught to imagine for themselves are so imbedded in "the fibers of the self" that fighting against them can seem impossible.

Those authors who want to create a new narrative, Williams says, must embody and perform "latent, momentary, and newly possible consciousness."[7] In other words, they must imagine characters living radically different lives.

Williams and DuPlessis would agree with what Frantz Fanon says about authors striving for liberation: they can't do it alone but must work in conjunction with other change agents. Participating in political struggles and imagining new narratives, then, go hand in hand. DuPlessis writes that once women have "the economic, political, and legal power" to challenge the many ways they are subordinated, then "novelists will begin to 'write beyond' the romantic ending."[8]

Just as Fanon sees authors as vital allies in the fight for freedom, so do many literary feminists. With their *Madwoman* book, Gilbert and Gubar showed how the landscape changes once women start telling their own stories, and they followed it up with their groundbreaking *Norton Anthology of Literature by Women: The Traditions in English*. The anthology has become a staple in Women's Studies classes, and *Ms Magazine* named Gilbert and Gubar "Women of the Year" in 1986, an award not normally bestowed upon scholars.

For all the efforts of great women authors to challenge the marriage plot, whether covertly or directly, the fact remains that the story remains a core element of the "mass produced fantasies" that continue to sell millions of copies. Is this proof, then, that pop lit is bad?

Southern California University scholar Tania Modleski (b. 1949) doesn't think so, even though she acknowledges that courtship novels, gothic romances, soap operas and "chick lit" all owe their success to their rigid adherence to a predictable partnership plot (especially Harlequins). Since she will go on to defend them, it's worth noting how much she initially concedes.

For instance, she admits that they appear prime examples of the Frankfurt School's cultural opiate of the masses, brainwashing women into thinking that marriage, not activism, is their only salvation. She partially agrees with author and publisher Elizabeth Merrick, who sounds as though she is channeling Frankfurt School's Herbert Marcuse or Theodor Adorno in the preface to her anthology *This Is Not Chick Lit* (2005). Modleski quotes Merrick declaring that the chick lit formula,

> numbs our senses. Literature by contrast, grants us access to countless new cultures, places, and inner lives. Where chick lit reduces the complexity of the human experience, great literature increases our awareness of other perspectives and paths. Such works employ carefully crafted language to expand our reality instead of beating us over the head with clichés that promote a narrow worldview. Chick lit shuts down our consciousness. Literature expands our imaginations.[9]

Merrick especially targets Helen Fielding's *Bridget Jones's Diary* (1996), which many regard as the novel that launched contemporary chick lit. Fielding's wildly successful romance distressed those feminists who desired more woke heroines. For her part, Modleski describes Bridget in such a way as makes her appear as one of the marriage plot's victims. Fielding, Modleski writes, "created a ditzy character who is hilariously skeptical of marriage but hoping against hope to evade the fate of 'singletons'—dying alone at the end of their lives and, not being immediately missed by anyone, are finally discovered half eaten by their Alsatian dog." Bridget, she notes, is "obsessed with controlling her weight and limiting her alcohol and tobacco intake, and throughout much of the novel she is embroiled in an unhealthy relationship with her boss, an attractive cad."[10]

Despite her reservations, however, Modleski nevertheless believes that critiques of chick lit and mass-produced women's fantasies don't do justice to the complexity of their readers, who she believes are far angrier than such depictions acknowledge. For instance, Harlequins often feature a scene in which the future Mr. Right insults the heroine (just as Jane Austen's Darcy insults Elizabeth on their first encounter). Harlequins also feature a revenge fantasy (the self-sufficient hero becomes sick and dependent) and a power fantasy (the woman takes over). Modleski insists we should not overlook that momentary rebellion, pointing out that "the very fact that the novels must go to such extremes to neutralize women's anger and to make masculine hostility bearable testifies to the depths of women's discontent. Each novel is as much a protest against as an endorsement of the feminine condition."[11]

The anger finds even more dramatic expression in gothics, with the heroine often finding herself imprisoned by a tyrannical man. "Because the male appears to be the outrageous persecutor," Modleski writes, "the reader can allow herself a measure of anger against him yet at the same time she can identify with a heroine who is entirely without malice and innocent of any wrongdoing."[12] Modleski says that the gothic also allows women readers to vent their anger at "the mother, for allowing herself to be a victim and for (as often happens) taking out her own anger and aggressive impulses on the helpless child."[13]

Ann Radcliffe's *Mysteries of Udolpho* (1794), the gothic that enthralls Catherine Morland in Jane Austen's *Northanger Abbey*, is a textbook example of such energies at work. The villainous female in this case is the grandmother, not the revered (and dead) mother. The virtuous Emily St. Aubert finds herself locked up in a mysterious castle because her grandmother has irresponsibly married an Italian brigand.

To be sure, Modleski must admit that women don't stay angry in these mass-produced genres. In Harlequins, the abusive hero eventually succumbs to the heroine's goodness and beauty and his behavior is rationalized away: he was only obnoxious because he was struggling against a growing attachment for her. In the gothics, meanwhile, marriage also rides in to save the day. Having vented her anger, the heroine learns that the murderous male protagonist is not a Bluebeard after all but actually a more or less admirable man.

To cite a well-known example, author Daphne du Maurier in *Rebecca* finds a way to rationalize away the fact that Mr. Right has shot his first wife. It so happens that this awful woman, knowing she was dying of cancer, manipulated him into it. This in turn somehow means that he is not guilty, thereby clearing the way for the deserving heroine to have confidence in him. In other gothic novels there is sometimes a bad brother and a good brother, one providing the opportunity to vent, the other to console.

Modleski's point is that, despite their succumbing to the marriage plot, mass-produced Harlequins and gothics are more nuanced than they first appear. As a result, they help women manage difficult relationships. After all, not everyone is in a position to walk away from a dominating husband. Sometimes you must grab help where you can, and sometimes that help comes in the form of a book.

Yet Modleski, like DuPlessis, ultimately wants women to break out of problematic marriages, not enable them. When mass-produced fantasies allow women to rationalize away male aggression and paper over their anger, they are not doing them a favor. Therefore Modleski, again like DuPlessis, would prefer that women read literature that makes them aware of their condition, not merely endure it.

HANS ROBERT JAUSS

CHALLENGING THE HORIZON OF
EXPECTATIONS

A literary work is not an object which stands by itself
and which offers the same face to each reader in each
period. It is not a monument which reveals its timeless
essence in a monologue. It is much more like an orches-
tration which strikes ever new chords among its readers and which frees the text from the substance of the
words and makes it meaningful for the time...A literary
work must be understood as creating a dialogue...

— **Hans Robert Jauss,** "Literary History as a Response to Literary Theory" (1967)[1]

ALL THE THINKERS IN this section see themselves engaged in a battle against a worldview (Brecht's *"Weltanschauung"*) that subjugates,
demeans, or otherwise writes off large swatches of the population,
whether they be people of color, workers, former colonized peoples,
or women. In the late 1960s a University of Konstanz scholar earned
his 15 minutes of academic fame by describing what happens when a

great work of literature collides with the prevailing worldview—or, as he called it, the "horizon of expectations." If you want to see literary audiences on the cusp of significant transformation, Hans Robert Jauss contended, look at how a literary masterpiece makes them uncomfortable.

Jauss (1921–97) was one of the pioneers of Reception Theory, an approach to literature that shifted the focus from text to reader. Jauss had a dark past, having spent two years on the Russian front during World War II as a youthful member of the SS, a fact he managed to keep hidden until shortly before his death. After the war, he fled from his past by immersing himself in French literature, and his belief that great literature can rewire its readers in a progressive direction may owe something to his own metamorphosis from one possibly involved in war crimes to scholar. The transformational power that Jauss ascribes to literature is what attracts scholars like me to his theory.

During Jauss's Konstanz career, he and his colleague Wolfgang Iser changed the way literary scholars see readers engaging with texts. As Iser saw it, reading is a collaborative process, with the reader filling in the gaps left by the author. Iser was particularly interested in the opportunities for audience creativity in works where the ending is left open.

The more historically minded Jauss, on the other hand, looks at how a work interacts with a reader's existing assumptions or "horizon of expectations." Potentially, following immersion in a masterpiece, one's assumptions or expectations can change—which is to say, one can become a different person, with a broader and more complex view of the world.

Jauss is most interested in works that confront or unsettle audiences. When readers encounter a work that demands they change their view, they will often kick back, sometimes angrily. Jauss owes a debt to Brecht's theories about confrontational theater, as well as to avant-garde art, which in the 1920s judged itself by how thoroughly it scandalized the bourgeoisie. The more, the better.

If certain works we now consider great were attacked when they first came out, Jauss explains, it's because they took readers out of their comfort zones. Many of us don't like abandoning traditional modes of thinking for new and broader frameworks.

Jauss therefore looks at a work's reception to chart its dialogue with readers: what new demands does it put on them and how do they react? To determine this back and forth, reception historians resort to everything from personal diaries to published reviews to (in certain cases) trial transcripts and political attacks. They also check book sales and other indirect ways of assessing impact. Finally, they find implicit acknowledgement of the author-reader dialogue in subsequent works by the author (how has he or she changed because of audience reactions?) and in works by his or her contemporaries (how are *they* writing differently because of the work?).

As for literature that does *not* challenge readers' horizons, Jauss, borrowing from Brecht, calls it "culinary."[2] Culinary works do not stretch readers' visions of what the form or genre could accomplish but merely satisfy what they expect. It's as though culinary authors provide a literary Big Mac to readers who have ordered a Big Mac. More to the point, readers who come expecting, say, a formulaic crime novel will be irritated if they are served anything different. Imagine their distress, or at least confusion, if after ordering Agatha Christie's enjoyable but lightweight *Partners in Crime* they were instead served with Fyodor Dostoevsky's *Crime and Punishment*.

A great work may challenge readers in ways they cannot perceive. By focusing on horizon changes, Jauss's theory resembles philosopher of science Thomas Kuhn's influential idea of paradigm shifts, found in his landmark work *Structure of Scientific Revolutions* (1962). Because people see reality in a certain way, Kuhn says, they cannot accept new ideas, even when faced with compelling scientific evidence. For the longest time, Europe could not accept Copernicus, Kepler, and Galileo's view of the solar system because the reigning paradigm had humankind at the center of creation. Only with incessant challenges did the paradigm eventually change.[3] Jauss's horizons are his version of Kuhn's paradigms. Great artists, like great scientists, hammer away at our understanding of reality until we come around to seeing things through their eyes.

Jauss's major example of a horizon-changing work is the one lionized by Herbert Marcuse, only Jauss looks at Flaubert's *Madame Bovary* (1857) from the vantage point of its reception. When it first appeared, the novel was taken to trial on charges of indecency, which Jauss notes at first glance does not make sense. Although *Madame Bovary* features adultery, a similar treatment of the subject appearing the same year had a dramatically different reception. Georges Feydeau's all-but-forgotten novel *Fanny* was a smash success, going through 13 editions.

A lengthy account of Jauss's *Madame Bovary* example is warranted given the insight it provides into literature's potential to change what passes for reality. Jauss first focuses on the similarities between *Bovary* and *Fanny*. Both "understood how to give a sensational twist to the conventional, rigid triangle which in the erotic scenes surpassed the customary details." In Flaubert's novel, the wife of a provincial doctor has a sordid affair with a local landowner, runs up debts, and commits suicide after he dumps her. Feydeau, meanwhile, "has the youthful lover of [a 30-year-old woman] becoming jealous of his lover's husband, although he has already reached the goal of his desires, and perishing over this tormenting situation." Despite the similarities, however, *Madame Bovary* shook the very foundations of French society whereas *Fanny* did not.[4]

Jauss locates the difference in the way the stories are told. *Fanny* might depict immoral actions in a titillating way, but the reader is aware of what's right and what's wrong and, more importantly, knows that the author is making the same moral distinctions. While social rules get broken, the underlying moral structure remains intact. Because *Fanny* makes no real demands upon the reader's value system—it has just provided a temporary illicit thrill before returning the reader to familiar moral ground—the novel is a comfortable, culinary read. No horizon having been challenged, none is expanded.

Flaubert, by contrast, disturbs readers with a new style of story-telling, called "impersonal telling" or "*le style indirect libre.*" Instead of signaling a value system by which to judge the action, the author appears to have absented himself. Accustomed though we are to impersonal telling now (think Ernest Hemingway), it challenged the 1857 horizon of expectations. One can see why Flaubert was taken to court by examining how the public prosecutor responded to Emma's ecstasy over having a lover. The following passage from the novel was presented as evidence of indecency:

> But when she saw herself in the glass she wondered at her face. Never had her eyes been so large, so black, of so profound a depth. Something subtle about her being transfigured her. She repeated, "I have a lover! a lover!" delighting at the idea as if a second puberty had come to her. So at last she was to know those joys of love, that fever of happiness of which she had despaired! She was entering upon marvels where all would be passion, ecstasy, delirium.[5]

As the prosecutor saw it, Flaubert glorifies adultery. Jauss notes that he "regarded the last sentences as an objective description which included the judgement of the narrator and was upset over this 'glorification of adultery,' which he considered to be even more dangerous and immoral than the misstep itself."[6]

When we read the passage today, we recognize this as Emma's belief, not Flaubert's opinion. We know the author has taken us into her mind. The defense in fact made exactly this argument. Readers of the time, however, were not accustomed to having the responsibility of judgment thrown upon them. After all, in earlier novels omniscient authors make clear how we should assess characters and events. To cite a random example, Charles Dickens intrudes to reassure readers following the heartbreaking death of Little Nell at the conclusion of *The Old Curiosity Shop* (1841):

> Oh! it is hard to take to heart the lesson that such deaths will teach, but let no man reject it, for it is one that all must learn, and is a mighty, universal Truth. When Death strikes down the innocent and young, for every fragile form from which he lets the panting spirit free, a hundred virtues rise, in shapes of mercy, charity, and love, to walk the world, and bless it. Of every tear that sorrowing mortals shed on such green graves, some good is born, some gentler nature comes. In the Destroyer's steps there spring up bright creations that defy his power, and his dark path becomes a way of light to Heaven.[7]

The problem with Flaubert was more than a new storytelling technique. If that's all it was, then there would probably have been no trial. When indirect style shifted power to the reader, however, it appeared to undermine society's moral guardians. Without an author to guide them, Flaubert's readers felt as though they were wandering in an amoral world. Looking at the case through the prosecutor's eyes, Jauss asks, "To what authority should the case of *Madame Bovary* be presented if the previously valid standards of society, 'public opinion, religious beliefs, public morals, good manners,' are no longer sufficient for judging this case?"[8] Given France's experience with revolutions that overthrow the established order, the French court saw Flaubert's novel as the latest entry into that field.

As with the scientific breakthroughs that challenge Thomas Kuhn's paradigms, masterpieces don't change horizons all at once. For a while, novelists continued to write as they had in the past. Victor Hugo's *Les Misérables*, which appeared five years after *Madame Bovary*, features an author who regularly intrudes to comment on the action and draw moral lessons. Nor did a significant number of French citizens stop looking to society's reigning social guardians for guidance in how to live their lives. But wheels had been set in motion for significant changes, both in the way stories were told—*showing* rather than *telling* eventually became all the rage—and in how people regarded traditional institutions.

Whether *Madame Bovary* made French lives better depends on who's making the call. The court, tasked with upholding public morality, agreed with the prosecution that the novel undermined prevailing social standards. Without these, it feared, society would slide into the anarchy that Matthew Arnold feared. On the other hand, if those institutions had become so problematic or debased that society, to renew itself, needed citizens capable of thinking outside the prevailing horizon of expectations, then we can regard *Madame Bovary* as a force for social progress. We've seen Marcuse praising the novel for exposing one-dimensional capitalism, challenging readers through its "great refusal" not to settle for less but to keep imagining the possibilities for a more fulfilling society. If Flaubert prodded people to better understand the source of Emma's frustrated longings, then he helped set forces in motion that would make their lives better.

Jauss's model doesn't work for all literature since not all works cause a ruckus, let alone make court appearances. The model may prove more flexible, however, if we replace "horizons" with a term imported from political science. Political theorists sometimes talk about "the Overton window," which the Mackinac Center for Public Policy describes as "a model for understanding how ideas in society change over time and influence politics." As the Center explains it, "The core concept is that politicians are limited in what policy ideas they can support — they generally only pursue policies that are widely accepted throughout society as legitimate policy options." If, on the other hand, these policies lie *outside* the Overton Window, then politicians risk losing popular support if they champion them.[9]

That literary works might shift the Overton window rather than lead to instantaneous horizon changes is less dramatic, but it's also a plausible explanation for how change happens. It therefore explains why defenders of the status quo had some reason to fear a work like *Madame Bovary*. They realized that allowing contrary ideas to be taken seriously—such as judging for oneself rather than relying on authorities—changed the landscape, even if not all at once. Once the public ventures out upon such slippery slopes, who knows what will happen?

Jauss's idea may be most useful for understanding the controversies that arise over works, including those works under attack in American school systems today. In each battle, one can ask about the horizons being challenged. Even when one doesn't agree with the attackers, one can construct their horizon by studying their responses. If Jauss is right that great literature leads to foundational changes in readers, then reading is indeed akin to playing with dynamite. The thinkers in this section, along with many of their antagonists, have understood this well.

TRAINING GROUND FOR CITIZENSHIP

Terry Eagleton

Literature and Classroom Socialization

In the early 1920s it was desperately unclear why English was worth studying at all; by the early 1930s it had become a question of why it was worth wasting your time on anything else. English was not only a subject worth studying, but the supremely civilizing pursuit, the spiritual essence of the social formation.

— **Terry Eagleton,** *Literary Theory: An Introduction*
(1983)[1]

ONCE MATTHEW ARNOLD PROCLAIMED that general literature instruction would usher in a new epoch marked by "a national glow of life and thought," teachers enter our picture. In Arnold's vision, they were to be the new missionaries, replacing clergy in inculcating foundational social values. Teachers were to introduce students to poetry, the new sacred texts, and make sure they drew the proper conclusions. A new Renaissance beckoned.

In his influential *Literary Theory: An Introduction* (1983), Terry Eagleton focuses on Arnold in his historical chapter on "The Rise of English." I've already cited Eagleton in my Marx-Engels chapter but turn to him here because he explains what schools over the past 150 years have seen as literature's benefits. While Eagleton uses class and gender politics to explain why we teach literature as we do, non-Marxists may still find his summation useful.

That's because Eagleton is not doctrinaire. Born in 1943 into a working-class Irish Catholic family with Irish Republican sympathies, Eagleton served as an altar boy at a local Carmelite convent and at one point considered becoming a priest. He studied literature at Cambridge under the noted Marxist scholar Raymond Williams and also edited a Catholic leftist periodical called *Slant*. Although a socialist, Eagleton, like his American counterpart Fredric Jameson, criticizes leftists who judge literary works by their class politics, calling them "vulgar Marxists." As we have seen, he has not hesitated to defend conservative artists such as Joseph Conrad, T.S. Eliot, and D.H. Lawrence. His same dislike of narrow ideology has led him, in later years, to go after atheists like Christopher Hitchens and evolutionary biologist Richard Dawkins, accusing them of being just as blinkered as the Christian fundamentalists they attack. Eagleton is a daunting opponent, in part because of his razor-sharp wit.

While English teachers don't normally see themselves as political when they teach literature, Eagleton points out that 19th century school authorities had politics very much on their minds. English literature became a general field of study at precisely the time when working class men and women were being admitted into schools. After all, as Arnold had noted, existing class and gender relations could be reenforced this way. In the Mechanics' Institutes, Eagleton notes, the "poor man's Classics" were used to stress solidarity between the social classes, cultivate "larger sympathies," install national pride, and transmit "moral" values (27).

Women followed workers as people for whom an English education was deemed appropriate. Eagleton points out that early proponents of literary study regularly spoke of its "softening" and "humanizing" effects. The rise of English in England, he points out, "ran parallel to the gradual, grudging admission of women to the institutions of higher education; and since English was an untaxing sort of affair, concerned with the finer feelings rather than with the more virile topics of *bona fide* academic 'disciplines,' it seemed a convenient sort of non-subject to palm off on the ladies, who were in any case excluded from science and the professions."[2]

World War I changed all this. If before the war the English ruling class saw literature as a way to soften striving women and rough working-class men, after the war sweetness and light seemed like a good idea for everyone, a way to make England whole again. Eagleton remarks that "it is a chastening thought that we owe the University study of English, in part at least, to a meaningless massacre." Chief among literature's advocates was George Stuart Gordon, Professor of English Literature at Oxford, who in 1922 trenchantly wrote, "England is sick, and ... English literature must save it. The Churches (as I understand) having failed, and social remedies being slow, English literature has now a triple function: still, I suppose, to delight and instruct us, but also, and above all, to save our souls and heal the State."[3]

The view of literature as salvation for a diseased West motivated the influential critic and scholar F. R. Leavis, whose focus on "closely reading" the literary canon helped shape how we still study literature today. In the 1920s, before Leavis, many saw literature as a pleasurable pastime. After Leavis, by the 1930s, they saw it as "the supremely civilizing pursuit, the spiritual essence of the social formation."[4]

As we have seen, Leavis was not the first literature enthusiast to make such broad claims—remember Percy Shelley's description of poets as "the unacknowledged legislators of the world"—but his influence spread through literature programs everywhere. For his part, Eagleton has his doubts. Although passionately committed to literature, as a Marxist he believes that literature must be allied with political action for it to have real effect. Whatever one thinks of this stance, his response to Leavis is both witty and scathing:

213

Was it really true that literature could roll back the deadening effects of industrial labor and the philistinism of the media? It was doubtless comforting to feel that by reading Henry James one belonged to the moral vanguard of civilization itself; but what of all those people who did not read Henry James, who had never even heard of James, and would no doubt go to their graves complacently ignorant that he had been and gone? These people certainly composed the overwhelming social majority; were they morally callous, humanly banal and imaginatively bankrupt? One was speaking perhaps of one's own parents and friends here, and so needed to be a little circumspect. Many of these people seemed morally serious and sensitive enough: they showed no particular tendency to go around murdering, looting and plundering, and even if they did it seemed implausible to attribute this to the fact that they had not read Henry James.[5]

Leavisites, Eagleton declares, were "inescapably elitist," betraying "a profound ignorance and distrust of the capacities of those not fortunate enough to have read English at Downing College [Cambridge]."[6]
Eagleton then adds another twist. Just as there are people who appear unharmed from not having read literature, there are others that literature has actually damaged, or at least failed to improve:

For if not all of those who could not recognize an enjambement were nasty and brutish, not all of those who could were morally pure. Many people were indeed deep in high culture, but it would transpire a decade or so after the birth of [Leavis's journal] *Scrutiny* that this had not prevented some of them from engaging in such activities as superintending the murder of Jews in central Europe. The strength of Leavisian criticism was that it was able to provide an answer...to the question, why read Literature? The answer, in a nutshell, was that it made you a better person. Few reasons could have been more persuasive than that. When the Allied troops moved into the concentration camps some years after the founding of *Scrutiny*, to arrest commandants who had wiled away their leisure hours with a volume of Goethe, it appeared that someone had some explaining to do.[7]

Eagleton's cautions are useful for those who expect literature to accomplish miracles. Skepticism is always necessary when assessing literary impact. But in combatting one extreme, Eagleton goes to another. Sure, it's easy to cite instances where literature has proved ineffective. One thinks of tyrants who, despite having encountered literature when young, still grew up to become tyrants. For instance, there's Liberia's mass-murdering dictator Charles Johnson, who attended an American liberal arts college. You haven't proved much when you have said that, however.

Let's look at the Nazis-reading-Goethe example since Eagleton uses it to dispute claims that literature makes us better people. We've cited previous thinkers who, while lauding literature's salutary effects, offer qualifications. Sir Philip Sidney, for instance, acknowledges that poetry—like physic, swords, and the Bible—can be used for ill as well as for good, depending on who is wielding it. An example of wielding literature for ill would be those Nazis who attempted to fashion Goethe into a proto-fascist writer. For instance, in at least one instance his Faust was depicted as "the archetypal German hero, whose efforts to win land from the sea in the final act of *Faust, Part Two* prefigured the Nazis' own drive for more *Lebensraum* [historically destined expansion territory] in the East."[8]

That Nazis would fixate on Faust, as they did on Nietzsche's Über-mensch (Super Man), makes sense given Faust's soaring ambitions. And it's true that Faust, like Hitler, claims as his higher purpose the reclamation of new land for his emperor, dominating the sea to do so. When his ambitions are opposed by a rival emperor, Faust unleashes the devil Mephistopheles and three thugs to carry out the dirty work. Then, having built himself a seaside castle, he becomes obsessed with a neighboring plot of land and orders Mephistopheles to seize that as well. What's there for a fascist not to like?

The play then turns in a different direction, however. The land that Faust covets is owned by the kindly Baucis and Philemon. In classical mythology, the couple are the quintessential good hosts, sharing the little they have with gods disguised as wandering beggars. Further-more, Mephistopheles and his henchmen exceed Faust's orders and kill the couple, along with a guest, in a mini-Holocaust of their own. Faust is so appalled at the consequences of his desires that the play takes a non-fascist direction: he renounces his magical powers, gives over his imperial ambitions, and devotes himself to being of service to others. As a result, Goethe's Faust, unlike Christopher Marlowe's Faustus, gets his soul back and the play ends with celebrations of nature and divine love. One can only wish that German fascists had followed suit.

More to the point, Goethe's humanism helped provide a founda-tion for much that is positive in German culture. That he was hijacked by the forces of intolerance may reveal the limitations of Enlighten-ment thinking, but it doesn't wipe away the good that he did.

If concentration camp commandants had employed Leavis's close reading strategies, they could not have seen Goethe as a kindred soul. I'm of course joking when I say that. It could well be, however, that they were just reading selected excerpts of Goethe. Or, what I suspect is most likely, they didn't so much engage with Goethe as genuflect before him, regarding him (as some Brits regard Shakespeare) as a cul-tural marker or fetish of national greatness. They lionized him to signal their national superiority. I imagine German teachers were expected to teach very narrow versions of him in school.

German novelist Klaus Mann, who fled Hitler, describes something like this happening in his 1936 novel *Mephisto,* where a talented director modifies Shakespeare's *Hamlet* so that the protagonist appears strong and decisive as opposed to tormented and uncertain. The director is applauded by the Nazis but at the cost of his artistic soul. Nor does this negate Shakespeare's positive impact.

Back to the classroom. When Matthew Arnold, who had been a school inspector, looked to schools to emphasize class harmony and placate the masses, he probably didn't envision teachers teaching, say, Percy Shelley's "Men of England" ("Men of England, wherefore plough/ For the lords who lay ye low?") or William Blake's "The Grey Monk" ("'I die, I die!' the Mother said,/ 'My children die for lack of bread'"). He would want teachers teaching *his* favorite works with *his* intended message. When we explore Leavis's claims that literature makes us better people, to some extent we must look at who is teaching and what they consider as better.

I suggest we divide those teachers believing in literature's life-changing powers into three categories, determined by political leaning: conservative Arnoldians, liberal Arnoldians, and radical Shelleyites. Conservative Arnoldians use literature to affirm traditional values, liberal Arnoldians to instill humanist values, and radical Shelleyites to fight for economic and social justice. (A fourth category would be ideologues, right and left, who don't care for literature other than as an indoctrination vehicle.) All committed teachers may see it as their mission to use literature to produce good citizens and good people, but their criteria for "good" will vary.

Of course, there can be a gap between what teachers want students to take away and what students actually take away. If literature has the explosive power that Plato and others have attributed to it, then even the most careful attempts to circumscribe and manage it may not succeed.

I think of the Wife of Bath's fifth husband and his failed educational strategy in Geoffrey Chaucer's *Canterbury Tales.* To transform his rebellious wife into a docile and submissive woman, every evening he reads to her *Stories of Wicked Wives*. After a few nights of this, she leaps to her feet, tears three pages out of the book, and pushes him into the fire. And while, in response, he shifts from soft power to hard power, delivering a blow that renders her deaf in one ear, in the end she reasserts control and tells her own story. By imagining a woman who, in the face of relentless medieval misogyny, appropriates Biblical stories and fairy tales to find a voice of her own, Chaucer has created one of British literature's greatest characters, on a par with Shakespeare's finest.

In other words, no matter what teachers hope students will take away from assigned literature, students will do with it what students do.

THE CULTURAL
CONSERVATIVES

LITERATURE AS ESSENTIAL BEING

Men may live more truly and fully in reading Plato and
Shakespeare than at any other time because then they
are participating in essential being and are forgetting
their accidental lives.

— **Allan Bloom,** *The Closing of the American
Mind* (1987)[1]

TO UNDERSTAND CULTURAL CONSERVATIVES like Allan Bloom,
Harold Bloom, and E.D. Hirsch, it's important to distinguish them
from political and social conservatives, even though the latter have
sometimes championed them. Their assumption, more or less in line
with F.R. Leavis, is that the classics are a good thing because they make
us deeper and more well-rounded people.

Trumpeting the classics in the 1950s would not have caused them
to stand out since, at the time, most literature professors thought this
way. By the 1980s, however, the political environment had changed,
with progressive literary scholars transforming the literary canon—lit-

erature's sacred works—into a battlefield. Once those responsible for the canon allowed more diversity, it was inevitable that standards for inclusion would be reexamined and often challenged. Overlooked writers were elevated and long revered names were sometimes downgraded. Horrified, cultural conservative pushed back, especially the two Blooms. For them, the new barbarian at the gates was not the working class (as it had been for Matthew Arnold) but multiculturalism.

Raised in a Yiddish speaking household, Harold Bloom (1930–2019) didn't learn English until he was six, but after that there was no holding him back. There are stories of him having memorized the entirety of Milton's *Paradise Lost* at an early age and challenging professors by reciting and asking them to identify long passages from obscure epics. A Fulbright scholar at Cambridge, he went on to teach in the Yale English Department and to author over 40 books, along with hundreds of anthologies and essay collections.

For a while, Bloom was most famous for "the anxiety of influence," a theory that authors, in their determination to be original, are haunted by those who come before them and with whom they see themselves as competing. Indeed, Bloom himself was obsessed with ranking authors. Of these, Shakespeare tops the list, and *Shakespeare: The Invention of the Human* may be his most lasting contribution.

Seeing himself as a modern-day Samuel Johnson, whose *Preface to Shakespeare* (as we have noted) is "one of the landmarks in the history of literary criticism,"[2] Bloom contends that Shakespeare "pragmatically reinvented" us,[3] changing the way we see others and ourselves and even how we experience feelings.[4] Whereas fellow playwrights Marlowe produced "cartoons" and Ben Jonson "ideograms,"[5] Shakespeare created characters like Hamlet and Falstaff, thereby inventing "human inwardness."[6] Personality as we understand it, Bloom explains, is "a Shakespearean invention...Insofar as we ourselves value, and deplore, our own personalities, we are the heirs of Falstaff and of Hamlet, and of all the other persons who throng Shakespeare's theater..."[7]

By "deplore," Bloom is particularly thinking of Shylock, the money lender in *Merchant of Venice* who literally demands a pound of flesh for an unpaid debt. The depiction is so powerful, Bloom believes, that it may have incited more anti-Semitism than *The Protocols of the Learned Elders of Zion*, the infamous 1903 Russian tract about "Jewish global domination" that played a role in the Holocaust.[8] The vivid characters that Shakespeare unleashed upon the world, in other words, didn't always have a positive effect. Bloom here departs from Percy Shelley, who along with Johnson is Bloom's great model and who believes that Shakespeare moved history toward social and political liberation with his art. Bloom is more skeptical about history's forward direction.

Both agree that Shakespeare changed history, however. To use Hans Robert Jauss's framework, the Bard shifted our horizon of expectations. "Even if we never attend a performance or read a play," Bloom writes, Shakespeare has "made us theatrical,"[9] changing our ideas "as to what makes the self authentically human."[10] Unlike the angry and confused audiences in Jauss's model, however, 17th century British theatergoers loved how *Hamlet* upended conventional expectations of what to expect from a revenge tragedy. They were so enthralled by the wild ramblings of Hamlet's mind that the play's revenge plot seemed almost incidental. They were similarly fascinated by Falstaff, Othello, Rosamond, Macbeth, Lear, Cleopatra, and others. For them, it was as if the world had gone from black and white to color.

One other way Bloom is like Shelley is in the way he uses the greater authors as a cudgel to beat up on the lesser, especially those concerned with local matters. Just as the Romantic poet dismisses Voltaire, so Bloom waves off those authors who are included in the canon merely for the sake (as he sees it) of diversity and inclusion.

He's particularly hard on those scholars arguing on their behalf. In *The Western Canon: The Books and School of the Ages* (1994), he complains about "the Balkanization of literary studies" and contends, "We are destroying all intellectual and esthetic standards in the humanities and social sciences, in the name of social justice."[11] The destroyers, whom he characterizes as "the School of Resentment," include "Feminists, Marxists, Afrocentrists, Foucault-inspired New Historicists and Deconstructors." Regarding them as doctrinaire ideologues, he says they want to sacrifice literature on the altar of politics.[12]

Bloom doesn't altogether ignore these lesser authors, as his "Critical Views" series and his many anthologies make clear. After all, he has published close to a hundred collections of critical essays devoted to such authors as Toni Morrison, Alice Walker, Amy Tan, August Wilson, Gwendolyn Brooks, Jamaica Kincaid, James Baldwin, Langston Hughes, Maya Angelou, Richard Wright, Robert Hayden, W.E.B. Du Bois, Zora Neale Hurston, Hispanic-American writers, Native American writers, and others. But while he sees these writers as worthy of our attention, he also believes they should know their place.

Like Harold, Allan Bloom (1930-92) believes that the traditional classics expand notions of what it means to be human, although occasionally he gets more specific as to how exactly the works can improve lives. He himself was ready to be so improved when, as a teenager, he recognized the University of Chicago's fabled "Great Books" program as an elite club that he was determined to join. He began taking classes there at 13 and eventually earned both a B.A. and a Ph.D., the latter in Chicago's Committee on Social Thought. He would go on study under the legendary political philosopher Leo Strauss and to write about Shakespeare and Plato. After teaching stints at Yale, Cornell, and the University of Toronto, he returned to Chicago. He unexpectedly gained a popular following with *The Closing of the American Mind* (1987), which sold half a million copies.

Sounding sometimes like Marcuse in his complaints about American one-dimensionality, Bloom accuses American higher education of "failing democracy and impoverishing the souls of America's students." As Bloom sees it, humanities departments, hamstrung by cultural relativity and a false egalitarianism, fail to fully appreciate the masterpieces. They don't acknowledge that popular culture renders us mediocre while the classics provide true fulfillment. When we read Plato and Shakespeare, Bloom says, we, like they, participate in "essential being" and forget our "accidental lives." That "this kind of humanity exists or existed, and that we can somehow still touch it with the tips of our outstretched fingers," he writes, "makes our imperfect humanity, which we can no longer bear, tolerable. The books in their objective beauty are still there, and we must help protect and cultivate the delicate tendrils reaching out toward them through the unfriendly soil of students' souls."[13]

Like Percy Shelley, Bloom sees us longing for some deeper perfection, and, like Harold, he does not associate this perfection with social liberation movements. Rather, he wants us to focus on great men and women (usually men) because they inspire us to excel. "The real community of man," Bloom asserts,

> is the community of those who seek the truth, of the potential knowers, that is, in principle, of all men to the extent that they desire to know. But in fact this includes only a few, the true friends, as Plato was to Aristotle at the very moment they were disagreeing about the nature of the good. Their common concern for the good linked them; their disagreement about it proved they needed one another to understand it...This, according to Plato, is the only real friendship, the only real common good. It is here that the contact people so desperately seek is to be found.[14]

In other words, rather than teaching down to students—patronizing them, as Bloom would see it—we should present them with culture's greatest hits and give them a chance to rise to the occasion. Bloom's framing of the issue excited intellectually ambitious students that longed to be tested and to join the Academy's version of Plato's philosopher kings.

Bloom says that these are the students he wants leading America. Those "who are most likely to take advantage of a liberal education," he writes, are those who will have "the greatest moral and intellectual effect on the nation."[15]

In *Closing of the American Mind* Bloom is frustratingly vague about what exactly this moral and intellectual effect looks like. He's more specific in a work written 23 years earlier, *Shakespeare's Politics* (1964). Among the plays he examines is *Julius Caesar,* which he says presents a workshop on political leadership. As Bloom sees it, Caesar, drawing on the wisdom of both the high-minded Stoics and the material-focused Epicureans, represents an ideal mixture of idealism and pragmatism. Meanwhile, Brutus, "the noblest Roman of them all," is driven by high ideals that will inspire future defenders of freedom. Unfortunately, he and Cassius fail to grasp Caesar's genius, which is to combine "the high-mindedness of the Stoic with the Epicurean's awareness of the low material substrate of political things." Caesar, he says, "seems to have been the most complete political man who ever lived."[16]

Yet in Bloom's political science lesson, Brutus and Cassius also have an important role to play, having become "the eternal symbols of freedom against tyranny. They showed that men need not give way before the spirit of the times; they served as models for later successors who would reestablish the spirit of free government. Their seemingly futile gesture helped, not Rome, but humanity."[17]

Echoing Aristotle's contrast between literature and history but extending it to philosophy itself, Bloom says that literature can deliver such training as the latter cannot. "The philosopher cannot move nations; he speaks only to the few," Bloom writes, whereas the poet "can take the philosopher's understanding and translate it into images that touch the deepest passions and cause men to know without knowing that they know." Whereas Aristotle's description of heroic virtue "means nothing to men in general," Homer conveys that virtue in ways that are "unforgettable." In short, poetry's ability "to depict the truth about man and to make other men fulfill that truth is what raises [it] to its greatest heights..."[18]

This means, Bloom adds, that the poet has a double task: "to understand the things he wishes to represent and to understand the audience
to which he speaks. He must know about the truly permanent human
problems; otherwise his works will be slight and passing."[19]

Bloom appears to have taken lessons from several of the thinkers
we have discussed. While he doesn't agree with Plato's suspicion of
poetry, like Plato he believes that life should devote itself to a search
for the true and the good. Like Aristotle, he sees literature as essential
to the life of the state. And he appears to channel Horace when he
writes that poetry's mission is to simultaneously delight and instruct.
Shakespeare, he says, "wrote at a time when common sense still taught
that the function of the poet was to produce pleasure and that the
function of the great poet was to teach what is truly beautiful by means
of pleasure."[20]

Bloom draws on Sir Philip Sidney when he talks about poetry
inspiring heroic virtue. He also takes up Johnson's challenge to se-
lect "a system of social duty" from Shakespeare: The Bard, Bloom
says, "shows most vividly and comprehensively the fate of tyrants, the
character of good rulers, the relations of friends, and the duties of
citizens."[21] When Shakespeare does so, Bloom asserts, "he can move
the souls of his readers, and they recognize that they understand life
better because they have read him; he hence becomes a constant guide
and companion."[22] Or at least, Bloom says, that's the way it was in the
old days, when people turned to Shakespeare "as they once turned to
the Bible."[23]

Finally, Bloom uses the same descriptor for today's students that
Matthew Arnold applies to those in the middle class who, while eco-
nomically successful, are culturally illiterate. Because the classic authors are no longer "a part of the furniture of the student's mind,
once he is out of the academic atmosphere," Bloom says that today's
graduates are "technically well-equipped, but Philistine."[24]

Bloom's celebration of the traditional canon attracted two political
figures when the "culture wars" went national: Secretary of Education
William Bennett (under Ronald Reagan) and National Endowment

of the Humanities Chair Lynne Cheney (under Reagan and Herbert Walker Bush). Neither Bennett nor Cheney can, by any stretch of the imagination, be regarded as rigorous seekers of truth. Bennett's prefaces to his children's anthology *Book of Virtues: A Treasury of Great Moral Stories,* for instance, are sanctimonious and platitudinous. Bennett and Cheney thought, however, that if they allied themselves with the classics while denigrating works not in the traditional canon, greatness would be thrust upon them.

Such thinking fit well with Republican concerns that the traditional dominance by upper class White men was being threatened. The rich Western literary tradition became one of their ideological arguments: women and other races couldn't claim as many luminaries in the pantheon of greats as White men, whiteness now being defined as European. These conservatives described other races and genders who wanted to crash the party as inferior interlopers, beneficiaries of literary affirmative action. Some even directed the charge at America's most recent Nobel laureate, Toni Morrison. Others, meanwhile, urged English departments to teach "Austen, not Alice Walker," a move that they regarded as open-minded since it showed they counted at least one woman amongst the greats.

The cultural right also embraced the ideas of E. D. Hirsch (b. 1928), even though, as a self-described Jeffersonian Democrat teaching at Thomas Jefferson's University of Virginia, he believed that universal education is a pathway for disenfranchised groups to achieve the American Dream and that a republic cannot survive without an educated citizenry. I group him with the Blooms because he sees the traditional classics as an integral part of the national culture. Programs of "cultural literacy," he contends, will give Americans a collective national identity while also showing underprivileged groups the language they must master if they hope to be successful.

Hirsch's formulation resembles Matthew Arnold's but with a difference that reflects the difference between the United Kingdom and the United States. Whereas Arnold believes that the working classes, if they attain a classical education, will be content with their position at the bottom of the class hierarchy, Hirsch argues that it will give them opportunities for advancement *into* the middle class.

Hirsch describes culture more broadly than Arnold does, using it to include not only the arts and the humanities but knowledge generally, including science. Cultural literacy, he writes, is "the network of information that all competent readers possess. It is the background information, stored in their minds, that enables them to take up a newspaper and read it with an adequate level of comprehension, getting the point, grasping the implications, relating what they read to the unstated context which alone gives meaning to what they read."[25]

We risk becoming the Tower of Babel if we fail. "The complex undertakings of modern life," he observes, "depend on the cooperation of many people with different specialties in different places." His literacy project, therefore, is "to foster effective nationwide communications."[26]

Hirsch doesn't overtly privilege literature in his definition of culture, and his expansion of Arnold's understanding of the word means that literature, for him, comprises a smaller proportion of what students should spend their time with. Hirsch also doesn't limit himself to instilling values but adds skills competency as well. I include him in this book, however, because, like Arnold, Hirsch sees literature as particularly effective at reaching into the minds of citizens and raising them up.

We can see this in the work that serves as the model for Hirsch's own project. In 1783 the Scottish scholar Hugh Blair published *Lectures on Rhetoric and Belles Lettres,* which would go on to become (as Hirsch describes it) "one of the most influential textbooks ever issued in Great Britain or the United States," with 130 editions appearing between 1783 and 1911. While some of Blair's book looks at historical and philosophical writing, most of it focuses on Greek, Roman, British, and French literature. Above all, *Lectures on Rhetoric* signals that to be cultured requires a grasp of great literature.[27]

Hirsch himself dramatizes the centrality of literature with an anecdote about how his father, a commodities trader, used Shakespeare in his profession. In his business letters, the elder Hirsch would often allude to Shakespeare, sometimes applying (without further elaboration) the phrase, "there is a tide." The line is from Brutus's observation to Cassius in *Julius Caesar* that now is the most propitious time to attack their enemies:

> There is a tide in the affairs of men
> Which taken at the flood leads on to fortune;
> Omitted, all the voyage of their life
> Is bound in shallows and in miseries.
> On such a full sea are we now afloat,
> And we must take the current when it serves,
> Or lose our ventures.[28]

"Those four words," Hirsch explains, "carried not only a lot of complex information, but also the persuasive force of a proverb." Using the phrase, he says, is "better than saying 'Buy (or sell) now and you'll cover expenses for the whole year, but if you fail to act right away, you may regret it the rest of your life.' That would be twenty-seven words instead of four, and while the bare message of the longer statement would be conveyed, the persuasive force wouldn't." Hirsch concludes that, by no longer sharing "literate background knowledge," middle-level executives no longer communicate effectively.[29]

By focusing on how a knowledge of Shakespeare can lead to making money, Hirsch is speaking the language of the middle class, but he implies certain higher values as well. Entrepreneurial citizens like Hirsch's father, using Brutus's inspiring words, conjure up an image of themselves as members of a heroic band, prepared to take daring action as part of a higher enterprise. The in-group feeling that such an allusion communicates is part of its appeal—we get it, others don't—and it can very easily lead to Allan Bloom's elitism. In the hands of certain conservatives, such an embrace of Shakespeare affirms exclusionary tendencies.

That's not how Hirsch sees it, however. For him, *all* Americans should aspire to joining this heroic band, and we sell people short if we don't give them substantive literature. Hirsch became interested in these issues when he saw the large reading gap between students at the prestigious University of Virginia, where he taught, and a local community college. His famous list of "what every American needs to know" has led to a series of textbooks, often used by parents home-schooling their children: *What Your First Grader Needs to Know, What Your Second Grader Needs to Know,* etc. He also established and now heads the non-profit Core Knowledge Foundation. Cultural literacy, Hirsch asserts, "constitutes the only sure avenue of opportunity for disadvantaged children, the only reliable way of combating the social determinism that now condemns them to remain in the same social and educational condition as their parents.[30]

To cite at random a somewhat mixed endorsement of Hirsch's vision, writer Phuc Tran, whose family fled Saigon after its fall, reports turning to a comparable project. Encountering racist bullying in Carlyle, Pennsylvania, he concluded that he needed some special key to become "American." Clifton Fadiman's *The Lifetime Reading Plan,* comprised of "over one hundred of the greatest writers and thinkers of Western civilization's literature," seemed to provide that key. As Tran reports, Fadiman

lamented the times, the customs: the iconoclasm of the sixties, the upheaval and overthrow of social institutions, the audacity to question the Western canon. Nothing was sacred anymore. This was the result of tuning in and turning off. He bemoaned that no one was interested in being an "all-American" boy or girl anymore but declared that these books were the foundation for being "all-American." He wrote with a zealot's fervor. Fadiman was not soft-pedaling or excusing himself. I trembled as I read the entire introduction in the basement. He was speaking to me. All I wanted was to be well-read and all-American, and now—now I had the book.[31]

Tran would discover and fall in love with multicultural authors when he reached college, but one can understand why Fadiman's list meant so much to him in high school.

For his part, Hirsch bristles at charges that he is elitist. Rather, he wants "mature literacy for *all* our citizens."[32] He therefore avoids wading into the debates we have seen over high culture vs. low culture, and he is careful to state that he is not "advocating a list of great books that every child in the land should be forced to read."[33] Despite his protestations, however, he implies that high culture is good for you and low culture is not by the works he does and does not include in his lists. For instance, the list that initially appeared in 1987 included certain niche writers like Gertrude Stein and Edith Wharton (although they have since been dropped). Meanwhile, age-old children's classics, often adapted and retold, make up the bulk of the "language arts" readings in his textbooks. For first graders he recommends *Mother Goose*, Edward Lear, Aesop, Charles Perreault, Beatrix Potter, the Grimm Brothers, Hans Christian Andersen. For fourth graders, he lists Henry Wadsworth Longfellow, Carl Sandberg, Ralph Waldo Emerson, Jonathan Swift, and Robert Louis Stevenson.

Like Plato, whom he cites approvingly (he doesn't mention the philosopher's attacks on Homer), Hirsch assumes that he knows what is good for people and what is bad. Plato, he writes, "believed that the specific contents transmitted to children are by far the most important elements of education." Quoting Socrates in *The Republic*— "Shall we carelessly allow children to hear any casual tales which may be devised by casual persons, and to receive into their minds ideas for the most part the very opposite of those which we shall wish them to have when they are grown up?"—Hirsch says that Plato was right to be concerned with the specific contents of schooling and their ethical outcomes. Again quoting Plato, he writes, "For great is the issue at stake, greater than appears—whether a person is to be good or bad."[34]

In short, be careful about letting children encounter "casual tales...devised by casual persons." There is no answering for the consequences.

Once again we encounter someone contending literature determines "whether a person is to be good or bad." As we have seen, feminists like Tania Modleski, loathe to dismiss works that have a large popular following, twist themselves into knots to defend popular romances. The two Blooms and Hirsch, by contrast, don't shy away from charges of elitism and argue that they are honoring disenfranchised groups by offering them the best of what has been thought and written.

To his credit, Hirsch is more open than the Blooms to shifting notions of what constitutes "the best." He acknowledges that his lists can change as society changes, and his textbooks now include a smattering of Native American and African folktales, as well as poems by minority authors. Allan Bloom, by contrast, sticks to the belief that the Western classics provide all the foundation that one needs.

WAYNE BOOTH

THE BEST BOOKS BUILD CHARACTER

You [literature] lead me first to practice ways of living that are more profound, more sensitive, more intense, and in a curious way more fully generous than I am likely to meet anywhere else in the world. You correct my faults, rebuke my insensitivities. You mold me into patterns of longing and fulfillment that make my ordinary dreams seem petty and absurd. You finally show what life can be...to anyone who is willing to work to earn the title of equal and true friend.

— **Wayne Booth,** *The Company We Keep: An Ethics of Fiction* (1989)[1]

OF THE VARIOUS THINKERS I survey in this book, Wayne Booth (1928–2005) is among my favorites. Although, like the cultural conservatives, Booth believes that great literature is good for us and pop lit not so much, he acknowledges that even masterpieces can contain noxious elements. Booth calls for us to compare our interpretations and, if we disagree, to understand why we do so. Not afraid to rethink his own opinions, Booth contends that reading and discussing literature together can become the basis for a new, vibrant, and ever-evolving community. Booth laid out his vision in his important book *The Company We Keep: An Ethics of Fiction* (1989).

Booth was born of Mormon parents and, while he didn't continue in the faith, the Mormons' strong commitment to community shows up in his theoretical work. He taught for a while at Earlham College, a Quaker school that also focuses on community, before moving on to the University of Chicago, where he spent his career. Most famous for *The Rhetoric of Fiction,* in which he pioneered the notion of the "implied author" (the author that readers infer while reading a work), he turned to readers in *Company We Keep.*

Booth acknowledges the difficulty of figuring out if and how literature changes readers. We've seen Jauss make the case that great literature changes an epoch's horizon of expectations while culinary literature reaffirms existing values and world views. Booth, by contrast, focuses on individual readers. While he, like Jauss, describes readers as being in dialogue with works, for him literature operates more as a companion. The literary "company we keep" influences us the way an actual acquaintance influences us so that, just as some friends are good for us and some are bad, so it is with literature. The question, then, is how exactly our book acquaintances change us.

Booth draws on Aristotle to understand the potential for the fullest friendship, saying that it arises "whenever two people offer each other not only pleasures or utilities but shared aspirations and loves of a kind that make together worth having as an end in itself."[2] Such friends, Booth continues, "love to be with each other because of the quality of the life they live during their time together." Good book friends can deliver similar rewards:

> The fullest friendships, the "friendships of virtue" that the tradition hails as best, are likely to be with the works that the world has called classics. When I "perform"

for myself or attend a performance of *King Lear, The Misanthrope,* or *The Cherry Orchard,* when I read *Don Quixote, Persuasion, Bleak House,* or *War and Peace,* I meet in their authors friends who demonstrate their friendship not only in range and depth and intensity of pleasure they offer, not only in the promise they fulfill of proving useful to me, but finally in the irresistible invitation they extend to live during these moments a richer and fuller life than I could manage on my own.[3]

It's as though great literature is saying to us, "You've never had a friend like me." Booth imagines himself having a conversation with a great work, saying that "if I choose to ignore you, I lose something more precious than any one point I could make *about* you and your kind; your company is in some ways superior even to the best company I can hope to discover among the real people I live with. Certainly it is superior to what is usually provided by those 'inner resources' we are all advised to fall back on when bored."[4]

Above all, Booth says, great literature speaks to "our desire to improve our desires—to *desire better desires.*"[5] Just as we may seek out certain people because they help bring out the best in us, so we seek out book friends. We long to fulfill our potential and are looking for ways to bring that about.

Unfortunately, we can also be drawn to false friends. In Booth's mind, for instance, Norman Mailer's *Executioner's Song,* about murderer Gary Gilmore, is a false friend. To make his point, he contrasts Mailer's book with Anne Tyler's *Dinner at the Homesick Restaurant,* even while acknowledging that this is his subjective opinion:

"My" Tyler's range and daring are much more limited that "my" Mailer's, but I feel that she is giving me everything she's got, and she cares a great deal about what will become of me as I read. My Mailer, in contrast, is simply playing games with me; he does not care a hill of beans for my welfare—he would obviously be happy to sacrifice me and any other reader to further his own ends. This does not mean that he is not worth talking to—but it may mean that I finally regret spending quite so long with him, when I might have been reading more of Anne Tyler.[6]

To judge Mailer, however, Booth admits that he must enter into a relationship with him, which sets up precisely the dynamic that worries Plato. Booth even goes Plato one better, noting that the very act of reading always acknowledges an emotional surrender to the work. He refers to the George Poulet passage I quote in the introduction about readers delivering themselves "bound hand and foot, to the omnipotence of fiction."

While agreeing with Plato to a point, Booth then says this is a danger we must face. After all, if we don't surrender, we will emerge "comfortably unharmed but no better off than if we had spent our time playing checkers."[7] In other words, reading, like close friendship, always involves a risk.

Booth's solution involves a two-stage process like the one I lay out in the introduction, where I discuss "immersion" and "reflection." (I then add "action" as a third step.) The first involves "surrendering as fully as possible on every occasion," even if the surrender is to *Executioner's Song*. The second, however, calls for "deliberately supplementing, correcting, or refining our experience with the most powerful ethical or ideological criticism we can manage."[8]

Booth puts the process in terms of friendship. "To understand a book well enough to repudiate it," he writes, "I must have made it a part of me; I will have lived my hours with it, as friend, and to that degree I will have already experienced an ethical change, for better or worse."[9]

In stage two, however, we should step back and examine the work's ethical impact. It is our moral responsibility to do so. Also, we should teach our children and students to be ethical readers. Or as Booth puts it, "We must both open ourselves to 'others' that look initially dangerous or worthless, and yet prepare ourselves to cast them off whenever, after keeping company with them, we conclude that they are potentially harmful. Which of these opposing practices will serve us best at a given moment will depend on who 'we' are and what the 'moment' is."[10]

As concrete examples are always useful, Booth randomly asked people to "name fictions that changed your character—or made you want to change your conduct." The list is too long to cite in its entirety but the answers, Booth observes, range "all over the moral landscape" and include actions taken. In the following excerpted passage, we see both true and false friends at work:

> I am told that "Ken Kesey's *One Flew over the Cuckoo's Nest* led me to tell off my boss at the hospital and walk out on him." I am told that "Balzac's *Père Goriot* made a real difference in how I thought about and treated my father." I hear a tearful claim that "Toni Morrison's *Song of Solomon* made me feel really guilty about how I had been thinking about Blacks these days—you know, with all the headlines about crime—and I've really acted different toward them, you know, when I meet them in stores and things like that." I hear the claim that "Ignazio Silone's *Bread and Wine* made a Christian socialist of me—at least for a while." "Arthur Koestler's *Darkness at Noon* not only knocked any temptation to fellow-traveling out of my head; it firmed up my notions to what kinds of moral corner-cutting I would allow myself." "*The Man in the Grey-Flannel Suit* got me out of advertising." ... "Reading Ayn Rand's works when I was working in my first job led me, I'm sorry to say, to cancel all of my gifts to philanthropies—I bought a convenient version of her 'me-philosophy' hook, line

and sinker." ... "Reading Chinua Achebe's *Things Fall Apart* radically changed my view of—and my teaching about—African colonialism and its aftermath." "*Gone with the Wind* made me behave much differently towards southerners; I had previously dismissed them as vicious or stupid."[11]

In examining literary impact, Booth is willing to subject even the most revered works to ethical judgment, and the final part of his book looks at political critiques of three authors he admires: feminists who believe that Jane Austen's *Emma* and D. H. Lawrence's novels can have a negative impact on women and African Americans who believe that *Huckleberry Finn* strengthens noxious stereotypes. Modeling ethical criticism, Booth listens to the critics. And although he continues to admire all three authors, he admits to some new reservations and new insights.

For instance, *Company We Keep* is dedicated to an African American colleague at Chicago—perhaps Booth's *only* Black colleague in 1963—because he got Booth to change his opinion of *Huckleberry Finn*. As a junior faculty member in Chicago's humanities program, Moses took a controversial and courageous stand against Twain that Booth and his White colleagues dismissed out of hand but that Booth revisited later. Moses died before Booth wrote his book, but, speaking in Moses's voice, Booth reconstructs his fears about the damage the novel could do to students:

> It's hard for me to say this, but I have to say it anyway. I simply can't teach *Huckleberry Finn* again. The way Mark Twain portrays Jim is so offensive to me that I get angry in class, and I can't get all those liberal white kids to understand why I am angry. What's more, I don't think it's right to subject students, black or white, to the many distorted views of race on which that book is

based. No, it's not the word "nigger" I'm objecting to, it's the whole range of assumptions about slavery and its consequences, and about how whites should deal with liberated slaves, and how liberated slaves should behave or will behave toward whites, good ones and bad ones. That book is just bad education, and the fact that it's so cleverly written makes it even more troublesome to me.[12]

In Booth's imagined reconstruction, Moses appears to have in mind how Twain depicts Jim as an infantilized slave and how he goes for laughs when he has Tom Sawyer treat him like a toy or a pet.

Although it took several years, Booth came around to seeing validity in some of Moses's objections. While Austen, Lawrence and Twain remain Booth's good friends, he acknowledges that they have more blemishes than he once realized. Such reflective conversations with critics, he adds, lead to deeper insights into race and gender.

While the responses reported by Booth testify to the power of literature to impact and sometimes change lives, their variety once again highlights the difficulty of generalizing. Can one arrive at comprehensive theories from a welter of separate experiences? To be sure, we have seen Hans Robert Jauss contending that *Madame Bovary* challenged the horizon of expectations of mid-19th century France, thereby making lives better in the eyes of progressives and worse in the eyes of traditionalists. But what generalizations can we make if there are as many horizons as there are individual readers?

Booth would say, the better the literature, the more complex the resulting reflection process. This in turn leads to more humane ways of looking at the world. We may become more accepting of difference, more forgiving of human frailty.

Booth adds one other dimension to how we can benefit from our reading. Just as we should cultivate multiple friendships, so we should read a variety of masterpieces. After all, different friends fulfill different needs, with one helping us through immediate difficulties and another telling us things we may find useful years from now. We might go to some authors for comfort and reassurance, others for tough love. Booth observes that "every narrative, even one as comprehensive as *Remembrance of Things Past,* can claim to present no more than one of many possible worlds."[13] Don't limit yourself to a single friend, Booth says, warning that "serious ethical disasters" can occur when readers "sink themselves into an unrelieved hot bath of one kind of narrative." A "steady immersion at any age in any one author's norms is likely to be stultifying," he says, "even if they happen to be as broad and conventional as those of a Shakespeare or Tolstoy."[14]

As examples of such narrowness, Booth lists "idolators of authors I myself admire," such as "the 'gentle Jane-ite' who re-reads all of Austen's novels every year and thus risks living a narrower life than Austen herself ever led" and "the total Lawrentian who still in the 1980s tries to enact in dress and behavior the roles that for Lawrence were genuinely exploratory in the 1920s..."[15]

A multicultural democracy, Booth believes, will benefit if its citizens read widely. People must supplement the perspective put forward by one work with perspectives put forth by others. A single author cannot get as close to the truth as many authors because "all statements of truth are partial," which means that we should embrace "the very plurality that from other perspectives may seem threatening. We not only recognize that there are many true narratives; we celebrate the multiplicity, recognizing that to be bound to any one story would be to surrender most of what we care for." He adds that any one of our "ever-expanding collection of metaphoric worlds" will be "at best a half-truth; some of them may be downright falsehoods..."[16]

Since we are seeking for fictions that will lead us to "the most precious truths we ever know," Booth counsels us to try different works on "for size," comparing each with "the other worlds we have tried to live in." Each new encounter with a powerful narrative, he says, "throws a critical light on our previous collection. We can embrace its additions and negations vigorously, so long as we remember that, like all the others, this is a metaphoric construction: a partial structure that stands in place of, or 'is carried over from,' whatever Reality might be."[17]

Thus, each new poem or story we read becomes "either a decisive rival to or a reinforcement of the world in which we have previously led our lives."[18] The process is dynamic, not static.

In short, while literary works can change readers' lives for the better, it is up to readers to make sure they do so with optimal effect. Read widely and freely and choose books that challenge you as well as books that comfort you. At the same time, don't hesitate to question even revered works since you may learn something important when you do so. A varied group of book friends will help you build a good character and bolster you throughout your life.

Martha Nussbaum

Literature, Indispensable Tool for Citizenship

Narrative art has the power to make us see the lives of
the different with more than a casual tourist's interest—with involvement and sympathetic understanding, with anger at our society's refusals of visibility.

— **Martha Nussbaum,** "Cultivating Humanity: A
Classical Defense of Reform in Liberal Education"
(1998)[1]

MARTHA NUSSBAUM (B. 1947), one of America's most prominent
philosophers, has a humanist's perspective very much like Wayne
Booth's, and the two University of Chicago colleagues cite each other
regularly. She can also be compared to Sir Philip Sidney in that she
sees great literature inculcating virtue, although virtuous behavior for
her involves becoming a better citizen and a better voter. To improve
in these areas, one must think outside one's own framework, and
Nussbaum believes that no activity encourages this more than reading
great literature.

Early on, Nussbaum was more interested in literature than in philosophy. She dropped out of Wellesley College her junior year to try out an acting career, joining a repertory company that performed Greek tragedies. Then she transferred to New York University, graduating with majors in theater and classics. She shifted to philosophy in graduate school, receiving her PhD at Harvard, but never left literature. In the Aristotle chapter I noted how, in *The Fragility of Goodness*, Nussbaum sees Greek tragedy as having played an important role in Athenian citizenship. She has also delved deeply into novelist Henry James's moral philosophy.

Determined to make philosophy and literature applicable to everyday life, Nussbaum has written extensively about human rights, animal rights, sexual orientation, grieving, aging, and other subjects. She is not afraid to mix it up with others and has taken aim at her Chicago colleague Allan Bloom for what she sees as his simplistic depictions of non-Western cultures and his reductive caricatures of humanities departments.

Despite her disagreement with Bloom, however, Nussbaum too believes that literature should be at the core of what college students read. Unlike Bloom, however, she doesn't believe students should just sit at the feet of the great authors and absorb their wisdom. She is more like Booth, prepared to question even revered classics if they warrant it. More on this in a moment.

First, however, let's look at how she views literature's role in forming good citizens. In her highly regarded essay "Cultivating Humanity: A Classical Defense of Reform in Liberal Education," Nussbaum draws on the Stoic Marcus Aurelius to set forth her case. The Roman philosopher, she says, stressed the need to "cultivate in ourselves a capacity for sympathetic imagination that will enable us to comprehend the motives and choices of people different from ourselves, seeing them not as forbiddingly alien and other, but as sharing many problems and possibilities with us." Literature, as she sees it, is ideal for bridging "differences of religion, gender, race, class, and national origin."[2]

Nussbaum observes that literature makes "an especially rich contribution" to cultivate our "capacities of judgment and sensitivity." That's because (here she draws on Aristotle's *Poetics*), literature shows us "not something that has happened, but the kind of thing that might happen. This knowledge of possibilities is an especially valuable resource in political life."[3]

Nussbaum shows the sympathetic imagination at work in Sophocles's *Philoctetes*, a play about the great Greek archer who is stricken by a lingering disease after stepping on a serpent guarding a sacred shrine. Because of his cries of pain and his wound's stench, he is marooned upon a desert island. A seer informs the Greeks, however, that they cannot win the Trojan War without his archery skills. Because of Philoctetes's bitterness against his former comrades, Odysseus believes he must trick the archer into rejoining them, and he uses Achilles's son Neoptolemus in the deception. Neoptolemus initially goes along but then, after much agonizing, blows up the plan by telling Philoctetes the truth.

Nussbaum observes that the play shows us two different ways to treat people. Odysseus doesn't care anything about Philoctetes the man, regarding him merely as the means to an end. The soldiers who make up the chorus, however, have a different response, expressing compassion for him:

Chorus

Think how
with no human company or care,
no sight of a friendly face,
wretched, always alone,
he wastes away with that savage disease,
with no way of meeting his daily needs.
How, how in the world, does the poor man survive?[4]

This is the narrative imagination at work. "Unlike their leader," Nussbaum writes, "the men of the chorus vividly and sympathetically imagine the life of a man whom they have never seen, picturing his loneliness, his pain, his struggle for survival. In the process they stand in for, and allude to, the imaginative work of the audience, who are invited by the play as a whole to imagine the sort of needy homeless life to which prosperous people rarely direct their attention."[5]

As Nussbaum sees it, Athenian society, through sympathetic identification, is being taught the political and moral benefits of seeing people in their full complexity, not as mere tools. "Although the good of the whole should not be neglected," she writes, the audiences see that "that good will not be well served if human beings are seen simply as instruments of one another's purposes."[6]

Nussbaum's other example is Ralph Ellison's *Invisible Man*. By judging the protagonist only by the color of his skin, Nussbaum points out, society cannot see him for who he really is. Instead, they see "various race-inflected stereotypes: the poor, humiliated black boy who snatches like an animal at the coins that lie on an electrified mat; the good student trusted to chauffeur a wealthy patron; the listening ear to whom the same patron unburdens his guilt and anxiety; the rabble-rousing activist who energizes an urban revolutionary movement; the violent rapist who gratifies the sexual imagination of a woman brought up on racially charged sexual images—always he is cast in a drama of someone else's making, 'never more loved and appreciated' than when he plays his assigned role."[7]

Or as Ellison puts it, "You go along for years knowing something is wrong, then suddenly you discover that you're as transparent as air." Invisibility, the narrator says, is "a matter of the construction of their inner eyes, those eyes with which they look through their physical eyes upon reality."[8]

Nussbaum then links *Invisible Man* with *Philoctetes*. While the two worlds seem poles apart, both are concerned with "social stratification and injustice, manipulation and use, and above all invisibility and the condition of being transparent to and for one's fellow citizens." Like

Philoctetes, Invisible Man "invites its readers to know and see more than the unseeing characters."[9]

Nussbaum's essay argues that the very functioning of democracy is at stake, with novels being of utmost importance in the formation of good citizens. Ellison, she points out, "explicitly linked the novelist's art to the possibility of democracy," contending in the novel's introduction that it "could be fashioned as a raft of hope, perception and entertainment that might help keep us afloat as we tried to negotiate the snags and whirlpools that mark our nation's vacillating course toward and away from the democratic idea."[10]

At a time when, in rightwing discourse, immigrants can be reduced to "rapists and murderers" and "vermin," women to beauty ratings, Muslims to potential terrorists, and Black urban communities to "hellholes" (I write this following the Donald Trump presidency), literature is no mere luxury. As Nussbaum summarizes her argument, "Narrative art has the power to make us see the lives of the different with more than a casual tourist's interest—with involvement and sympathetic understanding, with anger at our society's refusals of visibility. We come to see how circumstances shape the lives of those who share with us some general goals and projects, and we see that circumstances shape not only people's possibilities for action, but also their aspirations and desires, hopes and fears.[11]

She then spells out the implications of the narrative or sympathetic imagination for citizens attempting to do the right thing. For instance, understanding "how a history of racial stereotyping can affect self-esteem, achievement, and love," she says, "enables us to make more informed judgments on issues relating to affirmative action and education."[12]

Her belief in the powers of sympathetic identification sometimes puts Nussbaum at odds with scholars who practice "identity politics," which Nussbaum defines as the belief "that only a member of a particular oppressed group can write well or, perhaps, even read well about that group's experience. Only female writers understand the experience of women; only African American writers understand Black experience." Nussbaum does concede that, if we want to understand the situation of a group, we do well to begin with "the best that has been written by members of that group."[13] In other words, we must expand the canon in ways that would appall figures like Allan and Harold Bloom.

That being acknowledged, however, Nussbaum then points out, "We could learn nothing from such works if it were impossible to cross group boundaries in imagination." She declares that "any stance toward criticism that denies that possibility seems to deny the very possibility of literary experience as a human social good."[14]

Therefore, rather than seeing the "citizen body" as "a marketplace of identity-based interest groups jockeying for power," she advocates for "the world-citizen." She concludes that "the great contribution literature has to make to the life of the citizen is its ability to wrest from our frequently obtuse and blunted imaginations an acknowledgment of those who are other than ourselves."[15] Even though we can never know fully what it is like to be of another race or gender or class, we can at least get an inkling from the literature we read.

Recent Psychological Studies

Literature's Psychic Impact

At a minimum, we can say that reading stories— those
with strong narrative arcs—reconfigures brain networks for at least a few days. [The study] shows how
stories can stay with us. This may have profound implications for children and the role of reading in shaping
their brains.

—**Gregory S. Berns,** "Short- and Long-Term Effects of
a Novel on Connectivity in the Brain" (2013)[1]

I CONCLUDE THIS SURVEY of different theories of literary impact
with a look at what contemporary psychologists have to say. What can
empirical studies of the brain and of the mind tell us about literature's
effect upon us? Three approaches in particular appear to have produced intriguing results: brain scans, Theory of Mind (ToM) tests, and
transportation theory.

Iris Murdoch, a notably cerebral novelist, once observed that literature "is concerned with visual and auditory sensations and bodily

sensations" and contended that, "[i]f nothing sensuous is present, no art is present."[2] The observation casts special light on scientific studies using functional magnetic resonance imaging or fMRI to detect such sensations in readers, as reported by journalist Annie Murphy Paul in a 2012 *New York Times* article.

After psychologists sent their subjects through the large tubes to have their brains scanned, Paul reports, they reached the surprising conclusion that the brain "does not make much of a distinction between reading about an experience and encountering it in real life; in each case, the same neurological regions are stimulated." A 2012 Emory University study, for instance, discovered that the sensory cortex, responsible for perceiving texture, becomes active when encountering metaphors like "velvet voice" and "leathery hands."[3]

If a stand-alone metaphor can have such an effect, imagine the impact of an entire poem, which piles image upon image to pull the reader into its imaginary world. To cite a random example, think of how poet Samuel Taylor Coleridge stimulates our sensory cortex, and makes us thirsty as well, with his vivid description of a drought-stricken mariner:

> And every tongue, through utter drought,
> Was withered at the root;
> We could not speak, no more than if
> We had been choked with soot.[4]

Along with the sensory cortex, language registers upon the motor cortex, which is the part of the brain involved in the production of skilled movements. According to Paul, cognitive scientist Véronique Boulenger of the Laboratory of Language Dynamics in France found that this part of the brain records changes when subjects read accounts of physical action.[5] Again, if the mere mention of action registers with that part of the brain, think of how much more our motor cortex will be stimulated when literature unleashes its powers. Think of the intensified sensations when we read, say, Jean Valjean's excruciating and seemingly interminable slog through the sewers of Paris in Victor Hugo's *Les Misérables*.

Moving from touch, hearing and movement to social interaction, researchers have discovered that, once again, the brain "treats the interactions among fictional characters as something like real-life social encounters." For instance, as Paul's *New York Times* article reports, a 2011 study by psychologist Raymond Mar, published in the *Annual Review of Psychology*, concluded that "there was substantial overlap in the brain networks used to understand stories and the networks used to navigate interactions with other individuals — in particular, interactions in which we're trying to figure out the thoughts and feelings of others."[6] Having seen Aristotle emphasize a strong connection between literature and reality (*mimesis*), it seems logical to conclude that the linkage receives a boost if the brain literally thinks we are dealing with actual people when we read a book or watch a play. Perhaps the deeper we are immersed in a work of fiction, the more the brain is convinced. Recall that philosopher Martha Nussbaum contends that we engage in complex moral reasoning about real-life situations when we read.

Dr. Gregory S. Berns, director of Emory University's Center for Neuropolicy, confirmed in a follow-up study that readers essentially enter the world of the characters they read about. The study, described in the Dec. 9, 2014 issue of *Brain Connectivity,* was designed to figure out "whether reading a novel causes measurable changes in...the brain and how long these changes persist."[7] Berns had 21 undergraduates read Robert Harris's action-packed bestseller *Pompeii* over nine nights, scanning each of their brains for five mornings after completing the novel. He discovered over these five days that, after the reading sessions, the brain was stimulated to perform better in the areas of language comprehension, sensation, and movement.

Because he limited his study to five days following the last reading, Berns couldn't say how long a novel's effects last but noted that the strength of the narrative arc and the age of the reader appear to be factors, with younger readers experiencing the deepest impact. It's noteworthy that Berns doesn't—and perhaps can't— elaborate on these profound implications, observing only that some part of the brain has been reconfigured for an indeterminate period. He does lend scientific support to those who talk about the emotional power of literary immersion, however.

Natalie Phillips, at the time a graduate student at Stanford, chose a more challenging novel than *Pompeii* in her own experiment, scanning students' brains as they were reading Jane Austen's *Mansfield Park*. A chapter from the novel was projected onto a panel inside an MRI machine and the subjects, all PhD candidates in literature, were asked to move between two styles of attention: sometimes they were instructed to read Austen for pleasure, at others "with a heightened attention to literary form."[8] In other words, sometimes they engaged in immersive reading, sometimes in reflective reading.

Preliminary results revealed "a dramatic and unexpected increase in blood flow to regions of the brain beyond those responsible for 'executive function,' areas which would normally be associated with paying close attention to a task, such as reading." According to Phillips, the increased blood flow suggests that "paying attention to literary texts requires the coordination of multiple complex cognitive functions."[9] She noted that, although there was increased blood flow during pleasure reading as well, it occurred in different areas of the brain.

Magnet resonance imaging is only one method psychologists have used to detect differences in literature's impact. David Comer Kidd and his advisor Emanuele Castano at the New School turned to the Theory of Mind (ToM) test to examine readers after they read literary fiction, popular fiction, and non-fiction and found very different effects for each.

As Kidd and Castano explain it, Theory of Mind is "the human capacity to comprehend that other people hold beliefs and desires and that these may differ from one's own beliefs and desires."[10] We have seen philosopher Nussbaum applauding how literature gets us to see the world through others' viewpoints, and Kidd and Castano designed ToM tests to measure such a change.

According to their article in *Science,* the two represented literary fiction by excerpts from recent National Book Award finalists and winners of the 2012 PEN/O. Henry Prize for short fiction. For popular fiction they turned to Amazon.com bestsellers and an anthology of recent popular fiction. *Smithsonian Magazine* provided the non-fiction works. The researchers used several tests, including the "Reading the Mind in the Eyes" test, where participants must indicate the emotion expressed by the eyes in a black-and white photograph; and the Yoni test, which looks at changes in the reader's eye gaze and mouth. Kidd and Castano report that those assigned to read literary fiction performed better on the ToM tests than did those assigned popular fiction and non-fiction. The psychologists did not detect significant difference between the latter two groups.[11]

Another approach to measuring differences between reading greater and lesser literature and between reading fiction and non-fiction is transportation theory. Social psychologist Melanie Green has used transportation testing to measure the degree to which a reader becomes transported by a story. Her description sounds a lot like what I have been calling immersion. Most people, she notes, "have had the sensation of being swept up into the world of a story so completely that they forget the world around them. Instead of being aware of their physical surroundings, transported readers see the action of the story unfolding before them. They react emotionally to events that are simply words on a page."[12]

Green draws on psychological theories that describe the Self as an evolving narrative, quoting psychologists Kashima et al. that "both individual and collective narratives are central to the self, and furthermore, that the self resembles a narrative due to its dynamics and temporal nature."[13] Put another way, who we are—the Self, our core identity— is the story we imagine we are living. When this Self then interacts with literature, that literary story can modify the story of the Self and therefore change who we believe ourselves to be and consequently how we behave. This is big news, though not entirely unexpected for those of us who have made literary studies our life's work.

Green is interested in how this interaction between the Self and the story occurs. Most commonly, the reader identifies with the protagonist, seeing events from that perspective and experiencing the same emotions. If we like a character, the "attitudes implied by the story" become more persuasive.[14] Persuasion can occur either directly (by making one more positively disposed toward the story) or indirectly (by reducing internal counterarguing). This, as we have seen, is exactly what Samuel Johnson feared would happen to young people upon reading a racy novel like *Tom Jones* and why many German parents were distressed by Goethe's *Sorrows of Young Werther*, which seemed to glorify suicide. Becoming immersed in or transported by Tom's hijinks made it easier for young people to override the parental voices within (reduce their counterarguing). Or to use a more current example, Green mentions studies showing that negative attitudes towards condoms are linked to romance novels that fail to mention contraception.[15]

When one is identifying with a character, Green says that one loses a certain amount of self-awareness. One's Self is temporarily replaced with the emotional and cognitive connections one has with the character. If the character is positive, then one may adopt that character's goals and model one's behavior on that character. If negative, one views his or her actions with distaste.[16]

In another study, Green and psychologist Timothy Brock delved further into the power of immersion, discovering that the more a story grips us, the more (to borrow Coleridge's phrase) we suspend our disbelief. According to Green and Brock, "highly transported readers found fewer false notes in a story than less-transported readers."[17] Perhaps Plato, if he were writing today, would cite such a study to back up his fear that literary immersion subverts rational clarity.

A noteworthy use of transportation theory is Thor Magnus Tangeras's *Literature and Transformation: A Narrative Study of*

Life-Changing Reading Experiences (2020). Tangeras does a deep dive into readers' accounts of meaningful encounters with literature, leaning on a Kuiken et al. study that uses such terms as "absorption" and "expressive enactment" to capture reader immersion. Quoting the study, Tangeras notes that expressive enactment is "a form of reading that penetrates and alters a reader's understanding of everyday life" and that "modifies feeling, and reshapes the self."[18]

To chart the process, Tangeras conducted extensive interviews with 16 people who claimed that a literary work had changed their lives. He then shared and analyzed five of the transcribed interviews. Reviewing recent research on the emotions, Tangeras argued that we only change if the emotions are deeply involved—we move only if we are moved—and that literature, because it reaches deep into our emotional lives, is a particularly effective means of transformation. One of his subjects, for instance, reported that D. H. Lawrence's *Lady Chatterley's Lover* gave her the clarity and the resolve to break free of a dysfunctional relationship and to live life on her own. As Tangeras described the process, "in being moved new movement is created: that which was stuck is loosened, that which was frozen melts, that which was in the dark is brought into light and so on." While life does not necessarily become "easier or free from suffering" when our sense of self is transformed," we do discover that "the muddled, restrictive, unclear or shallow self-experience" is "given greater depth, clarity, connectedness and openness." We achieve a "renewed vitality and sense of direction,"[19] and with these come breakthroughs. In this case, once the woman integrated Lawrence into her own self-narrative, she was able to break up with her partner, which she did six months later.

To do justice to his subjects' experiences, Tangeras pushed the bounds of conventional psychological language. He found useful American psychologist William James's exploration of religious conversion, in which crisis is followed by surrender and redemption and which, Tangeras wrote, might better be described as a religious transformation. He also compared his readers' experiences to the medieval practice of *Lectio Divina,* where religious figures would see themselves tasting and digesting the Scriptures to inscribe them on their hearts.[20] Reporting on his subjects, Tangeras observed that

> at some point these readers unreservedly give them-
> selves over to, and surrender to, the experience, and
> become fully involved, body, heart and mind. Further-
> more, in this evolving and deepening devotional trans-
> action, these readers are deeply moved. The experience
> of a panoply of feelings that traditionally have strad-
> dled aesthetic and religious domains – such as won-
> der, awe, tenderness, jubilation and faith – come into
> full awareness. When this happens, the expanded af-
> fect-consciousness allows for an altered sense of self in
> which the crisis can be resolved.[21]

Tangeras mentioning the aesthetic, spiritual and existential dimen-sions of the reading experience is a tacit acknowledgement that the study of literary impact cannot be limited to psychology. While some of the findings mentioned in this chapter appear to support the philosophers, poets, and literary theorists that we have encountered, psychology can only supplement, not supplant, humanistic attempts to determine the impact of reading literature. Even when fMRI scans of readers do record brain activity and when Theory of Mind tests reveal significant results, these results only touch on tiny parts of the experience. The psychology of reading can give us insight and even some hard evidence, but nothing will ever substitute for the subjective experience of reading itself and our reasoned reflection about it. In other words, we will always need the theorizing we have encountered in these pages.

PART THREE: Literature's Impact—In Practice

Has JANE EYRE Made the World a Better Place?

Having surveyed what great minds think about literature's life-changing powers, it's useful to bring them together and imagine what they would say about a single classic. Doing so illuminates what the theories have in common while accentuating key differences. Always before us are the questions we have been raising throughout: does great literature improve individual lives, does it impact history, is it necessarily progressive, and how does its impact differ from the impact of pop lit?

I have chosen Charlotte Bronte's *Jane Eyre* in part because it checks multiple boxes. It's a work that straddles the scholarly/popular divide, achieving canonical status while, at the same time, retaining a large popular following. For instance, it regularly appears amongst the top three of books that librarians cite as their favorites (along with *To Kill a Mockingbird* and *Pride and Prejudice*), and it has been adapted for stage, film, and television over 50 times.

Causing both a positive and a negative sensation when it originally appeared, *Jane Eyre* also had an historical impact over a century later, providing the 1970s feminist movement with one of its central images. Yet it has also been criticized by progressives, many of whom realized that it traffics in various colonialist stereotypes only after they read Jean Rhys's *Wide Sargasso Sea* (1967), which imagines Rochester's mad Creole wife telling her side of the story. (In other words, a White British woman has created a crazy woman of color to embody her anger.) Finally, because *Jane Eyre* invites comparison with lesser romances and gothics, I contrast it with Stephenie Meyer's *Twi-*

light Saga, the vampire tetralogy that for a while was wildly popular amongst teenagers.

Literary impact always starts with individual readers. To dramatize such humble origins, I begin by examining the memoir of a reader whom no one outside my own family has heard of, my great grandmother Eliza Scott. What I imagine to have been her positive experience, however, differs from that of 19th century reviewer Elizabeth Rigby, who penned one of the most virulent reviews ever launched against a work destined to become a classic. In the contrast one sees two different ways that women of the time processed the novel.

In my account of Eliza, I must acknowledge one difficulty: in the memoir that has passed down to us through our family, Eliza never specifically mentions *Jane Eyre.* Nevertheless, I pick up small indications that the novel played a key role in one of her most momentous decisions—that, in fact, Eliza had internalized Bronte's narrative so thoroughly that she instinctively framed her own world view accordingly. Even if I read too much into these indications, however, at the very least Eliza represented a class of women who drew inspiration from *Jane Eyre.* Some background into Eliza's life and her reading habits makes clear how.

Born in 1857 in Barton, England, Eliza was a spirited girl and an avid reader. Novels helped her grapple with various identity issues, as is clear in her response to *The Mill on the Floss.* As she looks back, she uses George Eliot's novel to justify her childhood departures from the feminine ideal:

> When, some years later I read *The Mill on the Floss* I saw myself in Maggie Tulliver, running wild, thinking my own thoughts imaginative and somewhat secretive, delighted when the boys would let me follow on one of their bird nest or rabbit hunting expeditions, and playing cricket. I could climb trees, walk on high walls, jump as high as any of them, and run as fast, but only

for a short distance, a pain in my side always interfering with my reaching the goal.[1]

In other words, literature can validate aspects of ourselves that society overlooks or even censures.

Literature also helps us cope with loss, as it did when Eliza's mother was dying. Together they read Susan Warren's *Wide, Wide World,* a now-forgotten novel about a girl who loses her mother. It gave her strength to cope with the looming tragedy, toughening her emotionally for the heartbreak to come. Nellie is Eliza's older sister:

> On my 10th birthday, Mother gave me the *Wide, Wide World* and as a new baby arrived a few days later, she and I read it together while she was confined to her room. We both thought Ellen cried too much, but I thought she was very wonderful. Mother did not get well and during the summer went to the seashore for a while, Nellie coming home from boarding school to help care for the little ones.[2]

Other novels stepped in to help with the subsequent domestic unhappiness. Forbidden by laws of the time from marrying his wife's sister, whom the family loved, Eliza's father instead hired a housekeeper. When Miss Wyburn tried to set the children against their beloved aunt, Eliza turned to novels to navigate the fraught waters:

> Nellie, Richard and Robert being away at school, I had no companions of my own age, excepting in vacations. I had little to do that was interesting. I read all the books I could get and amused myself with the young children, but had to spend most of the time with Miss Wyburn, for whom for diplomatic reasons I pretended to have an affection, which I did not feel. I really mistrusted and

disliked her, and was becoming as deceitful as she, but Charlotte Yonge's books, particularly *The Daisy Chain* and *The Heir of Redcliffe*, our good Vicar's preparatory lessons before confirmation, and later Miss Drake's influence [a teacher] helped restore me to normal thinking. Miss Yonge's characters were human and natural, with faults which by persistent efforts, though with frequent failures, they were finally able to overcome. They lived with me and were a continual inspiration. I was also reveling in Dickens' and George MacDonald's books at that time.[3]

Eventually the housekeeper was dismissed and Eliza grew to adulthood. Given her extensive reading and the enduring popularity of *Jane Eyre*—which was enhanced by Elizabeth Gaskell's 1857 biography of the author—there is little likelihood that she would *not* have read *Jane Eyre*. Add to this Eliza's ambition to become a governess and it becomes a near certainty, given that *Jane Eyre* and Anne Bronte's *Agnes Grey* were regarded as the quintessential examples of the governess novel. Eliza tells us that her governess ambitions occurred over the objections of her father. "Father made strenuous objections at first," she writes, "but I was glad to have the prospect of a change and of earning a little money." And then she adds, in a remark that I am convinced channels Bronte's novel, "I was not needed at home and was restless at having nothing to do."[4]

Eliza fits the profile of many of the young women-turned-governesses that scholar Nora Gilbert, in an article about Jane Eyre as governess novel, has constructed from historical evidence. "When we look at the language of the way real women talked about their entry into the profession in their letters, journals, and memoirs," she reports, "we find, in fact, a knotty combination of anxiety and excitement, of trepidation and anticipation, of acquiescence and moxie."[5]

Eliza's use of the word "restless" confirms—at least for me—the importance of *Jane Eyre* for her as there are few words more important in the novel than "restlessness." Jane uses it when, as a governess at Thornfield, she chafes against her rural isolation and imagines visiting "the busy world, towns, regions full of life I had heard of but never seen." She desires, she says, "more of practical experience than I possessed; more of intercourse with my kind, of acquaintance with variety of character, than was here within my reach." Then comes the passage that I think Eliza internalized:

> Who blames me? Many, no doubt; and I shall be called discontented. I could not help it: *the restlessness was in my nature; it agitated me to pain sometimes*. (Emphasis mine)[6]

This passage echoes an earlier one in the novel that, while it doesn't use the word "restlessness," nevertheless captures the same sentiments as it speaks to a situation very much like the one in which Eliza found herself. A teacher at Lowood, where she has spent her entire childhood, Jane first expresses fears of stagnation and her longing for contact with "the real world":

> My world had for some years been in Lowood: my experience had been of its rules and systems; now I remembered that the real world was wide, and that a varied field of hopes and fears, of sensations and excitements, awaited those who had courage to go forth into its expanse, to seek real knowledge of life amidst its perils.[7]

After reviewing her regimented life and her lack of "communication by letter or message with the outer world," Jane concludes with a desperate plea. "I tired of the routine of eight years in one afternoon," she tells us. "I desired liberty; for liberty I gasped; for liberty I uttered a prayer..."[8]

I'm convinced from studying my great-grandmother Eliza's memoir that Bronte's novel helped give her—and many young women like her—the courage to venture out into the world. In Jane's case, sensing that her request for liberty is too bold since women were supposed to be content with their lot in life, she ratchets her desires down. Nevertheless, she is still flaunting convention:

> [Liberty] seemed scattered on the wind then faintly blowing. I abandoned it and framed a humbler supplication; for change, stimulus: that petition, too, seemed swept off into vague space: "Then," I cried, half desperate, "grant me at least a new servitude!"[9]

To round out my great grandmother's story, her own "new servitude" proved to be a fortunate one. Mrs. Martin, her employer, was the eldest daughter of Mark Lemon, whom Eliza notes was "the well-known editor of Punch [a fabled literary magazine], an intimate friend of Charles Dickens, Macauley, and all the literary men of the day." Like Jane, Eliza would receive two marriage proposals within a year. She chose the more daring one, turning down a man with a steady job and choosing instead my great grandfather, Edwin Fulcher, a bookkeeper who would take her to America, then to South Africa (where she would meet "the great imperialist" Cecil Rhodes), and then back to America. They would suffer periodic reversals of fortune before settling down in Evanston, Illinois, where they finally found stability.

In the feminism chapter, I mention the debate over whether one should focus more on Jane's heroic quest or the marriage that Jane triumphantly announces at the end of the book ("Reader, I married him"). Looking at the effect I think the novel had on Eliza, the answer could well be "both."

On the one hand, *Jane Eyre* may have supported Eliza's desire for independence, confirming her decision to leave her father and enter the world. In the end, she traveled to corners of the globe that Jane could only dream of.

On the other hand, Eliza also appears to have embraced the marriage plot. At least in her memoir, Eliza accepted the prevailing patriarchal structures of the time and was proud to have become a wife and a mother. In other words, *Jane Eyre* didn't get her to challenge the institution. Literature in this case bolstered the time-honored practice, serving the more conservative cultural role that Horace, Sir Philip Sidney, Samuel Johnson, Matthew Arnold, Allan Bloom, and E. D. Hirsch assign to it.

For instance, *Jane Eyre* shows traditional Christian values triumphing when the protagonist is put to her severest test. Jane turns to the Bible when she finds herself torn between illicit love and social morality. Reviewer Elizabeth Rigby, a contemporary of Bronte's who lambasted the novel for pretty much everything else, at least commended the author for her handling of this struggle. She approves of Jane's actions:

> Now follow scenes of a truly tragic power. This is the grand crisis in Jane's life....There is no one to help her against him or against herself. Jane had no friends to stand by her at the altar, and she has none to support her now she is plucked away from it. There is no one to be offended or disgraced at her following him to the sunny land of Italy, as he proposes, till the maniac should die. There is no duty to anyone but to herself, and this feeble reed quivers and trembles beneath the overwhelming weight of love and sophistry opposed to it. But Jane triumphs; in the middle of the night she rises—glides out of her room—takes off her shoes as she passes Mr. Rochester's chamber;—leaves the house, and casts herself upon a world more desert than ever to her...[10]

"Thus," Rigby concludes, "the great deed of self-conquest is accomplished; Jane has passed through the fire of temptation from without and from within; her character is stamped from that day..."[11]

I can well imagine Eliza having the same response as Rigby, applauding as Jane resists temptation. Like many readers, Eliza probably also applauded when Jane returns to marry the injured Rochester and nurse him back to health. For her, the novel had confirmed traditional values.

If Eliza Scott found inspiration in Jane Eyre, however, the conservative Rigby did not, and her review reveals how radical the novel is. Some biographical background is useful to understand the significance of Rigby's response.

A remarkable woman in her own right, Elizabeth Rigby was a privately taught arts aficionado. A travel book she authored earned her an invitation to write for the *Quarterly Review,* and while working in this predominantly male environment, at 37 she once mused in her diary that unmarried women have their own compensations.[12] Nevertheless, three years later she would marry Sir Charles Lock Eastlake, director of London's National Gallery, assist him in finding acquisitions for the collection, write prolifically about German art, author an important early book on photography, and host impressive gatherings of notable people.[13] If there was a woman who would sympathize with Jane's desire for independence—the *Jane Eyre* review was written before her marriage—one would think it would be Rigby.

Instead, her review is one of the most slashing attacks in literary history. As such, it is a perfect illustration of Hans Robert Jauss's thesis that great works challenge the prevailing horizon of expectations. Jauss theorizes that if a reader is offended and reacts badly, it is because the work is presenting a radical new way of seeing the world, one that undermines comfortable certainties. Given the intensity of Rigby's reaction, *Jane Eyre* confronted her expectations to the max.

Among other things, Rigby attacks *Jane Eyre* for being both anti-Christian and communist (a.k.a. Chartist):

> Altogether the autobiography of Jane Eyre is pre-eminently an anti-Christian composition. There is throughout it a murmuring against the comforts of the rich and against the privations of the poor, which, as far as each individual is concerned, is a murmuring against God's appointment—there is a proud and perpetual assertion of the rights of man, for which we find no authority either in God's word or in God's providence—there is that pervading tone of ungodly discontent which is at once the most prominent and the most subtle evil which the law and the pulpit, which all civilized society in fact, has at the present day to contend with. We do not hesitate to say that the tone of mind and thought which has overthrown authority and violated every code human and divine abroad, and fostered Chartism and rebellion at home, is the same which has also written *Jane Eyre*.[14]

If that weren't enough, Rigby also finds the author to be unladylike. The Bronte sisters had published under androgynous pennames that carried their initials (Currer, Ellis and Acton Bell), and while their identity and gender were still unknown at the time, Rigby is fairly certain about Currer. "[I]f we ascribe the book to a woman at all," she writes, "we have no alternative but to ascribe it to one who has, for some sufficient reason, long forfeited the society of her own sex." Whew!

In mid-century Victorian England, women were expected to be self-sacrificing angels, to cite the image made famous seven years later by Coventry Patmore's lengthy poem *Angel in the House* (1854). Contemporary scholar Lucasta Miller, in her book *The Bronte Myth*, provides insight into why *Jane Eyre* would have unsettled Victorian readers. By foregrounding Jane's individual psyche— "unheard of in the novel at the time"—Bronte's work was revolutionary:

> Charlotte had found a way of relocating the Romantic individualism that had shaped her literary ambitions in the outcast figure of the small, plain, shabby-genteel governess, the social persona into which she herself had often felt boxed. Instead of trying to emulate male writers in her quest for literary identity, she had found a path of her own, distinct from the exhibitionism of a Byron. Disbarred by her gender from the public posturing of the man of genius, she instead poured her egoism into a new and specifically female form of self-expression. In Jane, she let out the pent-up emotions of a woman who feels the world against her, and in doing so she indicted the society that had told her to suppress her passions and ambitions in the interests of womanly duty.[15]

Perhaps no passage in *Jane Eyre* sums up such a revolutionary vision, or threatened Rigby as much, as the declaration that follows Jane's admission of restlessness. It may be what triggered Rigby's passing allusion to Thomas Paine's *Rights of Man*, written in defense of the French Revolution in 1791 and again in circulation fifty years later as labor conflict mounted. One sees clearly why Jane's words would put a conservative on edge. Jane declares,

> It is in vain to say human beings ought to be satisfied with tranquility: they must have action; and they will make it if they cannot find it. Millions are condemned to a stiller doom than mine, and millions are in silent

revolt against their lot. Nobody knows how many re-bellions besides political rebellions ferment in the mass-es of life which people earth. Women are supposed to be very calm generally: but women feel just as men feel; they need exercise for their faculties, and a field for their efforts, as much as their brothers do; they suffer from too rigid a restraint, too absolute a stagnation, precisely as men would suffer; and it is narrow-minded in their more privileged fellow-creatures to say that they ought to confine themselves to making puddings and knitting stockings, to playing on the piano and embroidering bags. It is thoughtless to condemn them, or laugh at them, if they seek to do more or learn more than custom has pronounced necessary for their sex.[16]

That a literary work containing such passages should emerge on the eve of the 1848 European revolutions and the publication of Marx's *Communist Manifesto* had the effect of linking female discontent with general worker unrest. Although modern audiences may like the young Jane confronting the tyrannical Mrs. Reed and the adult Jane proclaiming female equality, early readers such as Rigby saw such outbursts through the lens of social upheaval. Rigby even goes so far as to defend the oppressive and sanctimonious Mrs. Reed and Rev. Brocklehurst, saying of young Jane, "It pleased God to make her an orphan, friendless, and penniless—yet she thanks nobody and least of all Him."[17]

In *Bronte Myth* Miller points out that others shared Rigby's discom-fort. *The Christian Remembrancer* (April 1848) "castigated the book's 'masculine hardness, coarseness, and freedom of expression' as inappropriate in a female author," and Miller notes that "[t]he question of Currer Bell's gender was soon being used by critics as an occasion for pontificating on what was acceptable 'feminine' writing and what was not."[18] Likewise a *Spectator* review, grouping *Jane Eyre* together with Anne Bronte's *Tenant of Wildfell Hall*, wrote, "There is a coarseness of tone throughout the writing of all these Bells, that puts an offensive subject in its worst point of view."[19] Even Elizabeth Gaskell, whose 1857 biography of Charlotte would elevate the author to enduring stardom, apparently wouldn't let her eldest daughter read *Jane Eyre* until she was twenty.[20] Clearly under assault is the prevailing horizon of expectations for women.

As an independent, professional woman, Elizabeth Rigby would have been particularly attuned to Bronte's discontent. One doesn't write such a scathing review unless one feels a personal connection, and it is unclear whether she was disturbed because Bronte has articulated a deep anger that she herself had repressed and didn't want to acknowledge—or because she was afraid that *Jane Eyre* would spoil the prospects for women like her who had found ways to circumvent male insecurities. Once one had read *Jane Eyre*, however, women no longer looked the same, no matter how much Victorian poets such as Patmore and others framed them as household angels. Indeed, Patmore's poem may have been in part a reaction to works like *Jane Eyre*.

My ancestor Eliza Scott would have read *Jane Eyre* some twenty or thirty years after Rigby's review, by which time something had changed. It may be that the novel had in fact helped shift the horizon of expectations so that enterprising young women were no longer seen as quite so threatening. If this is the case, then Jauss's model is borne out.

There's another possible explanation, however, which may have us turning to Percy Shelley rather than to Jauss. Shelley wrote that great works may be so far ahead of their time that it takes decades, centuries, or even millennia for people to really hear them—and only when they do, when the time is ripe, can activists use them to their advantage. By this reasoning, Bronte's radical vision of female anger and female selfhood could be seen for what it was only for a brief moment, appearing as it did in radical times. Once the revolutionary threat subsided, however, there was strong incentive for readers to focus once again on the marriage plot.

Bronte's friend Elizabeth Gaskell bears some responsibility here, with her 1857 biography of Bronte feminizing her image. In *Bronte Myth*, Miller says that Gaskell came to the Bronte biography "eager to uncover evidence of self-sacrifice and femininity precisely because she feared that 'Currer Bell' was lacking in these qualities."[21] Rather than focus on Bronte's strong assertion of self, which Gaskell too found coarse, the biographer focused on Bronte's suffering, "propagat[ing] the misleading notion that Charlotte's whole existence was one of unremitting martyrdom."[22] Gaskell's project was thus not unlike a similar clean-up job performed by Jane Austen's relatives. Both reclamation projects had the effect of robbing these revolutionary authors of their steely spines and strong personalities.

In short, the gravitational pull of women as wives and homemakers was so great that it was going to take more than one novel and one era to shake it up. In fact, another 130 years were required for people to stop reading *Jane Eyre* as primarily a courtship novel. For a senior project my student Kayla Waring, after researching theatrical adaptations of *Jane Eyre* and viewing as many of the film and television versions of the novel as she could, reported that all but the most recent version (2006) essentially ignore the second half of the book, which is where Jane steps into her intellectual and professional powers and asserts an independent identity. Instead, every one of them focuses on the love affair with Rochester.[23]

Bronte's strong feminist stance could not be buried forever, however, and during the 1970s feminist revolution literary scholars Sandra Gilbert and Susan Gubar picked up on the same confrontational vision that Rigby had detected. This time, however, they celebrated rather than condemned it.

As we have seen, in *Madwoman in the Attic* these scholars argued that the character of the madwoman Bertha Mason is the symbolic manifestation of Jane's restlessness. They pointed out that, when Jane is walking backwards and forwards in the third story corridor, she mirrors the walk of the madwoman in the attic, and they saw the following passage as Bronte linking Jane's longing for freedom with the madwoman's manic ravings:

> When thus alone, I not unfrequently heard [the madwoman's] laugh: the same peal, the same low, slow ha! ha! which, when first heard, had thrilled me: I heard, too, her eccentric murmurs; stranger than her laugh.[24]

Calling Bertha Mason the novel's "most threatening" avatar of Jane, Gilbert and Gubar point out that, whenever Rochester is overly domineering, Bertha Mason is sure to strike, at one point setting his bed on fire, at another tearing Jane's wedding veil (which Rochester has purchased for her despite her protests). In the end, Bertha all but emasculates him, destroying his right hand and his eyesight in a fiery conflagration.[25] The novelist and poet D. H. Lawrence, who in the early 20th century celebrated male sexual energy, was unnerved by the image of Rochester "burned, blinded, disfigured, and reduced to helpless dependence."[26] In Lawrence's mind, the fact that Jane comes to nurse him back to health is just a manipulative power move on her part. This woman in love has found a way to subjugate this formerly volcanic man.

In interpreting Bertha Mason as Jane's alter ego, Gilbert and Gubar drew on Freud's return of the repressed. To articulate socially prohibited rage—feelings that the author couldn't even fully admit to herself—Bronte shifts into the uncanny gothic genre, where monstrous women, locked up by imperious men, stalk through dark corridors at night. Bertha strikes out against patriarchy in ways that a proper lady could not. Or to apply Jung's symbolism, Bertha is a vampiric *anima* figure, rising up because male civilization, with its emphasis on control, cannot acknowledge that it has this passionate female side.

What was scandalous in the mid-19th century became a positive call to arms in the 1970s so that the "madwoman in the attic" image became a fitting way of capturing the discontent of women who, following World War II, had surrendered career ambitions—many unwillingly—to become wives and mothers. The energies that feminist pioneer Betty Friedan unleashed with *The Feminine Mystique* (1963) were verified with this new interpretation of *Jane Eyre*.

What of the fact that Bronte herself was not a feminist but one who opposed women's suffrage? She wasn't even a liberal as her politics leaned Tory, and she appears to have been ambivalent about the cultural and imaginative energies she released. Had she lived, she might well have approved of Gaskell's clean-up job of her reputation. Here the observations of those leftwing thinkers who prize truth over political correctness—Shelley, Marx and Engels, W. E. B. Du Bois, Terry Eagleton—come to our aid. Marx and Engels would have downplayed Bronte's politics, just as they did Balzac's royalism. After all, Bronte taps into historical forces that eventually will free women from patriarchy and workers from capitalism.

Meanwhile Eagleton, the modern Marxist scholar, would point out that Bronte's conservative politics made her all the more attuned to these forces because she didn't have to render them in politically correct ways. By conveying the deep truth of women's experience in the early 19th century rather than softening her depiction of female desire (which would make it easier to advance female-friendly legislation), Bronte captures (as Du Bois would characterize it) the rich complexity of those who have been stereotyped and kept down. Bronte herself claimed she was responding to a higher directive, which is how she excuses her sister Emily for having written the even more disturbing novel *Wuthering Heights*. "[T]he writer who possesses the creative gift," she wrote in her sister's defense, "owns something of which he is not always master — something that, at times, strangely wills and works for itself."[27]

Marxist philosopher Herbert Marcuse's idea of a "great refusal" is another way of framing how Jane fights against Rochester's domination and insists on following her own path. In Marcuse's eyes, however, a less conventional ending—say, the female suicides that conclude the novels *Madame Bovary* and Kate Chopin's *The Awakening*—would be more consistent with Jane's rebellion. In his 1964 eyes, anything short of full resistance to paternal capitalism is an artistic cop-out and a capitulation.

With the 1966 publication of the novel *Wide Sargasso Sea* by Dominica born-and-raised Jean Rhys, *Jane Eyre* would find itself challenged from another direction, one that has us turning to that key figure in post-colonialist theory, Frantz Fanon. Rhys exposes Bronte's racial and national biases by transforming Bertha Mason from a psychological projection into a three-dimensional major character, a mixed-race Caribbean woman. Rhys also graphically depicts the violence of British imperialism that leads to Bertha's disintegration. In doing so, Rhys undermines the dominant colonialist narrative in *Jane Eyre* in ways that would have gained Fanon's approval in his call for a new national literature.[28] Although she did not create such a literature per se, Rhys at least opened an imaginative space that activists could use to rethink prior assumptions and forge new alliances. For that matter, Rhys's revision of *Jane Eyre* helped women of color find a place in—and acceptance by—1970s feminism, which was initially mostly middle class and White.

If *Jane Eyre* contains such a blatant racial stereotype, does that diminish it? Wayne Booth and Martha Nussbaum address the question directly. For Booth, a work should drop in our esteem if it fails to grant a character her full humanity. Such a work becomes a friend with previously undetected flaws, just as his beloved *Huckleberry Finn* did when he looked at Twain's depiction of Jim through Black eyes. Having acknowledged that great works can contain imperfections, however, Booth points out that they can still be great. In fact, sometimes parts of a work can work as implicit critiques of other parts, which African American novelist Toni Morrison argues is the case with *Huckleberry Finn*[29] and which contemporary feminists argue also occurs in *Jane Eyre*. Bronte's blistering critique of patriarchy, after all, can be embraced by White women and women of color alike. To those involved in the early 1990s literary culture wars, Morrison offers a middle way when she says, "There must be some way to enhance canon readings without enshrining them."[30]

In any event, great works like *Jane Eyre* provide a rich site for discussing values, which will make us better citizens in a world made up of a wide array of views and experiences. As Nussbaum observes, by simultaneously appreciating and critiquing literary masterpieces, we find ourselves better able to negotiate the world's complex challenges.

If great literature benefits readers, does popular literature harm them. To answer that, I turn to a student of mine who contrasted *Jane Eyre* with Stefanie Meyer's *Twilight* series (2005-08) and whom I quote with her permission. Theresa (not her real name) contends that the teenage vampire books contributed to an abusive relationship in which she found herself whereas *Jane Eyre* helped her heal after she extricated herself.

In the *Twilight* books, 17-year-old Bella Swan falls in love with bad boy Edward Cullen, a beautiful boy who, like Rochester, is hiding something. Edward, it so happens, is a 103-year-old vampire in a 17-year-old body, and Theresa charts the worrisome relationship dynamics:

> Bella quickly falls in love with this golden eyed, pale teenage boy and completely ignores the warning signs that something very sinister is going on. All her new friends in Forks don't seem to like him or his family, and

they verbally warn her about him. One moment, he is incredibly interested in her and the next, he won't even talk to her. His eyes change color, something that she has a sneaking suspicion has to do with his eating habits. Sometimes he stares at her hungrily, as if she could become a part of those eating habits. The list of warning signs is endless, but Bella gets pulled in anyway.[31]

Even when she learns that "Edward is a vampire that is intoxicated with the smell of her blood," Bella is undeterred. Instead, she regards her continuing loyalty as a confirmation of true love. As Theresa sees it, the relationship works as

a very real metaphor for someone stuck in a horrible relationship. [Bella] sees Edward as someone who can love her and give her attention because she can't love herself. She is entirely reliant on him, to the point where it is dangerous. When Edward leaves her, she commits suicidal acts in order to "feel" him with her, and throughout the series she asks Edward to essentially kill her so that she can be a vampire and live with him forever.[32]

Jane Eyre too, Theresa notes, ignores the many danger signals—especially the madwoman in the attic—as she moves toward the idolatry of a "romantic" relationship with a man. Theresa cites Jane's response to Rochester's declaration of love:

My future husband was becoming to me my whole world; and more than the world: almost my hope of heaven. He stood between me and every thought of religion, as an eclipse intervenes between man and the broad sun. I could not, in those days, see God for His creature: of whom I had made an idol.[33]

The two works go in very different directions, however. Theresa notes that Bella is so caught up in her grand passion that she eventually gives up her life and becomes a vampire of her own volition. The author of the *Twilight* series, Theresa points out, compares Bella's love to Catherine Earnshaw's consuming passion for Heathcliff in *Wuthering Heights*. (In fact, Meyer's mention of Emily Bronte's 1847 novel turned it into a momentary teenage bestseller.) In dramatic contrast, Jane performs a heroic act of will by asserting the integrity of self. Theresa approvingly cites the scene where, having learned about Bertha Mason, Jane debates within herself whether to accept Rochester's proposal to move to the south of France and become his mistress. At first, she is willing to surrender all sense of self to make him happy:

> "Oh, comply!" [Feeling] said. "Think of his misery; think of his danger—look at his state when left alone; remember his headlong nature; consider the reckless- ness following on despair—soothe him; save him; love him; tell him you love him and will be his. Who in the world cares for *you*? or who will be injured by what you do?"[34]

Something deep within revolts against this self-abnegation, how- ever. Jane declares in response, "Still indomitable was the reply—'I care for myself. The more solitary, the more friendless, the more unsustained I am, the more I will respect myself.'"[35]

Tessa sees this as one of "the shining moments in literature" and notes that Jane, unlike Bella, realizes that the man "is not the only person who cares for her. She cares for herself." She says that reading *Jane Eyre* "has made me wish that, instead of having heroines like Bella Swan during my adolescent years, I had a heroine who was flawed but learned how to accept these faults, who taught herself how to survive not only on human compassion but on hard work and emotional strength, who realized in a circumstance as universal as a bad relationship that you need to find the will power to save yourself."[36] Unlike Elizabeth Gaskell, who withheld Bronte's novel from her daughter, Theresa says that Jane is someone she would recommend to her own daughters as a role model.

Our discussion of *Jane Eyre* has shown others turning to the protagonist for such a model. By means of compelling images and narratives, the novel has given readers a firm foundation upon which to stand. While not all works generate the controversies that *Jane Eyre* did, to the extent that great literature can access and communicate deep truths that challenge prevailing social mores, then it should be seen as having the potential to spur transformative change. To be sure, it may take time for a classic to work its magic—we saw Bronte's novel having a significant impact 130 years after its publication—but once such encounters take place, there is no answering for the consequences.

JANE AUSTEN ON POP LIT

ENJOY BUT BE WARY

THE CONTRAST THAT MY student drew between Charlotte Bronte's *Jane Eyre* and Stephenie Meyer's *Twilight*—that *Jane Eyre* bolstered her strengths while *Twilight* preyed upon her weaknesses—leads us to ask whether this is one way of distinguishing between great and not so great literature. Is great literature invariably good for us while lesser literature is less good, if not outright bad? Of course, one person's good can be another person's bad. Books that sustain a Somali prisoner or help a kidnapped American-raised Pakistani girl hang on to her identity are, from the point of view of the Somali authorities and the fundamentalist parents, by definition bad. In fact, it's why they sought to keep books away from Mohamad Barud and Shamyla.

In my own humanitarian view of the world, the best books are those that do the fullest justice to our intellectual, psychological, and spiritual selves—and that, by contrast, lesser literature sells us short. Pop lit demands less of us, perhaps by indulging us with shallow romantic or power fantasies or offering up cheap solutions. We turn to it the way we choose comfort food over a well-balanced meal, an analogy that Hans Robert Jauss's utilizes when he describes lesser literature as "culinary."

Calling such literature "popular" or "pop" is a useful but unfortunate designation since many works that we now regard as literary masterpieces were popular hits when they came out (*Hamlet,* for instance). But just because pop lit fails to put our full selves into play doesn't mean that it lacks power, and it is the nature of pop lit's particular power that I address in this chapter. I look first at the history of how

279

authors, critics, theorists, and others have regarded pop lit; then turn to three works of debatable literary quality that have had a significant historical impact; and conclude with Jane Austen's views (as indicated by her novels) about the dangers of pop lit and how we as readers should respond. Among the writers that Austen cautions us about are gothic writer Ann Radcliffe, poets William Cowper, Sir Walter Scott, Lord Byron, and Robert Burns, and dramatist Elizabeth Inchbald. Not shy about calling out flawed works, Austen shows that, while they may appeal to us emotionally, they represent a threat when they downplay or discourage rational reflection.

Although we have seen how the Roman poet Horace already hinted at a low/high divide when he differentiated between works that merely entertain and works that simultaneously entertain and instruct, this distinction first became a major focus of interest with the 18th century's explosion of print, triggered by a rapidly expanding middle class that flocked to books. In the chapter on Samuel Johnson, I discussed how the role of professional critic came into being to help these new readers make informed choices. Johnson commended works that he saw as beneficial and warned against works he considered harmful.

Johnson, along with other leading lights, feared that the flood of works by "hack writers" was debasing social standards. The mock epic satires of John Dryden (*Mac Flecknoe,* 1682), Jonathan Swift (*The Battle of the Books,* 1704), and Alexander Pope (*The Dunciad,* 1728, 1743) called out these writers by name, with Pope expressing apocalyptic fears that their lowbrow content would overwhelm the good authors. *The Dunciad* melodramatically concludes,

Nor public flame, nor private, dares to shine;
Nor human spark is left, nor glimpse divine!
Lo! thy dread empire, Chaos! is restored;
Light dies before thy uncreating word:
Thy hand, great Anarch! lets the curtain fall;
And universal darkness buries all.[1]

Pop lit thrives because it speaks to deep appetites so we can't casually dismiss it or close our eyes to why we read it. Often these so-called hack writers are in touch with marginalized groups and repressed passions, rushing in (to borrow a line from Pope's *Essay on Criticism*) where angels fear to tread. In fact, sometimes they open creative avenues for more celebrated authors. Although Jonathan Swift looked down upon the middle-class novelist Daniel Defoe, the novel *Robinson Crusoe* (1719) clearly influenced Swift's *Gulliver's Travels* (1726). Member of the gentry Henry Fielding, who had high art aspirations for his novel *Tom Jones*, found models for his boisterous bastard in Defoe's pulsating thief Moll Flanders and his resilient prostitute Roxana, protagonists of novels sold under the counter. In *Beggar's Opera* (1728), John Gay creates one of the world's first and greatest musicals by tapping into street songs and imagery of the criminal underworld, and Pope's *Dunciad* comes alive thanks to the manic energy of the dunces.

We continue to see this fertile relationship between high and low. Pulp science fiction featuring bug-eyed monsters gave novelist Kurt Vonnegut the tools he needed to write his masterpiece *Slaughterhouse Five* (1969), through which he processed the PTSD he suffered from witnessing the British firebombing of Dresden in 1945, where he was being held as a prisoner of war. Margaret Atwood's novel *Alias Grace* (1996), shortlisted for the Booker Prize for literature, draws on the energies of the penny dreadful and the sensationalist press as she fictionalizes a famous 1843 murder. While much genre fiction is eminently forgettable, even the worst instances sometimes open the way for substantive exploration while the best popular works have been admitted into the literary canon—witness various works of science fiction, fantasy, crime fiction, the gothic, and young adult fiction now enshrined as "classics" in their own right.

In fact, there are any number of works that, regarded as merely popular in one age, have risen to classic status in another. (W. W. Norton's ever-evolving literature anthologies chronicle these changes.) This has been especially true of the novel, which in the 18th century was regarded as a formless mess, not as real literature. In an attempt to gain literary respectability for his genre, Fielding defensively associated his novel *Tom Jones* with previously well-established genres (epics, romances, plays, histories) and thought he could, through hybridization, retain the prestige of the classics. (He claimed *Tom Jones* to be "a heroic, historical, prosaic poem.")[2] It took a while for his dream to be realized, however, as it wasn't until the 20th century that literary scholars began taking novels seriously. The landscape has shifted, however, so that we now recognize the so-called hack writer Defoe, for instance, as a genius author. Meanwhile, certain once-applauded authors have fallen out of favor, such as Joseph Addison, Dorothy Richardson, Joseph Hergesheimer, and John Barth.

Scholarly study of pop lit began with the Marxist-oriented Frankfurt School in the period between the two world wars. At the time, culture critics regarded such writing with contempt and suspicion, and Marx-influenced Herbert Marcuse and Theodor W. Adorno described it as an opiate of the masses, used to seduce workers into accepting their subordinate status. Like Pope, Marcuse believed such literature contributes to a one-dimensional society, which he hoped could be countered by classics like Gustave Flaubert's *Madame Bovary*. Those are the works, he believed, that really challenge capitalism.

Jauss's belief that pop lit is culinary arose out of the Frankfurt School as he distinguished between literature that confirms the prevailing horizon of expectations and literature that challenges it. He was also influenced by playwright Bertolt Brecht, who attacked plays that allow people to placidly accept an unacceptable world. By prompting middle class theatergoers to have a good cry (catharsis) over depictions of poverty, Brecht said that the theater of his time allowed them to expunge their feelings of guilt without having to act or change their lives. As an alternative to this "Aristotelian theater," Brecht proposed his own "epic theater," a form of art that prods people into constructive action.

A similar conversation about "high" and "low" has been a significant part of feminist discourse since the 1980s, as I noted in the feminism chapter. Many have argued that "mass produced fantasies for women" (to cite the subtitle of Tania Modleski's *Loving with a Vengeance*) seduce women into accepting patriarchy, especially the institution of marriage—unlike the work of great women writers like Virginia Woolf and Adrienne Rich, who break with the marriage plot. While Rachel Blau DuPlessis holds this view, however, feminists like Modleski and Janice Radway (*Reading the Romance: Women, Patriarchy, and Popular Literature*) worry that dismissing pop lit out of hand fails to acknowledge the real needs of women readers. In their books, they demonstrate that even formulaic Harlequins, gothic romances, and domestic dramas push against patriarchal oppression far more than most critics once thought. In other words, rather than being simplistic indoctrination vehicles, these works help women cope with their real-world challenges. Having made such arguments, however, Modleski in the end acknowledges that women probably would benefit even more from Woolf and Rich.

Wayne Booth, practicing what he calls ethical criticism, approaches the issue from a different angle. If books are friends, then our best friends increase our desire "to desire better desires."[3] Put another way, they prod us to expand what we want from life. Pop lit, by contrast, functions like a shallow friendship because it doesn't prompt us to aspire to anything greater. In fact, it gets us to desire *less*, as is the case with Peter Benchley's titillating and bestselling novel *Jaws*. Booth complains that "it is on the scales of otherness and range that this friend really lets me down. The range is extremely narrow—physical survival and physical pleasure are good; physical destruction or self-denial are bad. And whatever is really 'other' is simply to be feared, not understood."[4] He concludes that *Jaws* "tries to mold me into its limited shapes, giving me practice, as it were, in wanting and fearing certain minimal qualities and ignoring all others."[5]

A Freudian reading would see in Benchley's shark the return of the repressed or a battle with the forces of the id: as men push under fears of vulnerability, those fears return in the form of an emasculating monster or, specifically, a *vagina dentata* or toothed vagina.

Similarly, Jungians would see the shark as an anima, men's "female" side. Until the Self accepts this side of itself and becomes whole, such monsters will haunt their nightmares. That *Jaws* emerged in 1974 at the height of second wave feminism, when White men's hold on power was slipping, is not surprising as it embodies and articulates many anxieties. This was also the decade when America's period of the Great Prosperity was coming to an end, stymying expectations of rising living standards, and when the country lost the War in Vietnam.

Just as Modleski defends chick lit on the grounds that it helps women cope with patriarchy, so one could say that dick lit (the novels of Tom Clancy, Lee Child, and John Grisham join Benchley's here) give men a way to reclaim some of their dignity in a capitalist world that strips them of it. After all, a common plot of such fiction is a man-of-the-people hero triumphing over shadowy forces that seek to compromise, humiliate, or otherwise undermine him. When beleaguered men immerse themselves in such works, they (1) experience a symbolic reenactment of their frustrations and (2) imagine conquering them in a bloody finale. The man with the bigger boat conquers the monster, often achieving a sweet measure of revenge in the process.

Unfortunately, the macho bravado by which the fears are vanquished is what gives rise to the fears in the first place. As with a dope high, the satisfaction of reading such books is fleeting, perhaps driving readers to more such books in search of another fix. And just as unreflecting immersion in chick lit can enable submission to patriarchy, so immersion in dick lit can encourage toxic masculinity. I'm not saying that we should altogether stop reading such books, no more than we should swear off all junk food. We just must be aware of their effects and balance them off with more healthy fare.

Imagining victories over malevolent sharks and other shadowy adversaries may seem harmless enough, but too often the hatred of a fictional foe can be transferred to vulnerable populations, as was the case with the 1973 fascist novel *Camp of the Saints* by France's Jean Raspail. An apocalyptic nightmare about immigrants of color overrunning Europe, the book received some positive reviews when it first appeared (including from noted French playwright Jean Anouilh). It then played a role in fueling the rise of the anti-immigrant right. For instance, it "terribly impressed" Ronald Reagan when he was given a copy by the head of France's Intelligence Services (SDECE). More recently, it has found fans in Steve Bannon and Stephen Miller, Donald Trump advisors who helped shape the president's attacks on Muslim and Central American immigrants.[6] *Huffington Post's* summation makes clear how the novel feeds on the self-pity and fear of the Other that characterizes much of the world's extreme right:

> The French government eventually gives the order to repel the armada by force, but by then the military has lost the will to fight. Troops battle among themselves as the Indians stream on shore, trampling to death the left-wing radicals who came to welcome them. Poor black and brown people literally overrun Western civilization. Chinese people pour into Russia; the queen of England is forced to marry her son to a Pakistani woman; the mayor of New York must house an African American family at Gracie Mansion. Raspail's rogue heroes, the defenders of white Christian supremacy, at-

tempt to defend their civilization with guns blazing but are killed in the process.[7]

Raspail's book makes use of images common amongst White supremacists, including that of immigrants as a seething, bestial mass defined by their stinking bodies. Raspail writes,

> What struck the Western observers the most—those few who would speak to historians later—was clearly the smell. They all described it in much the same terms: "It stunk to high heaven ... It bowled you over, wouldn't let you breathe ..." As the decks sprang to life with their myriad bodies—as the hatchways puked out into the sunlight the sweating, starving mass, stewing in urine and noxious gases deep in the bowels of the ships, the stench became so thick you could practically see it.[8]

Anti-immigrant and racist sentiments, of course, predate Raspail's novel. When a compelling literary narrative like *Camp of Saints* emerges, however, racists and xenophobes find their views confirmed and bolstered. As political scientists put it, they are given a permission structure. Having immersed themselves in a story, they are able to speak with a renewed confidence that impresses many who are ambivalent but, perhaps because of their own unconscious racism, susceptible to such appeals.

Ayn Rand's perennially popular novel *Atlas Shrugged* (1957) poses a different kind of challenge to liberal visions. In the work, various corporation heads, including billionaire John Galt, are at war with the regulatory state. In retaliation, they shrug off social responsibilities and go on strike. Without their entrepreneurial spirit, society collapses, at which point the billionaires return to build a new world on the ruins. The work is an exercise in libertarian thinking that indulges various infantile fantasies, including that people can make it on our own without help from anyone, that they are not properly appreciated, and that the world will miss them when they're gone. Blogger John Rogers's witty and much-quoted observation about the novel captures some of its appeal:

> There are two novels that can change a bookish four-teen-year old's life: *The Lord of the Rings* and *Atlas Shrugged*. One is a childish fantasy that often engenders a lifelong obsession with its unbelievable heroes, leading to an emotionally stunted, socially crippled adulthood, unable to deal with the real world. The other, of course, involves orcs.[9]

Despite its simplistic vision, however, the novel has been a favorite of numerous conservative politicians, including former Speaker of the House Paul Ryan, who gave it to staff members and used it to bolster his attacks on social welfare programs. ("We don't want to turn the safety net into a hammock that lulls able-bodied people to lives of dependency and complacency," asserted the politician, who himself benefitted from Social Security survivor benefits as a child.)[10] As with *Camp of Saints*, those who immerse themselves in *Atlas Shrugged* can come out speaking with absolute certainty, even though the novel's vision, if put into practice, would lead to either anarchy or fascism.

The third work I highlight is the one whose literary merits are the most debated. Stylistically, *Uncle Tom's Cabin* (1852) has its defenders as well as its detractors, and its ambiguous status makes it an ideal text for the high vs. low debate. Literary quality aside, however, Harriet Beecher Stowe's novel undoubtedly had a major historical impact. Its reach was immense as, in its first year, the novel sold over 300,000 copies in America and over 1.5 million in Britain. Its influence was then further extended by means of theatrical versions, known as Tom shows. In *Mightier than the Sword: Uncle Tom's Cabin and the Battle for America*, Scholar Davis S. Reynolds makes a strong case that the book made civil war more likely and then influenced its subsequent progress.

Reynolds says that the novel rejuvenated and united the abolition movement, which until its publication had been scattered and on the defense. He also believes it enhanced the chances of an anti-slavery candidate winning the presidency while hardening southern attitudes, both of which were key factors in the outbreak of hostilities. Furthermore, in a key development, he believes *Uncle Tom's Cabin* undermined British sympathy for the southern cause so that, despite Britain's reliance on southern cotton, it did not intervene on the South's behalf. The power of the work was such, Reynolds adds, that it probably strengthened Lincoln's resolve when it came to signing the Emancipation Proclamation. While there were sound political reasons to do so anyway—by 1863, the border slave states of Delaware, Maryland, Kentucky, and Missouri were safely in union hands—a powerful narrative can push through final action.[11]

Political scientists might say that *Uncle Tom's Cabin* shifted "the Overton window," which we defined in the chapter on Jauss as the range of policies that politicians feel can be legitimately entertained at the time. Before the novel, many abolitionists were regarded as wild-eyed radicals. While many were still regarded as radical afterwards, debating the evils of slavery became acceptable.

As far as its literary qualities are concerned, Reynolds says that *Uncle Tom's Cabin* functions as effective narrative because of the way it combined, for the first time in American history, two of the era's favorite strains of popular fiction: the sensational and the sentimental. Sensational novels, he says, were usually published as pamphlets and featured "criminals, pirates, or other social outcasts involved in nefarious deeds that were often bloody or transgressive."[12] Sentimental fiction, meanwhile, often was about people who had visions of angels and heaven. As we have seen, for authors to draw on pop lit as inspiration doesn't automatically make their work merely culinary. The determinative question is whether the work limits itself to emotional appeals or also encourages substantive reflection. *Camp of Saints* and (despite its intellectual pretensions) *Atlas Shrugged* provide little in the way of nuanced reflection, what with their cardboard characters, resentment-fueled narratives, and black and white plotting. So is Stowe is guilty of the same?

If Stowe had only used an emotional appeal to advance the abolitionist cause—say, by providing us with saccharine sentimental caricatures of African Americans—she would have engaged in another version of denying them their full humanity. African American author James Baldwin has accused her of exactly that infraction, especially in her depiction of Uncle Tom, the saintly slave who dies being whipped by his unrepentant master.[13] It's worth noting, however, that others have praised it, with Langston Hughes calling it a "moral battle cry" as well as "a good story, exciting in incident, sharp in characterization, and threaded with humor."[14]

It's worth recalling Shelley's words about great authors adapting their vision to local customs and habits in order that "mortal ears" may hear "the planetary music." So is *Uncle Tom's Cabin* "universal" or merely "local?" Did Stowe sacrifice truth to advance a cause which, however noble, also had the effect of perpetuating certain noxious stereotypes (especially of a docile Black man acceptable to White audiences because he doesn't threaten them)? Or did she accurately describe slaves, slave owners and the slave system in such a powerful way that the truth of her novel shifted her era's horizon of expectations? If culinary lit, *Uncle Tom's Cabin* did some harm; if great lit, the benefits of the novel supersede the limitations.

The debate over whether a work is great or pop is more than an empty academic exercise. If literature has the power to change lives, then we must have a clear sense of what we are dealing with by understanding the implications of these labels. If we recognize a work to be culinary, for instance, we can guard against its pitfalls, perhaps seeing it (to use Booth's formulation) as a shallow or dangerous friend who will, nevertheless, possibly benefit us if we take proper precautions. That's how Frederick Douglass saw *Uncle Tom's Cabin* when, as mentioned earlier, he defended it against his co-editor at the *North Star*.[15]

Immersing ourselves thoughtlessly in pop lit, on the other hand, can cause us to fall prey to its facile ploys and to sell humanity short. How we read, Booth reminds us, is an ethical act.

As we have seen, this observation about the negative impact of pop lit has found some scientific backing in the work of psychologists David Comer Kidd and Emanuele Castano, whose Theory of Mind test discovered that reading substantive literature yielded higher scores than reading popular fiction. I would predict that reading *Camp of the Saints* or *Atlas Shrugged* would also lead to low scores. I'm less sure with *Uncle Tom's Cabin*, which I suspect has some redeeming value and might score somewhat higher than lesser kinds of lit. In any event, the debates about high and low are very productive because they force us to ask how deeply a work honors us as human beings.

The dangers of pop lit is a concern in Jane Austen (1775–1817), showing up in four of her six completed novels and in the unfinished *Sanditon* as well. The problem in each case is how the passions unleashed by reading bypass rational thought, which was Plato's concern as well. To be sure, Austen was not averse to passion. She was, after all, a contemporary of Wordsworth and Coleridge, and her heroines are passionate women. But she disliked how Romanticism sometimes substituted cheap feelings for genuine thoughtfulness.

The daughter of a rector in a small village, Jane fell in love early on—it appears that the man's relatives thwarted the match—and she never married, living as a dependent on her family for the rest of her life. Scholars argue, however, that her novels increasingly embodied the ideals of Romanticism, with her heroines becoming more assertive and with love playing a greater role than class status in their choices. Unfortunately, Austen did not begin to achieve income and recognition from her work until the last six years of her life, dying at 42.

Austen addresses pop lit's pitfalls most directly in *Northanger Abbey* (completed in 1803 but published posthumously), where we see protagonist Catherine Morland led astray by Ann Radcliffe's gothic potboiler *The Mysteries of Udolpho* (1794). Radcliffe was the immensely popular author of gothic romances in the 1790s, earning unheard of sums for *Udolpho* and *The Italian*. In *Udolpho*, orphaned Emily St. Aubert finds herself captive in the mysterious castle of the Italian brigand Signor Montoni. After various adventures, some involving dead bodies in underground passages, she finally escapes and reunites with her lover, the valiant Valancourt.

In Austen's novel, meant to be a parody of the genre, the Radcliffe-obsessed Catherine falls in love with Henry Tilney, whose family lives in a restored medieval abbey. Primed by her reading to expect a gothic mystery when she visits the place, Catherine concludes that Henry's dictatorial father must be a gothic villain who has either killed his wife or locked her away in some back bedroom. What else would one expect from a family that lives in an ancient abbey? Mrs. Tilney, however, has simply died, and son Henry Tilney, who is in love with Catherine, rebukes her upon learning of her suspicions. "If I understand you rightly," he scolds, "you had formed a surmise of such horror as I have hardly words to—Dear Miss Morland, consider the dreadful nature of the suspicions you have entertained. What have you been judging from?"[16]

It is likely that Austen is satirizing some of her own youthful enthusiasm for Radcliffe. At any rate, she captures the attraction of such reading, including how (as *Harry Potter, Twilight,* and *Hunger Games* fans can testify) it can serve as a bonding experience. When Catherine's friend Isabella Thorpe asks her about what she thinks is "behind the black veil"—"Are not you wild to know?"—Catherine answers, "Oh! Yes, quite; what can it be? But do not tell me—I would not be told upon any account. I know it must be a skeleton, I am sure it is Laurentina's skeleton. Oh! I am delighted with the book! I should like to spend my whole life in reading it. I assure you, if it had not been to meet you, I would not have come away from it for all the world."[17]

It could well be that Austen once considered writing gothics herself. Certainly, she would very much have liked Radcliffe's fame and wealth for herself. *Northanger Abbey,* however, suggests that Austen found the gothic too confining and perhaps too frivolous for the issues she wanted to explore.

Having said this, however, I should note that Austen is able to use the gothic genre, even parodied, to explore serious issues. A number of feminist critics have come to her heroine's defense, noting that gothic novels haven't totally misled Catherine. General Tilney may not have locked in wife in a dungeon, but she has in fact been locked in an unhappy marriage with a tyrannical man. Catherine's paranoia about the general, in other words, corresponds to a real-world source. In her defense of the popular gothic, Modleski notes that such paranoia fuels the genre, emanating as it does out of disturbed power relations. She could be describing General Tilney's family as she cites psychologist William Meissner's study of *The Paranoid Process.* Meissner, she summarizes, "claims that the paranoid usually comes from a family whose power structure is greatly skewed: one of the parents is perceived as omnipotent and domineering, while the other is perceived (and most usually perceives him/herself) as submissive to and victimized by the stronger partner..."[18]

Because women have been socialized to be submissive wives, Modleski says that gothic novels provide them with a way to secretly rebel. Reading these novels, they can retain plausible deniability as they express their hostility towards men.

To Modleski's theory of paranoia should be added Freud's theory of the uncanny, which explains that we are spooked by what we have repressed. The repressed in the gothic is often female anger. Catherine doesn't allow herself to admit that she's angry—anger in a woman is considered so abhorrent that she has learned to push it under—but she experiences a thrill of recognition when she sees female characters in *Udolpho* being mistreated. Literature portrays and helps us process what cannot be faced in real life.

To be sure, Austen doesn't explore repressed female anger to the degree that Ann Radcliffe and Charlotte Bronte do. Yet her character Catherine has plenty to be angry about. At one point, in a parody of a gothic abduction, the wannabe rake John Thorpe carries her off against her will. She also sees how General Tilney domineers over his son Henry and his sister, and she herself suffers when he expels her from Northanger Abbey with no explanation given. Her aversion to acknowledging her anger is so great, however, that she goes to almost comic lengths not to express it: in Austen's dry understatement, the most Catherine can bring herself to think about this horrid man is to "believe [him], upon serious consideration, to be not perfectly amiable."[19]

Of the literature available to Catherine, the gothic best captures her sense of vulnerability, just as Meyer's gothic *Twilight* series today helps teenage girls articulate anxieties about male violence.

But do popular gothics assist Catherine as much as Jane Austen's more serious novels would? It's as though Austen has seen a void and then writes the novels she thinks young women need. Repeatedly we see Austen women negotiating their vulnerability in patriarchal society—the Dashwood sisters in *Sense and Sensibility,* the Bennet sisters in *Pride and Prejudice,* Fanny Price in *Mansfield Park,* Jane Fairfax in *Emma,* Anne Elliot in *Persuasion.* If Catherine needs a guide for the world in which she lives, wouldn't serious, well-crafted novels like these serve her better? Following Tilney's reproof, Catherine's eyes are opened to Radcliffe's limitations:

> Charming as were all Mrs. Radcliffe's works, and charming even as were the works of all her imitators, it was not in them perhaps that human nature, at least in the Midland counties of England, was to be looked for. Of the Alps and Pyrenees, with their pine forests and their vices, they might give a faithful delineation... But in the central part of England there was surely some security for the existence even of a wife not beloved,

in the laws of the land, and the manners of the age. Murder was not tolerated, servants were not slaves, and neither poison nor sleeping potions to be procured, like rhubarb, from every druggist.[20]

While the Austen novels that would have aided Catherine had not yet been written, Austen holds up for approval another novel that she believes will help young people. In the contrast between Radcliffe's gothics and Samuel Richardson's comedy of manners *Sir Charles Grandison* (1753), we see the difference between a work that just triggers an emotional response and one that helps a young woman negotiate life's challenges.

Grandison, reportedly Austen's favorite novel, is not without its thrills in that it features a kidnapped heroine (saved by Grandison) and the various complications that ensue. Yet Grandison is a more complex man than is to be found in gothic romances, and his relations with protagonist Harriet Byron are far more nuanced. Indeed, the novel functions as a litmus test for character depth: Catherine's shallow friend Isabella regards it as "an amazing horrid book," while Catherine, despite her love for gothics, likes it. So does her sensible mother, which could be a turnoff for some teenagers but not for Catherine.[21]

Austen's positive mention of this novel is illuminating. *Charles Grandison* was Samuel Richardson's response to Henry Fielding's popular *Tom Jones,* the novel which (as we have seen) Samuel Johnson feared would corrupt young men by making vice seem attractive. Austen appears to agree with Johnson's assessment, at least later in life, and in *Northanger Abbey* makes *Tom Jones* the favorite novel of Isabella's doltish brother, who undoubtedly enjoys Tom's drinking and womanizing. In fact, the two Thorpes stand in for the shallow readers that Austen was worried about. By contrast, Richardson provides us a sensitive and noble protagonist that men should emulate and women should desire. While proving his manhood in rescuing Harriet, Grandison then reveals his elevated ethical sense by refusing to fight a duel with her captor. Although he is capable of holding his own in a fight, he considers the practice immoral.

In *Northanger Abbey*, Henry Tilney proves that he is the right man for Catherine in that he resembles Grandison rather than Jones. Austen, in other words, subtly leads the reader toward the conclusion that popular novels can lead you into trouble while great ones lead you out of it.

She's unwilling to throw out pop lit entirely, however. Rather than deny the very real pleasures that come with reading gothic novels, she suggests, just recognize them for what they are. After all, one sign that Catherine's beau Henry Tilney is a Grandison-type hero is because he enjoys reading Radcliffe's novels. For Jane Austen, real men are not afraid to admit they love *Udolpho*. Catherine is surprised to learn this:

"But you never read novels, I dare say?"

"Why not?"

"Because they are not clever enough for you—gentlemen read better books."

"The person, be it gentleman or lady, who has not pleasure in a good novel, must be intolerably stupid. I have read all Mrs. Radcliffe's works, and most of them with great pleasure. *The Mysteries of Udolpho*, when I had once begun it, I could not lay down again; I remember finishing it in two days—my hair standing on end the whole time."[22]

We have in Tilney, therefore, Austen's perspective on pop lit: enjoy but reflect.

So what's the difference between Radcliffe and Austen? Basically, Radcliffe just captivates the reader with one uncanny plot twist after another while Austen explores the dangers as well as the joys of fictional immersion. If Austen can persuade her young female readers to value the Henry Tilneys of the world over the dashing rakes, they, like Catherine, will do well for themselves. In fact, Austen admirers may note that Grandison-type heroes prevail in pretty much every novel: Colonel Brandon wins out over John Willoughby in *Sense and Sensibility,* Fitzwilliam Darcy over George Wickham in *Pride and Prejudice,* and Edmund Bertram over Henry Crawford in *Mansfield Park.*

Yet joining up with Mr. Right will not altogether banish the problems of skewed power relations within 19th century marriage. Women will need more great literature—they will need Emily, Charlotte, and Anne Bronte, George Eliot, Willa Cather, Zora Neal Hurston, and others—as they continue to search for happiness and fulfillment in the real world.

Returning to Austen's view of pop lit, she mentions other authors whom she regards as potentially dangerous in *Sense and Sensibility, Mansfield Park, Persuasion,* and *Sanditon.* In each case, we see characters swallowed up or led astray by literature that (as Austen sees it) encourages readers to wallow in emotion and bypass reason.

Sense and Sensibility tells the story of rational 19-year-old Elinor and passionate 16-year-old Marianne as they negotiate the challenges of courtship. Pop lit poses a serious threat to Marianne, who throws herself into poetry the same way she throws herself into music and into love. She and the charismatic but callow Willoughby cement their relationship by reading together the poetry of William Cowper and Sir Walter Scott. Meanwhile, they admire Alexander Pope "no more than is proper" (as sister Elinor comically characterizes Marianne's tastes).[23]

This contrast and choice of writers is significant: Pope, whose heroic couplets in *Essay on Man* assert that passion must be balanced with reason, might seem like a tiresome moralist to a 16-year-old in love. Scott and Cowper, on the other hand, celebrate losing oneself in larger emotions, Scott in chivalric love, Cowper in nature and melancholic self-absorption.

The dashing Willoughby encounters Marianne in the most romantic of circumstances —he rides up on his horse after she has sprained her ankle and carries her home—and they continue this romantic fantasizing by means of Scott's narrative poetry. (At the time of Austen's writing, he hadn't yet written his novels.) Perhaps they read together *The Lay of the Last Minstrel*, a romance set in the 16th century where a border clan feud has separated "Flower of Teviot" Lady Margaret Scott of Buccleuch and Baron Henry of Cranstoun. It's easy for anyone, but especially young readers, to get lost in such a tale.

In some ways, Marianne and Willoughby resemble Dante's Paulo and Francesca, the adulterous lovers who get caught up in an Arthurian love story and end up in the second circle of hell. The passion of Dante's lovers, which drowns out everything including thoughts of God, illuminates the danger that threatens the Austen couple. Dante shows the two lovers blown about perpetually by the winds of their desire, with nothing spiritual to ground them, which is why they are in hell despite their "love." Here is Francesca's account of what happens when she and Paulo read of Lancelot's adulterous affair with Guinevere:

> Full many a time our eyes together drew
> That reading, and drove the color from our faces;
> But one point only was it that o'ercame us.
>
> When as we read of the much-longed-for smile
> Being by such a noble lover kissed,
> This one, who ne'er from me shall be divided,
>
> Kissed me upon the mouth all palpitating.[24]

In the case of Austen's Marianne, she can think of nothing but Willoughby and grows listless when he is absent.

Marianne and her lover also read together the poetry of Cowper, whom Austen herself reportedly loved. Cowper is a fine poet so one hesitates to put him in the pop lit category. Austen, however, sees potential problems when a moody teenager encounters Cowper's romanticized melancholy. In the Ang Lee movie of *Sense and Sensibility* (1995), we see the two lovers reading Cowper's "The Castaway," in which a young man falls overboard and is drowned. It's heady stuff for young people:

> No voice divine the storm allay'd,
> No light propitious shone;
> When, snatch'd from all effectual aid,
> We perish'd, each alone:
> But I beneath a rougher sea,
> And whelm'd in deeper gulfs than he.[25]

Scott's celebration of chivalric love nearly ruins Marianne's reputation—she rejects stuffy convention when she is with Willoughby—while Cowper's love of nature nearly kills her. In the first instance, Willoughby proves to be no Walter Scott hero as he dumps Marianne for a woman with money. Then, depressed after the break-up, Marianne takes a long Cowper-like excursion into nature despite the threat of rain and comes down with a severe chill.

Through her characters' travails, Austen conveys that highly emotional literature in the hands of impressionable souls is potentially explosive. Adults may find themselves unsure how to handle their sons and daughters in such cases, which was also the case in ancient times. Horace, for instance, acknowledges the difficulties of guiding young people, whom he describes as "pliable as wax to the bent of vice," and notes that they will disregard "austere" poems imposed upon them by their grumpy elders.[26]

These elders, Horace notes, "rail against everything that is void of edification," and Austen gives us a character who fits the mold: Mr.

Collins. The insufferable rector in *Pride and Prejudice* insists on reading Rev. Fordyce's sermons to the Bennet sisters, and when Lydia turns away, Collins complains, "I have often observed how little young ladies are interested by books of a serious stamp, though written solely for their benefit."[27] While Austen doesn't reject altogether the idea that literature should be instructive, like Horace she believes it should be blended with entertainment. And when it comes to reading Radcliffe, Scott, and Cowper, all of whom speak to deep needs, she thinks such works must be supplemented, both with adult discussion and with better reading.

We see this balance throughout Austen. If Marianne doesn't lose herself entirely in a Paulo and Francesca passion, it is because she has, for guides, both a wise older sister and the poetry of Alexander Pope, which she has at least read. We have seen, in *Northanger Abbey*, how Catherine has Henry Tilney as guide and the novel *Sir Charles Grandison* as counterweights to *Udolpho*. And Theresa, my student who was once besotted with Stephenie Meyer's vampire series *Twilight*—so much so that she confused an abusive relationship with love—recommends Bronte's *Jane Eyre* as a gothic that is good for you. Smart parents and teachers, rather than banning or deriding *Twilight* (which after all articulates a genuine youthful state of mind) will wisely set it alongside and in dialogue with *Jane Eyre*.

Austen likewise wants her heroines to grow into sophisticated readers who can use literature to their full advantage. She would probably like Marianne to acquire the reading savvy of her heroine Charlotte Heywood, the protagonist of *Sanditon*. At one point Charlotte encounters an inept rake who rhapsodizes about Robert Burns in attempting to seduce her, declaiming, "Burns is always on fire. His soul was the altar in which lovely woman sat enshrined, his spirit truly breathed the immortal incense which is her due."[28]

Charlotte rationally replies that, while she enjoys the poet, his promiscuity casts doubt upon the depth of his affections for his poetic muse "Highland Mary." Her concluding summation of the poet is short, sweet, and deadly:

"I have read several of Burns's poems with great delight," said Charlotte as soon as she had time to speak.
"But I am not poetic enough to separate a man's poetry
entirely from his character; and poor Burns's known ir-
regularities greatly interrupt my enjoyment of his lines.
I have difficulty in depending on the truth of his feelings
as a lover. I have not faith in the sincerity of the affections of a man of his description. He felt and he wrote
and he forgot."[29]

Anne Elliot in *Persuasion* evinces a similar skepticism about emotional poetry when she learns about how Captain Benwick, a friend
of Anne's beloved Captain Wentworth, is using it to deal with grief.
Following the death of his fiancé, Benwick has turned for consolation
to long poems of high Romanticism, Scott's historical romances *The
Lady of the Lake* and *Marmion* and Lord Byron's orientalist fantasies
The Giaour and *The Bride of Abydos*. To be sure, one doesn't want to
criticize people's reading choices when they are grieving, and Anne is
in fact gentle. Unfortunately, however—as perhaps can be predicted
by the over-the-top melodrama of these particular poems—Benwick
makes himself the hero of his grief, enjoying it a bit too much. Anne
realizes she must suggest to him "the duty and benefit of struggling
against affliction" since he shows himself much more interested in
indulging in it. As they talk, Anne comments upon the dangers of
unreflective immersion:

He showed himself so intimately acquainted with all
the tenderest songs of the one poet [Scott], and all the
impassioned descriptions of hopeless agony of the other
[Byron]; he repeated, with such tremulous feeling, the
various lines which imaged a broken heart, or a mind
destroyed by wretchedness, and looked so entirely as if

he meant to be understood, that she ventured to hope
he did not always read only poetry, and to say, that she
thought it was the misfortune of poetry to be seldom
safely enjoyed by those who enjoyed it completely... [30]

British literature has a rich history of literature that would allow
Benwick to explore in more depth the sorrow he experiences—Shakespearean tragedies like *Hamlet* and *King Lear,* for instance—but he
has chosen the literary equivalent of Hallmark cards.

Of all Austen's protagonists, *Mansfield Park's* Fanny Price is the
most well-read and arguably the most thoughtful. A poor dependent
who is slighted by everyone but her cousin Edmund when she joins the
Bertram household as a young girl, Fanny, we learn, "has a fondness for
reading, which, properly directed, must be an education in itself."[31]
Edmund, six years her senior, coaches her reading in the early stages
although, by the end of the novel, teacher and pupil have exchanged
places as Fanny becomes the household's moral guide. We see Fanny
make good use of Cowper's poetry, at one point to condemn envi-
ronmentally destructive landscaping schemes, at another to weather
an intense period of uncertainty.[32] We also see her reading the poetry
of George Crabbe, a fine contemporary poet of Austen's with a social
sensibility very similar to her own.[33]

This reading education helps Fanny assess the emptiness of the
gentry society in which she lives and to accurately assess the character of the rake Henry Crawford, who first sets out to seduce her
and then pressures her to marry him. (Perhaps the novels of Samuel
Richardson, with their unredeemable rakes, support her in resisting
both Crawford's proposal and then the unimaginable pressure from
the Bertram family to accept.) Earlier in the book, it also allows her to
see the dangers of the play that the young and restless set of Bertrams
and visiting Crawfords decide to stage as a home performance after the
stern Sir Thomas Bertram leaves the country on business.

Lovers' Vows is a translation and adaptation by novelist Elizabeth
Inchbald, Austen's contemporary, of August von Kotzebue's steamy

melodrama *Love Child*. The play has two plot lines: in one, a young man, learning that he is a bastard and that the Baron Wildenham seduced his mother with a promise of marriage, attempts somewhat ineptly to kill his father. In the other, the daughter of the now-widowed baron falls in love with and makes advances to her tutor. These stories of illicit love inflame the imaginations of the young people. The church-bound Edmund, to be sure, initially resists, but he eventually succumbs to pressure from the others so that it is only Fanny, the poor dependent with no say in the decision making, who remains opposed. In her eyes, the wayward mother and the forward daughter "appeared to her in their different ways so totally improper for home representation—the situation of one, and the language of the other, so unfit to be expressed by any woman of modesty, that she could hardly suppose her cousins could be aware of what they were engaging in..."[34]

While many throughout the ages have accused Fanny of being narrowly moralistic—even Austen's mother found her "insipid"[35]—she accurately foresees the bad effect the play will have on the participants. The rakish Henry Crawford plays the two Bertram sisters off against each other and then essentially cuckolds Maria's stupid fiancé by casting Maria in a role where she can play out a tender scene with him. Meanwhile, the love scenes between the baron's daughter and her tutor allow the dazzling Maria Crawford to flirt with the principled Edmund in her effort to lure him away from a church career.

Fanny is appalled at their behavior, and their lack of a moral center soon plays itself out. Maria eventually ruins herself by having an affair with Henry Crawford, and he and his sister Mary blow their chances at soulful marriages, he with Fanny and she with Edmund. While *Lover's Vow's* may not be the direct cause of their aberrant behavior, there is little in the play to check them. In fact, like the Arthurian romance that lands Dante's Paulo and Francesca in hell, it does nothing but inflame them. Think of the play rehearsals as inferno in the drawing room, with the winds of passion blowing through and encountering no obstacle.

It's worth noting, in this discussion of these hollow young people, how the rakish Henry Crawford views Shakespeare: he treats the plays as prestige markers rather than as profound explorations, effectively turning them into culinary literature. When Edmund compliments him on how well he reads Shakespeare aloud—he even impresses Fanny with his performance—Henry replies that he hasn't actually read or seen the plays since he was a teenager:

> I do not think I have had a volume of Shakespeare in my hand before since I was fifteen. I once saw Henry the Eighth acted, or I have heard of it from somebody who did, I am not certain which. But Shakespeare one gets acquainted with without knowing how. It is a part of an Englishman's constitution.[36]

Pop lit has its pleasures, but when life poses real challenges—a tyrannical father, an inconstant lover, family pressures to marry, a death—it provides limited help. Such "culinary" lit may taste good, but it has the nutritional value of a donut. By contrast, great works are more substantive and satisfying. Like great relationships, they push us to new heights, teaching us to think and grow as well as to emote.

Austen's own fiction does this better than the pop lit read so avidly by many of her characters. It's not just her realism that's key since great works in other genres—the gothic *Jane Eyre,* for instance—also explore life's most urgent questions at a profound level. Setting Austen apart is the depth of her human understanding and her ability to capture it in finely crafted sentences, nuanced story lines, and exquisite comic satire. Pushing the courtship novel to new heights, Austen shows us what great art can do. At the same time, through the contrast, it shows us clearly where pop lit falls short. Perhaps that's why Austen continues to have a lasting readership while other popular writers of her era—Scott, Inchbald, Byron—are little read.

LITERATURE AS HEALING NARRATIVE

HOW BEOWULF HELPED ME GRIEVE THE DEATH OF MY SON

IN 1308, THE ITALIAN statesman and poet Dante Alighieri, living in exile and under threat of being burned at the stake should he ever return to his native Florence, famously finds himself "alone in a dark wood." "I never saw so drear, / so rank, so arduous a wilderness!" the narrator of Dante's book-length poem *The Divine Comedy* laments, adding, "Its very memory gives a shape to fear. / Death could scarce be more bitter than that place!"[1]

Initially Dante thinks he can simply rely on his faith in God to deal with the situation. His protagonist (let's call him "Pilgrim Dante" to distinguish him from the author) wants to march straight to the light that he sees glimmering in the distance, only to find himself blocked by fierce animals that represent inner doubts. These drive him back into his depression. Fortunately, Dante's favorite author is there to help him, guiding his harrowing travels through the underworld in Parts I and II of *The Divine Comedy*.

Literature, in other words, steps forth when we need it the most. Virgil's *Aeneid*, about the Trojan hero Aeneas putting his shattered life back together after the fall of Troy and journeying to start a new empire, gave Dante the model he needed to explore his own spiritual crisis. Aeneas's visit to the underworld in the original tale was especially important in shaping *Divine Comedy*. In the later poem, Virgil serves as pilgrim Dante's literal guide through Inferno and Purgatorio.

Significantly, pilgrim Dante doesn't initially recognize Virgil. That's another thing about literature: we don't always realize that it can serve as a resource. As pilgrim Dante gazes about in the darkness, only gradually does he detect Virgil's presence:

> And as I fell to my soul's ruin, a presence
> gathered before me on the discolored air,
> the figure of one who seemed hoarse from long silence.
> At sight of him in that friendless waste I cried:
> "Have pity on me, whatever thing you are,
> whether shade or living man.[2]

The authors we turn to are both shades and living people, shades in that they visit our imaginations, living people in that they become a part of our ongoing lives. Virgil reassures pilgrim Dante that he will help him grapple with his inner darkness. "I will be your guide and lead you forth through an eternal place," he tells him.

When I was lost in my own dark wood, I had my own guide in the 8th century Anglo-Saxon epic *Beowulf.* The darkness descended on April 30, 2000 when my 21-year-old son Justin died in a freak drowning accident. Justin was swimming in the St. Mary's River in a spot where we had often taken him and his two younger brothers to swim as children. In other words, he had every reason to think it safe. Unfortunately, the rainiest spring in decades had created dangerous currents, one of which caught him and dragged him under. He was gone in a matter of seconds.

The horror of the next twenty-four hours is still etched on my brain. First, there was my denial that the divers were looking for the body of *my* son: I remember feeling sorry for the parents of whomever it was, even though the victim could only have been Justin. Then there was the shock of identifying the body. I sang him a lullaby that I had sung to him when he was a child. Then they took him away.

Later that night, after our friends had left and my wife Julia and I had gone to bed, I recall waking up at 2 am and facing up to what had happened. Because the mind must go somewhere, I latched on to two phrases from poet Mary Oliver's "The Lost Children" and clung to them as if to a life raft, repeating them over and over to myself. Describing a father searching for a daughter who has gone missing, Oliver writes, "Pain picked him up and held him in her gray jaw." The other line was "when loss leans like a broken tree."[3] The phrases let me know that others had suffered as I was suffering, which suggested that maybe answers were somewhere to be found. It wasn't much to hang on to, but it was something. I didn't even realize at the time that the lines were from a poem about lost children. Deep in my unconscious, these words sensed I needed them and came to my aid.

Beowulf didn't enter the picture until two weeks later, after our extended families had come and gone, after the memorial service, after the college's commencement ceremonies—which I watched from afar—and the beginning of summer. I couldn't only stare into space so I returned to a book I was writing about Beowulf and other British classics.

Beowulf is about a young Geat warrior who journeys to the court of the Danish king Hrothgar to slay first Grendel, a destructive troll, and then the troll's vengeful mother. Following these successes, Beowulf returns to Geatland, eventually becoming its king. After a long and successful reign, he kills and is killed by an invading dragon.

In my writing, I found myself focusing on Beowulf's encounter with Grendel's Mother, which even before Justin's death I had interpreted as an archetype of warrior grief. A grieving warrior, I had told my students, would sometimes become a Grendel's Mother, lashing out in destructive rage as he sought to visit his own pain upon whomever came within reach. In the case of Grendel's mother, she inflicts maximal psychological hurt by killing Hrothgar's best friend. The *Beowulf* poet, I had surmised, chose a female figure to capture this particular rage because he could imagine no sorrow and no anger deeper than that of a mother who has lost her child. Grieving anger perpetually roiled real-world Anglo-Saxon society, seizing men and women alike in the form of blood feuds that could last for generations.

The passage that caught my eye after Justin's death was Beowulf's descent into the mere or lake in which Grendel's Mother lives. This mere is so forbidding that, we are told, a deer chased by hounds would rather be torn to pieces on the shore than leap into it to escape. It is infested with sea monsters and, though it is in "a frost-stiffened wood," the water burns at night, pitching "a dirty surge... towards the heavens."[4] A tiny detail that fascinated me was a tangled maze of tree roots that are reflected in the mere's surface.

Undoubtedly because of Justin, I felt inexorably drawn to Beowulf's journey into the depths. The mere can be seen as a metaphor for the grief-stricken mind, what John Bunyan in *Pilgrim's Progress* calls a "slough of despond." However cold the exterior—however much we try to freeze our feelings—it burns hot underneath. Like those tree roots, it is a tangled maze. Beowulf proves himself a hero because, unlike those who will passively allow themselves to be torn apart by their feelings, he is willing to face up to and grapple with them. Because I understood only too well the urge to passively succumb to depression, I was inspired by Beowulf's willingness to plunge into the turbulent waters and explore what is to be found there.

As he descends into the depths, sea monsters strike at the chest armor that encases his heart. Then Grendel's Mother seizes him and takes him off to her lair, with Beowulf helpless in her grasp. The regular sword he carries, the normal go-to resource for warriors, doesn't work. Nor does his strong arm, which worked against Grendel and symbolizes his strength of will. Grendel's Mother, meanwhile, stabs at his heart with her knife, and it is only a matter of time before she will break through. In other words, reading the scene as an inner struggle with grief, we are pulled into a realm of sorrow where our conventional coping mechanisms, including steeling our emotions and exerting our will power, don't work. I identified with how, for the first time in the epic, Beowulf finds himself at a loss.

We have an account elsewhere in the poem of what will happen if grief wins out. When the Geat king Hrethel loses his eldest son in a hunting accident, he crawls into bed, sings a lament, and never emerges.

Saving Beowulf from becoming permanently lost in sorrow is a giant sword, an ancient heirloom from the days of the giants, which he discovers in the depths of the mere—which is to say, deep within him. Symbolic of his core identity, the sword represents the warrior ethos that transcends all personal concerns, and Beowulf uses it to slay Grendel's Mother, that picture of destructive, raging grief. Sometimes, in our most dire moments, we find the resources within us that we need. At this point, peace returns. The sea monsters, symbolic of our inner tumult, vanish from the lake. "A light appeared and the place brightened," the poet tells us, "the way the sky does when heaven's candle is shining clearly."[5]

Much of this I worked out later. At that moment, two weeks after Justin's death, all I knew was that a story had been written that could help me negotiate my grief. My job was to dive in and take on my grief directly rather than allow my feelings to tear me apart as I stood helpless on the shore. Grief's journey, the poem helped me see, can take on an epic shape, which meant that I didn't have to flounder aimlessly. I also took to heart that the story promised a resolution. "I don't know where this grieving is going to take me," I remember saying to myself, "but I will follow her wherever she leads me." I also sensed that I had my own giant sword to turn to, which in my case was my commitment to my family, my college, and my community. These, I sensed, were counting on me, thereby giving me a firm foundation upon which to stand when I needed it.

I was so moved by this revelation of the poem's power to speak to me, which broke in upon me like heaven's candle, that I related the experience to Julia. In the act of explaining it to her, I broke down and cried for the first time in two weeks.

Following grief's lead, I was to discover, meant accepting whatever she dished out to me each day. Sometimes I was furious, sometimes I was sad, and often I was unimaginably tired, experiencing a bone fatigue that nothing could assuage. In each case I didn't fight it. I just figured that anger or depression or fatigue were on the menu for that day.

The poem's aid did not end there, however. At first, my way of handling grief was highly private. While I didn't entirely retreat from the world, I also didn't seek other people out but spent hours in my study working on my book project. I was offered grief counseling but figured I could handle things myself. After all, I told myself, I had literature. In *Beowulf*, however, thinking you can do everything on your own is associated with another of the poem's monsters. I learned upon reflection that I had dragon traits.

Dragons in *Beowulf* are associated with kings who lose themselves in depression and self-absorption. I've already mentioned Hrethel, the Geatish king who has lost his son and who refuses to leave his bed. There's also the legendarily bad king Heremod, a cautionary tale that King Hrothgar cites following Beowulf's victories. While "marked from the start for a happy life," Heremod becomes a "pariah king" in his old age, hoarding his wealth, venting his rage "on people he caroused with," and killing his comrades.[6] Although King Hrothgar tells the story of Heremod as a warning, he himself is in danger of withdrawing into dragon depression after Grendel's Mother kills his best friend. At one point he unnerves Beowulf by crying out, "Rest, what is rest? Sorrow has returned."[7] At this point, the young warrior reprimands him: "Endure your troubles today. Bear up and be the man I expect you to be."[8]

The most extended description we get of a human dragon is "the last veteran," a stand-alone character whom the poet inserts into the poem to account for the dragon's hoard. The last surviving member of an ancient race, the warrior sees nothing but emptiness as he gazes around him. "And so he mourned as he moved about the world," we are told, "deserted and alone, lamenting his unhappiness."[9]

The last veteran gathers his treasures around him and retreats into a funeral barrow, and it is into this barrow that Beowulf's dragon will move. "Then an old harrower of the dark ... Happened to find the hoard open ... The burning one who hunts out barrows," the poet recounts.[10] Seen from another perspective, the veteran's heart has become a funeral barrow and he a human dragon.

Dragons function as powerful archetypes for depression. Though they spend most of their time hunkered down, they can be triggered into outbursts of rage against anyone who violates what they regard as one of their prerogatives. Scaly hard on the outside, they will unleash inner fire upon anyone who seeks to intervene. Poison runs in their veins. The Dragon can be seen as the coin-flip side of Grendel's Mother. Where she lashes out in fury and then retreats into her lair, the Dragon emerges from its cave to burn down Beowulf's own home.

That Beowulf, the hero of the poem, would be threatened with dragon despondency at first comes as a surprise given that he has been a stellar king. By keeping enemies at bay and proving generous, he at first appears the polar opposite of the self-destructive Heremod. Yet like Heremod, he begins to regard his life as pointless. All he can see, as he looks back over his life, is a long series of meaningless deaths. In other words, even the best are prey to this monster of depression. Beowulf's resolution to deal with his depression alone, furthermore, is itself a dragon trait. Dragons can only be defeated with the help of others.

Beowulf is about to succumb to these dark thoughts when his nephew Wiglaf, disregarding orders and risking dragon fire—I interpret the fire here as Beowulf's harsh command to leave him alone—comes to his aid. Only by relenting and allowing his relative Wiglaf to help him can Beowulf defeat the monster and release the treasures that he has been holding inside him. In the final battle between armored antagonists, Beowulf accepts the help he needs and goes out a hero, not a dragon.

I'm not sure how much danger I was in of becoming a dragon as I buried myself in my writing project after Justin's death. I knew, however, that I wasn't reaching out to others as I once had. I remember experiencing a kind of crisis in mid-July, where all my determination to handle grief on my own seemed insufficient. Feeling a bit crazed, I told myself one afternoon I had to leave my cave and find a Wiglaf.

It so happened that my sons Darien and Toby were with friends and Julia was at work. I went into the college to find colleagues but found their offices were deserted. I finally stumbled upon some members of the housekeeping staff, whom I knew, and they generously allowed me to cry on their shoulders. They had known Justin and had a sense of what I was going through. It was profoundly comforting.

My story, I can now see, had an immersive, a reflective, and an active dimension. My initial interactions with the poem following Justin's death were deep and visceral. I felt that I *was* Beowulf descending into the depths of the monster-infested mere. Once I realized that the poem addressed my situation, I began using my tools of literary interpretation to move the insights to a more conscious level. I looked for themes and image patterns and analyzed the key symbols I have mentioned, thinking about what they might mean. I did so, not to please my profession, but because I wanted answers. I needed to know what to do next in my own life. And indeed, reflection provided me with options, which included seeking out help from others. When fall semester began, I also started looking for ways that I could assist others stricken with grief as Wiglaf assists Beowulf.

Partly for comparative purposes, I share two instances where I used the poem to aid suffering students, both in my "Literature in History I" survey. After reading *Beowulf*, a student named Charlotte (not her actual name) reported that, following the death of her teenage twin sister, she watched her father sink into a mental dark mere and never emerge. Thinking she could save him if she made him proud of her, Charlotte began studying hard and getting good grades. Her efforts proved fruitless, however, sending her into her own dark space.

Fortunately she discovered her own giant sword, which in her case was a determination to live her own life. Interpreting the poem as an affirmation of that resolve, she felt fortified in her life's goals, becoming the first member of her African American family to graduate from college. She went on to have a successful career in student services. When I chanced to run into her years later, I reminded her of her essay.

Another student, Erica, used *Beowulf* to process the recent news of her mother being diagnosed with terminal cancer. Her response is noteworthy because she used the work very differently than I did, pushing against the character of Beowulf rather than identifying with him. The contrast illustrates how each reader tailors a work to his or her own needs.

As she read *Beowulf* the first time, Erica found herself angry at its depiction of Grendel's Mother. Why should someone grieving for her son be seen as a monster, she wanted to know. She concluded that Anglo-Saxon warriors saw grieving as a weakness that must be pushed under and that, by repressing their fear, they made it monstrous. She therefore found significant the passage where Beowulf says he "can calm the turmoil and terror" in Hrothgar's mind when he is reeling from Grendel's nightly attacks.

"It seems to me," Erica wrote in her essay, "that the author is simply suggesting that grief is something Hrothgar can overcome with warrior-like brute force." Those who succumb to grief, on the other hand, are deemed unworthy. As a result, Erica notes, grief comes to be seen as an "end-all emotion," which you either conquer with "relentless strength" or to which you fatalistically surrender.

Erica took exception as well to Beowulf telling Hrothgar not to "indulge in mourning" after the king loses his best friend to Grendel's Mother. Mourning is not an indulgence, Erica protested:

> As far as my personal experience goes, it was a scary thing to really and truly open up to the grief over my mother for the first time. It marked the end of my denial—for the most part—and it is probably still the most emotionally intense experience I have had to date. I can personally say that when I chose to let grief in, I never expected to become as emotionally fragile as I did.

> In a way, Beowulf's calling mourning an indulgence
> is just another sign of his emotional inadequacies—his
> inability to let himself lose faith and then find it again.[11]

Although Erica did give Beowulf credit for diving into the lake, she was more critical than I was. As she saw it, he still holds part of himself back, hiding behind his warrior mask and his supernatural sword and not fully prepared "to face grief head-on, with his own emotions." The great sword solution also failed to satisfy her: she argued that the author of Beowulf, having "no real solution for the problem of grief, simply created the sword as a way to escape a real answer, a real struggle." Because "neither the poet nor the society understood or felt comfortable enough to really feel grief," she concluded, "Beowulf hid behind his armor and his weapons, under the pretext that he was on the good side and grief was on the bad side."[12]

Because he doesn't face up to grieving, Erica says that Beowulf merely delays the inevitable. Only at the end of the poem, when he is dying of dragon wounds, does she see him yielding appropriately to grief. From this she took away the lesson that "grief will get you. If not now, it will come later, and denying yourself the emotional freedom to be honest with your own heart will only work against you in the end." And she added, "Grief is not always a bad thing to feel; it allows you to come to terms with, and reconcile with, things in your life that cause you pain. In this way you grow and mature with greater wisdom, and even [develop] coping skills."[13]

Despite our differing readings, the poem gave both Erica and me the sense that we were on an epic journey, which bestowed significance on how we felt and how we acted. Even when beset by suffering and tragedy, we were not lost in an inchoate muddle. I suspect Erica was reacting against some inner (or maybe even outer) directive telling her to be warrior strong, advice she did not find to be helpful. She therefore used the poem to find an alternative way to grieve. As she wrote earlier in the essay,

> It has been a long while since my family received the diagnosis [of my mother's cancer], and, as any human would, I wrestle with grief and depression daily. Sometimes it gets the best of me while other times I subdue it. It is an everyday struggle, but in the end, I realize that it is something we must all face. Confronting such an event so early in my life may make me stronger than even Beowulf himself.[14]

And then, because the still-grieving Erica was determined to be scrupulously honest about how she felt, her essay ended with the following:

> Personally, I do not always believe what I say in the paragraphs above—grief does that to you sometimes—but now, as I reflect on this paper, I can see clearly how I have grown, learned, and experienced guilt (grief?) in a way that has made me, well, more aware of what I need in life, what I want, and who I love. If anything, there is that.[15]

Literature can support and guide us as we plunge into dangerous waters while also providing us with the weapons we need to slay—or come to terms with—our inner demons. Our great works seem all the more miraculous to me when I see them actually aiding young people whose lives are all before them.

In addition to being personally helpful, I believe that the epic poem can help us deal constructively with our current cultural and political situation. In the book I eventually published after Justin's death, *How Beowulf Can Save America: An Epic Hero's Guide to the Politics of*

Rage, I argued that the imagery in the poem speaks powerfully to three distinctive types of anger that I see at the heart of America's political polarization.[16]

In the resentment that prompts certain Americans to form rightwing militias and storm the U.S. Capitol, I see the archetype of Grendel, raging over what he regards as slights. For her part, Grendel's Mother is the archetype for the grief that our malcontents feel over having lost a cherished vision of America, one that is predominantly patriarchal, White, and Christian—and as with Grendelian resentment, they are determined to make others pay for their broken hearts. Finally, there is dragon depression, which is another response to a world that seems meaningless. Rather than lash out as the Grendels do, however, this rage goes underground, still hot and poisonous but out of view. When triggered, however, it can come charging out of its cave to burn down everything around it, proving no less formidable than Grendelian rage.

In my book, I argue that Beowulf represents an alternative and an antidote to each of these monstrous rages and that, by following his example, we can make inroads against them. Setting the interests of the community above himself, Beowulf defeats each of these social threats with strategies for which we can find modern equivalents. In the poem, he arm-wrestles Grendel into submission while we have the "strong arm" of the law: resentful bullies will often back down when society strongly asserts itself, as it has against those who stormed the Capitol and is currently doing so through indicting Donald Trump. While Beowulf discovers that grieving anger is harder to defeat—the emotions run deeper—modern Beowulfs find their giant sword in foundational documents that guide our values, including *The Declaration of Independence,* with its assertion that all people are created equal, and the *Constitution.* Whether our sword will always win out may be an open question—sometimes democracies backslide into autocracy and fascism—but it is still a potent weapon. Finally, to fight against the forces of cynicism and depression, there is collective action where Wiglafs come together to push back against dragon tyrants.

In the 8th century *Beowulf,* like all great literature, recognized the vulnerabilities of both individual warriors and society as a whole and delivered a compelling narrative in which people recognized themselves. When Anglo-Saxon warriors found themselves immersed in the story, which they must have found as frightening as our scariest movies, they didn't subject it to literary analysis. Rather, they instinctively recognized their fears, along with different ways to respond. Some of these responses were healthy, some not, but they learned they could make choices.

If the work still speaks to us today, it is because we are still subject to these psychological and social threats. And because we also have the tool of literary reflection, we can consciously identify the insights provided and (to use one of Henry David Thoreau's favorite words) *deliberately* apply them. I did so after Justin's death sent me reeling. Likewise, those discouraged by the current state of affairs may find themselves bolstered when they turn to various timeless classics.

Assessing Literature's Personal and Historical Impact

I HAVE BEEN TRACKING for years the different ways that literature influences our lives. On a personal level, I have been writing a daily blog essay since 2009 (at *Better Living through Beowulf*),[1] where I examine how literature helps me make sense of things going on in the world and in my own life. I also record what I call "literature sightings," meaning literary allusions that show up in the news, in articles, and in opinion columns. My purpose has been to demonstrate what I have always told my students, that literature is not a luxury or a side hobby but an essential life resource, as basic as food and shelter.

How do we go about looking more closely at the impact that literature has had on our own lives? We can all name works that have made a difference, but for those who want a more systematic understanding of the changes literature has wrought, I recommend undertaking some version of a "reading history" assignment that I have given my students, both at the introductory level in "Introduction to Literature" and in an advanced course entitled "Theories of the Reader."

The assignment involves a series of steps. First, I ask the students to choose a limited number of works (as few as three, no more than five) that have elicited strong reactions in them, either positive or negative. The works are to come from different times in their lives, starting with a poem, novel, or play from early childhood and ending with a work they've read recently. I tell them that more can be learned from works that left a strong psychological mark on them than books about which they were indifferent.

They are then to reconstruct everything they can remember about that reading experience. They must recall details about the work itself (enduring images, characters they liked or hated, plot twists, settings, illustrations if there were any) and describe external factors going on in their lives (Was the work read to them by parents? Was it assigned in a course?). I emphasize the importance of choosing an early work since those experiences will show us how literature works at a pre-rational level and how foundational a book or poem can be to our development. I also ask them not to revisit these books until *after* they have recounted their initial memories since, as many discover, sometimes how they misremember a work is itself revealing.

The next part of the assignment is the most challenging since it requires them to become sociologists, psychologists, and historians of their own lives. With each book they are *to figure out who they were at the time that explains why they had the reading experience that they did*. Doing this involves reconstructing those periods in their lives and matching them up with their reading memories. Out of that scrutiny emerge clues into how they were using literature to negotiate their challenges.

As an extra refinement, I sometimes ask the students to find a theme running through all their reading experiences. This helps them identify what Reader Response theorist Norman Holland calls an "identity theme."[2] Each of us, Holland says, has a characteristic way of engaging with the world, which becomes clearer when we see an emerging pattern amongst our reading responses.

I emphasize that the reading experiences do not have to be positive. I recall loathing J.D. Salinger's *Catcher in the Rye* when I was assigned it in Bill Goldfinch's 10th grade English class. I was particularly disturbed by Holden's encounter with a prostitute and her pimp, but that wasn't all. Holden's interchanges with his fellow students, his judgmentalism, his smoking and swearing, and his encounter with a pedophilic teacher all contributed to my feelings of distaste. I liked the scenes with his little sister Phoebe, but that was about it. Being a dutiful student, however, I read the novel to the end.

Looking back at the encounter with this book years later, I realize I hated *Catcher* because I recognized in Holden my own adolescent insecurities. I wanted to bury myself in fantasy such as *Lord of the Rings,* not confront life. It took rereading the novel when I was in my forties—in other words, when I was a safe distance from adolescence—to realize that Holden too hates having to grow up. He wants some "catcher in the rye" to save *him* as well as his sister Phoebe from tumbling over a cliff into adulthood. I missed this message when young, however, because my own anxieties overwhelmed me. As Holland observes, sometimes a work triggers such painful defenses that we shy away from it altogether.[3] Of course, defensive rejections can also tell us something about ourselves.

Similar self-insights await anyone embarking on a reading history. Often we will discover, for instance, that those books our parents read to us repeatedly addressed vital needs—and that we stopped demanding the books when our needs changed. A student of mine realized, upon probing his childhood obsession with Dr. Seuss's *Green Eggs and Ham,* that it related to severe food allergies he had at the time, which resulted in his being forced to eat certain unfamiliar foods. In even the best of situations, the dinner table can be the site of child-adult power battles, which helps account for the book's immense popularity, but this situation had extra intensity. For my student, the book's reversal fantasy was important: it is the smaller Sam-I-am that is doing the pestering about eating. He also loved the happy ending to the conflict ("I do so like/ green eggs and ham!/ Thank you!/ Thank you, Sam-I-am!"). Dr. Seuss acknowledged my student's emotional distress, offered him a way to deal with it, and assured him of a good outcome.

For those of you who are English teachers, you can employ a modified version of the reading history with each work you assign. In every class I teach, I allow my students to write about a personal concern that arises in conjunction with one of the works we have read. So that they don't simply collapse the work into their lives, I advocate what I call a "sandwich structure": they can write about themselves in the introduction and conclusion but must give over the body of the essay to analyzing the work itself. This has the effect of creating a conversation between the work and an issue they themselves feel to be important, with each being allotted its own space. Their personal issue allows them to push deeper into the work, which no longer seems so alien to them, while the literary work proves its worth by helping them discover new things about themselves.

I have given a sampling of the results of these kinds of assignments throughout the pages of this book, but to cite a few other examples (from my early British Literature survey), I have seen students use Chaucer's *Wife of Bath* to explore abusive relationships; *King Lear* to examine a grandparent's dementia; John Donne's poem "Valediction Forbidding Mourning" to process long distance relationships; Jonathan Swift's satirical novel *Gulliver's Travels* to look at a growing cynicism about politics; Alexander Pope's long poem *Rape of the Lock* to explore sexual harassment; and Jane Austen's *Pride and Prejudice* to look at the intricacies of dating following a divorce. Lest this sound more like therapy than a literature class, keep in mind that I insist on their doing traditional literary analysis in the body of the essay. They must respect the integrity of the work, I tell them. In this manner I seek to have them combine immersion, reflection, and action.

While personal reading histories and personalized interpretive essays certainly speak to the psychological impact of literature on readers' lives, I will sometimes assign an essay on how literature impacts history itself. Because studying history connects individuals with larger forces, this assignment provides students with a view of themselves as readers in a particular historical situation. Responses that we may consider personal to us take on new resonance when we realize many share them. My great grandmother Eliza Scott, whom I wrote about in the *Jane Eyre* chapter, thought she was just a lone young adult recognizing herself in Jane's "restlessness," but we now know that young women all over 19th century England (and probably other countries) felt the same way.

To prompt my students to think more broadly, in my "Theories of the Reader" course I ask them to choose a work that has "caused a commotion" in the culture at the time the work was published or rediscovered. I require that they find documentation about the historical incident to figure out why readers of the time responded as they did. If no such documentation exists, they are to draw upon what historians have written about that period. Here's a sampling of the possible topics I suggest to them:

- Why did the Earl of Essex pay for a special Globe performance of Shakespeare's *Richard II* on the eve of his rebellion against Queen Elizabeth—and why did she, in turn, order a performance of the same play on the eve of his execution?

- Why did the French church condemn Moliere's *Tartuffe* and why were his revisions insufficient to placate the authorities?

- Why were 19th century readers shocked when they discovered that *Wuthering Heights* was written by a woman?

- Why was the novel *The Picture of Dorian Gray* accused of corrupting young people (and why did certain of these young people have the novel all but memorized)?

- Why was Richard Sheridan's *School for Scandal* George Washington's favorite comedy?

- Why did Abraham Lincoln like *Macbeth* above all other Shakespeare plays? Why did President Teddy Roosevelt fall in love with the poetry of Edwin Arlington Robinson?

- Explain why Thomas Hardy made the changes he did to *Tess of the d'Urbervilles: A Pure Woman* for serial publication and then change them back when it appeared as a novel. Why did readers protest his subtitle?

Assignments like this help students realize that literature has always been part of history and can influence its outcome. The assignment also makes it easier for them to imagine that literature plays a similar role in our own time and place. Censorship battles, they learn, are nothing new.

Many choose to write about these modern battles, feeling themselves on familiar ground when they see Plato, Horace, Samuel Johnson, and others worrying about literature's impact upon impressionable young people. From the many essays I have received from students on instances of censorship, I have learned that some version of the following dynamic is usually at play: students turn to works like *Perks of Being a Wallflower* and *Are You There God? It's Me, Margaret* because they hunger for information. As they leave their family cocoons and enter a world that contains drugs, sexuality, race tension, suicide, gender and sexual identity confusion, and other major life issues, they want to know what is going on. Teachers and librarians, whose job it is to help them learn and mature, are generally sympathetic and will often assign such works, either during the school year or for summer reading. On the other hand, parents, who are programmed to keep their kids safe, sometimes fear losing their children to an uncertain world that is beyond their control. In too many cases they blame the books and sometimes the teachers themselves for prematurely plunging their sons and daughters into that world.

Conflict is often joined over these conflicting agendas. Predictably, my students usually side with the teachers and librarians. After all, the world *is* an uncertain place—even more so with easy access to the internet—so that it's virtually impossible to keep young people sheltered from uncomfortable realities. Those of us who love books know that they give us a way to negotiate that uncertain world, to try on different ideas, identities, and solutions to the problems we face. But even while my students know this, I tell them it's important for them to see the parents' point of view. While final agreement may not be possible, understanding the anxieties of parents along with the hunger of adolescents will heighten the possibilities for sensitive and reasoned dialogue between people with different educational philosophies.

A key objective of all these assignments is for students to realize that literature has played and can continue to play a critical role in readers' lives, including their own. Once they realize that poems and stories are a resource they can turn to in times of difficulty—and also a way of understanding the larger cultural trends and forces around them—they are likely to read more. Through further reading, they develop a greater love of books and an appreciation of the deep understanding they offer. To have students recognize, in a visceral way, that literature enriches our individual and collective lives—well, what more does a teacher want?

Conclusion

Unlocking Literature's Power

When people say that poetry is a luxury, or an option,
or for the educated middle classes, or that it shouldn't
be read at school because it's irrelevant, or any of the
strange and stupid things that are said about poetry and
its place in our lives, I suspect that the people doing the
saying have had things pretty easy. A tough life needs
a tough language – and that is what poetry is. That is
what literature offers – a language powerful enough to
say how it is.

— **Jeanette Winterson** (2008)[1]

DURING MY CHILDHOOD IN the 1950s and 1960s, people believed
that reading literature made one a better person. Between fiction
and drama's unique abilities to immerse us in imaginary worlds and
poetry's power to affix our minds with powerful images, literature
appeared to have life-changing potential. Granted, my own view of the
matter was skewed, raised as I was by bookish parents in the hometown

327

of the *Sewanee Review,* but that faith wasn't limited to the college educated. My wife's family, small farmers in southeast Iowa, subscribed to a Book of the Month club, from which they would regularly receive literary classics. Meanwhile, nationwide, *Reader's Digest* found an audience for a series of masterpieces made easily digestible through abridgement.

The country may well have turned to literature in those post-war years because we hoped that the creative imagination would counterbalance what had been one of the most traumatizing half centuries in human history. At some deep level, people recognized that poems and stories could push back against, or at least provide a counter perspective to, the bloodlettings of two world wars, a worldwide influenza outbreak, a worldwide depression, and murderous dictators in Italy, Germany, Spain, the Soviet Union, Japan and China. Because literature provides special insight into what it means to be human even in difficult circumstances, we thought that literature, perhaps, would help us rebuild a better world.

We were right to see literature as having life-changing potential. When the thinkers in this book testify to literature's ability to shape lives and sometimes history as well, they aren't engaging in detached theorizing but are instead basing their observations on their own transformative experiences with plays, poems, and stories. In these pages we've seen Plato theorize about what he sees as poetry's disturbing life effects because he was shaken to the core by *The Odyssey*. We've seen Aristotle, thanks to his cathartic experience with *Oedipus*, argue that tragedy is integral to a healthy society. *The Aeneid* so inspires Sir Philip Sidney that he regards it as must reading for men going into battle, and Samuel Johnson can argue for Shakespeare's profound knowledge of human behavior because of his own visceral encounters with the tragedies, *King Lear* especially.

And so it is with the others profiled here. Dante's depiction of Beatrice in *The Divine Comedy* moved Percy Shelley to such a degree that he believed the poem advanced the cause of women's liberation while John Stuart Mill, undergoing a major depressive episode when his Utilitarian philosophy appeared to have reached a dead end, was saved by the poetry of William Wordsworth, especially his poem "Intimations of Immortality." Karl Marx and Friedrich Engels attributed many of their insights into the nature of 19th century capitalism to Balzac's *Human Comedy* novels, which they deeply admired, and if Sigmund Freud is the founder of modern psychology and the primary developer of the process of psychoanalysis, it is in part thanks to his familiarity with *Oedipus* and *Hamlet*. Sandra Gilbert made major contributions to the feminist movement, especially the articulation of female anger and determination, thanks to her love affair with *Jane Eyre*, and Wayne Booth and Martha Nussbaum's compelling descriptions of how literature can promote multicultural democracy are rooted in their own immersive reading experiences, especially Jane Austen and Mark Twain for Booth and Sophocles, Euripides, Henry James, and Ralph Ellison for Nussbaum.

We've discussed some of the reasons why the surge of interest in literature following World War II subsided. Interest in literature hasn't disappeared altogether, however. In fact, since the rise of various liberation movements in the 1960s and 1970s, new voices have crashed the literary stage and insisted on being heard. Indeed, if multicultural literature became a target of conservatives in the culture wars of the late 1980s and early 1990s—and if it has become a target again today—it's because authors and teachers have demonstrated its explosive power. Literature has helped and is helping former colonized populations, women, African Americans, Latinos, Native Americans, LBGTQ+ folk, those with disabilities, and others find their voice while, at the same time, challenging reigning power assumptions. Perhaps literature teachers have been more successful than they realized in developing open-minded human beings resolved to think for themselves. Maybe that's a big reason why anti-Enlightenment forces are increasing their attacks on school libraries and classroom curricula, not to mention public schools themselves. Several times in these pages I've compared reading literature to playing with dynamite or waving a loaded gun, and many rightwing extremists would agree. They fear that once young readers—or readers of any age—immerse themselves in books, powerful feelings, ideas, and even movements will be unleashed.

In other words, rightwing book police, no less than liberals like myself, believe that books change us. It's just that we liberals contend that it's a good thing when poems and stories disturb and unsettle us, causing us to question and even challenge age-old traditions. As we have seen, the most audacious claims about literature's disruptive power were made by Percy Shelley when he argued that poets are "the unacknowledged legislators of the world."

To be sure, Shelley then had to admit that it sometimes takes centuries, if not millennia, for that "legislation" of psychological and moral influence to become actual law. Audiences may have caught a glimpse of female liberation in Greek tragedy's strong female characters, yet women were still being legally treated as second-class citizens two thousand years later. Yet it is also true that, when the time is right, certain works from the past suddenly speak with oracular power, providing aid and comfort to readers of a later age. When socio-economic conditions change, dramas that may have seemed safely ensconced in dusty museums suddenly take on a new significance. For instance, the women in Aeschylus's *Agamemnon*, Sophocles's *Antigone*, and Euripides's *Medea* can suddenly seem surprisingly modern. To apply the words of literary critic and philosopher Walter Benjamin, readers can "seize hold of a memory as it flashes up at a moment of danger" as past works are "blasted out of the continuum of history" and become "charged with the time of the now."[2]

So perhaps Shelley is right after all about literature's power to transform culture itself. By capturing humanity's "essential being" (Allan Bloom), the great authors of every age uncork a power that can never be entirely put back in the bottle. True, the Greek tragedians did not support equal rights for women, but this is no more relevant than America's founding fathers thinking they were excluding women, slaves, and non-landowners from full citizenship rights. Once you have said something memorable like "all men are endowed by their Creator with certain unalienable Rights, that among these are Life, Liberty and the pursuit of Happiness," historically marginalized groups will inevitably appropriate those same words and ideas and use them to direct future actions.

Given that W.E.B. Du Bois was a fan of Alexander Dumas's *Three Musketeers*, perhaps he thought of the musketeers' slogan "All for one and one for all" as he was founding the NAACP (1909), an organization that brought Blacks together so that they could resist the White terror that was undoing Reconstruction's gains. As noted in the chapter on African American criticism, Black poet Maya Angelou turned to Charles Dickens's abused Oliver Twist when figuring out how to process a particularly gruesome lynching that occurred in her community. In fact, throughout these pages we have noted one instance after another of literature stepping up when history unleashed its fury: *Anna Karenina* for an unjustly imprisoned doctor, *Little Women* for a Pakistani girl, various Shakespeare plays for imprisoned members of South Africa's African National Congress, Nabokov's *Lolita* for Iranian women thrown out of the universities by fundamentalist mullahs.

While literature played a role at these important historical junctures, it must be acknowledged that it cannot, by itself, change history. Reading a book will get one only so far. (Or as poet Seamus Heaney puts it, "No lyric has ever stopped a tank.")[3] But while true, it's also the case that literature doesn't sit passively on the sidelines when great change is happening. Marx and Engels's insights into the interaction of socio-economic base and ideological superstructure are important here: although there can be no significant historical movement without changes in the base, because base and superstructure are interwoven, economic actors come to know themselves through literature's images and narratives. Defoe's characters Robinson Crusoe and Moll Flanders, two indefatigable entrepreneurs, encouraged the rising middle class to overthrow or otherwise supersede age-old hierarchies, giving readers new visions of what was possible. So did Balzac's series of novels, even though he himself with a royalist. The British Romantic poets, meanwhile, by writing sympathetically about England's rural classes and about the natural world, opened new perspectives that have been expanding ever since.

Knowing this, postcolonial theorist Frantz Fanon welcomed authors as indispensable allies in the struggle against colonialism, speaking of a literature of combat. Feminist literary scholars in the 1970s played their own political role, showing how women were trapped inside certain narratives and finding alternative literature—or alternative ways to read literature—that provided them with ways of protest. *Jane Eyre* may have indirectly challenged Victorian patriarchy when it appeared in the mid-19th century, but the novel turned to full frontal attack a full 130 years later when readers identified with the central image of the madwoman in the attic.

While speaking of literature's contributions to the world stage, however, I would be remiss if I didn't mention how literature also speaks to smaller matters. Shelley's grand view, for all its lyrical power, downplays literature's more modest victories. Even if, at one moment, literature reassures us that we can defeat the cultural barbarians who are storming civilization's gates (Matthew Arnold, Allan and Harold Bloom), at the next it is helping us see our way through a marital spat or to stand up to playground bullies.

In these pages, I've recounted a number of these small stories. I've mentioned my own story of using *Huckleberry Finn* and *To Kill a Mockingbird* to negotiate my way through race hatred in the 1960s; my former marine student using *Sir Gawain and the Green Knight* to work through his Afghanistan War experiences; a student lacrosse student deciding to change his college behavior after identifying with the young man in *Rime of the Ancient Mariner*; and a student raised by Alabama fundamentalists using Christopher Marlowe's *Doctor Faustus* to sort through her conflicted feelings about religion and secular humanism. Teachers in any class in the nation can elicit such stories once their students realize, in Wayne Booth's framing, that books are friends who will encourage them to practice "ways of living that are more profound, more sensitive, more intense, and in a curious way more fully generous than [they are] likely to meet anywhere else in the world."[4]

If literature can indeed change our lives and sometimes change our world, then a special responsibility is laid upon those of you who connect others with books, whether you be a parent, a critic, a therapist, a social worker, a member of the clergy, a book discussion group leader, or just a friend recommending a good read. Think of yourselves as literature coaches. You are handling a rare, precious and, yes, sometimes dangerous substance, but any risks involved are worth it because the potential payoff is so great.

The reflective conversations that occur after one has immersed one-self in a work are particularly important. You can talk with your child about how a particular character negotiates a challenging situation and with your students about a work's insights into their own life situations. You can also talk about a work's blindnesses: is it hampered by race, gender, class, and other biases that keep it from acknowledging the full humanity of its subject or does it manage to transcend the prejudices of the author or of the age? One can regard these very discussions as citizenship training exercises since often they will arise when the work touches on hot button social issues. The best litera-ture, being as complex as life, will provide plenty of material for rich conversations.

Often in history, figures in positions of authority have hoped that literature would serve their particular agendas. The culture wars of the 1980 and 1990s were often over whether this or that work aided liberals or conservatives. The best literature, however, refuses to tamely submit to narrow political concerns, and readers faced with doctri-naire coaches will often rebel, either rejecting a work altogether or reappropriating it in ways that address their own situations. I have ref-erenced the fifth husband of Chaucer's Wife of Bath, an Oxford clerk who thinks he can turn his boisterous wife into a docile and submissive creature by reading to her nightly from *The Book of Wicked Wives*. Instead, he finds the book snatched from his hand and ripped apart and he himself pushed into the fireplace. That push is a metaphorical version of what teachers encounter when they try to use literature to indoctrinate their students, whether the messages are conservative, liberal, or radical.

Literature disturbs social censors because its impact is so unpredictable. I think of how Iranian students reappropriated *Pride and Prejudice* for their own purposes after they were forced back into veils and expelled from universities. Rather than interpreting the work as a romance trafficking in the conservative marriage plot, which is how American feminist Rachel Blau DuPlessis regards it, these women saw a heroine radically resisting social and parental pressure and standing up for her right to marry whom she chooses.

In other words, we cannot know how readers will employ the social dynamite we put into their hands. Our job, then, is to develop thoughtful and independent-minded men and women who will take stories and poems that catch their fancy and run with them. Once we've linked people up to the power source and directed their attention to the on-off button, the next step is to get out of their way.

If the literature is good, they will be okay. As we have noted, thinkers from Aristotle to Sir Philip Sidney to Samuel Johnson to Percy Shelley to Friedrich Engels to W.E.B. Du Bois to Martha Nussbaum have noted that the best authors are those who are most true to experience and do most honor to humanity's richness. In a 2018 essay, British-Indian author Salman Rushdie responded to the torrent of lies emanating from the Donald Trump White House by pointing out that the classics will always remain relevant because of their commitment to truth. Seeing literature as essentially a "no bullshit zone," Rushdie wrote that the job of contemporary writers was "rebuilding our readers' belief in reality."[5]

At some deep level, this is why people turn to literature. They intuitively recognize that masterworks, whether old classics or new arrivals, have the power to point us towards the individual and social transformation we crave. These works can turn us upside down and inside out as no other form of writing can. The culture wars forget this when they attempt to reduce literature to politics. When conservatives think that only older works are of value and that works by women or people of color have nothing to teach them, then they are circumscribing their vision of the world. The same is true for those radicals who think that writers and readers should stay within the bounds of their own communities. The thinkers we have surveyed in this book know literature is more powerful and challenging than any of these simplistic ways of thinking, as do good literature teachers, librarians and other of literature's advocates. They know—and you do as well—that a rich life opens before us the moment we pick up a book and immerse ourselves in its words.

ACKNOWLEDGEMENTS

I have spent my entire life researching this book, although I didn't realize that until 15 or so years ago. That's because I've been asking people about their favorite books for at least as far back as Carleton College, if not earlier. Nor did I limit myself to books people loved. When I became a college teacher myself, I started exploring why students disliked certain books. Antipathy was as interesting as love in revealing the dynamics at work, I quickly learned. My first acknowledgement, then, goes out to anyone who has ever shared a reading story with me. While I didn't start writing these accounts down until 15 years ago, many earlier ones are permanently lodged in my memory.

My next thank you goes out to all my students, at St. Mary's College of Maryland, Morehouse, the University of Ljubljana, and Sewanee, who put up with me as I asked them, incessantly, what in this poem or that story elicited a strong reaction, positive or negative, and why. I hope it was clear to them that I took each response seriously, figuring that both of us stood to learn something valuable if we explored it further. I particularly mention my senior project students because we spent a full year examining works that they found meaningful. But really, this exploration has occurred with every student I have taught, from first-year composition and Introduction to Literature to the first-year seminars, the historical surveys, and the topics courses.

I thank St. Mary's College for granting me sabbaticals that allowed me the time to research and write, and the students in my Theories of the Reader class for not complaining too much when I foisted drafts of the various chapters on them. I'm also grateful to those students who allowed me to share their work on my blog, *Better Living through Beowulf,* since many of the student responses I mention in these pages were first published (always with their permission) in that venue.

And then there are all of those who, over the years, have read portions of the book and given me feedback. With apologies to anyone I've forgotten, I include Carl Rosin, who teaches English and philosophy at Radnor High School; Professor Jason Blake in the University of Ljubljana's English Department; Glenda Cowen-Funk, who taught high school English in Idaho; John Gatta, Professor of English at the University of the South at Sewanee; Katie McDougall of the Porch in Nashville; Dr. Steve Obaid in Minneapolis; and Pastor Sue Schmidt at the Salem United Church of Christ in Harrisburg PA.

Special mention goes out the Rebecca Adams, my editor extraordinaire who provided the support I needed when I was ready to give up and who didn't allow anything to escape the scrutiny of her remarkable intellect.

Also, thanks to Matthew J. Distefano and Keith Giles at Quoir, whose encouragement and steady assistance were essential to bringing this book to completion.

And then there is my family. I must thank my sons—Darien, Tobias, and (in loving memory) Justin—for allowing me to read endlessly to them as children and query them about their responses. They didn't complain (at least openly) when their parents chose not to have a television since who needs anything besides books? I thank my late parents, who ushered me into the world of reading and who validated my own love of books by their own lifelong immersion, my father in poetry, my mother in the novels of Anthony Trollope. Finally, I thank Julia, who perhaps I was drawn to initially because she too is a passionate reader. We're still, after 50 years, reading and talking about what we read.

NOTES

Introduction

1. Warner, Greg et al. "He Was Imprisoned and Losing His Mind. *Anna Karenina* Saved Him." *Goats and Soda: Stories of Life in a Changing World.* March 29, 2019. https://www.npr.org/sections/goatsandsoda/2019/03/29/706870472/video-how-anna-karenina-saved-a-somali-prisoner-s-life.

2. Baker, Elna. "The Weight of Words: Go to the Mattress." *This American Life.* July 26, 2019. https://www.thisamericanlife.org/680/the-weight-of-words-2019.

3. Gosson, Stephen. *The School of Abuse.* London, 1579. Renascence Editions. http://www.luminarium.org/renascence-editions/gosson1.html.

4. Sidney, Sir Philip. *The Defence of Poesy.* Poetry Foundation. https://www.poetryfoundation.org/articles/69375/the-defence-of-poesy.

5. Wordsworth, William. "Observations Prefixed to *Lyrical Ballads.*" Poetry Foundation. https://www.poetryfoundation.org/articles/69383/observations-prefixed-to-lyrical-ballads.

6. Peacock, Thomas Love. "The Four Ages of Poetry." Poetry Foundation. https://www.poetryfoundation.org/articles/69387/from-the-four-ages-of-poetry.

7. Eagleton, Terry. *Marxism and Literary Criticism.* Berkeley: University of California Press, 1976, 28.

8. Wilde, Oscar. *The English Renaissance of Art.* Oscar Wilde Online. http://www.wilde-online.info/the-english-renaissance-of-art.html.

9. Auden, W. H. "In Memory of W.B. Yeats." *The Collected Poems of W.H. Auden.* New York: Random House, 1945, 48-51.

10. Maugham, W. Somerset. "Of Human Bondage, With a Digression on the Art of Fiction." Washington: Library of Congress, 1946, 7-8.

11. Williams, William Carlos. "Asphodel, That Greeny Flower." *Pictures from Brueghel and Other Poems.* New York: New Directions, 1962, 161.

12. Wimsatt, W. K. and Monroe Beardsley. "The Affective Fallacy." *Sewanee Review* 57, no. 1 (1949): 31-55.

13. Horace. *Art of Poetry*. In *Horace on the Art of Poetry*. Edited by E.H. Blakeney. Translated by C. Smart. London: Scholartis Press, 1928. Poetry Foundation. https://www.poetryfoundation.org/articles/69381/ars-poetica.

14. Yeats, W. B. "The Second Coming." *The Collected Poems of W. B. Yeats*. New York: Macmillan, 1956, 184-85.

15. Fitzgerald, F. Scott. *The Great Gatsby*. New York: Scribner, 1925, 179.

16. "Literary London during the Second World War." Imperial War Museums, London. https://www.iwm.org.uk/history/literary-london-during-the-second-world-war.

17. Vozzella, Laura and Gregory S. Schneider. "Fight over teaching *Beloved* book in schools becomes hot topic in Virginia governor's race." *Washington Post*. October 25, 2021. https://www.washingtonpost.com/local/virginia-politics/beloved-book-virginia-youngkin-mcauliffe/2021/10/25/e6157830-35d3-11ec-91dc-551d44733e2d_story.html.

18. Lopez, Brian. "Texas has banned more books than any other state, new report shows." *Texas Tribune*. September 19, 2022. https://www.texastribune.org/2022/09/19/texas-book-bans.

19. Associated Press. "Shakespeare Gets Caught in Florida's 'Don't Say Gay' Laws." NBC News. August 9, 2023. https://www.nbcnews.com/nbc-out/out-politics-and-policy/shakespeare-gets-caught-floridas-dont-say-gay-laws-rcna98970.

20. Hughes, Langston. "My Adventures as a Social Poet." *Phylon* 8, no. 3 (1947): 205. https://www.jstor.org/stable/272335.

21. Nafisi, Azar. *Reading Lolita in Tehran: A Memoir in Books*. New York: Random House, 2003, 48-50.

22. Schwalkwyk, David. "Reading Hamlet behind Bars." *Los Angeles Times*. Nov. 25, 2012. https://www.latimes.com/archives/la-xpm-2012-nov-25-la-oe-schalkwyk-robben-island-shakespeare-20121125-story.html.

23. *Grand Canyon*. Directed by Lawrence Kasdan. Twentieth Century Fox, 1991.

24. Yeats, "The Circus Animals Desertion," *Collected Poems,* 335-36.

25. Lee, Harper. *To Kill a Mockingbird*. Philadelphia: Lippincott, 1960, 117-18.

26. Twain, Mark. *The Adventures of Huckleberry Finn*. New York, 1885; Project Gutenberg, 1993. Chapter 31. https://www.gutenberg.org/files/76/76-h/76-h.htm.

27. Morrison, Toni. "This Amazing, Troubling Book." In *Adventures of Huckleberry Finn: An Authoritative Text; Context and Sources; Criticism*. Edited by Thomas Cooley. New York: W.W. Norton, 1999, 385–92.

28. Bates, Robin. *Better Living through Beowulf* (blog). https://betterlivingthroughbeowulf.com.

29. Hunter, J. Paul. *Before Novels: The Cultural Contexts of Eighteenth-Century English Fiction.* New York: W.W. Norton, 1990, 43.

30 Jauss, Hans Robert, "Literary History as a Response to Literary Theory." Translated by Elizabeth Benzinger. In *New Directions in Literary History.* Edited by Ralph Cohen. Baltimore: Johns Hopkins University Press, 1974, 17-18.

31. *Sir Gawain and the Green Knight, Patience and Pearl.* Edited and translated by Marie Borroff. New York: W.W. Norton, 1967, 28.

32. Bates, Robin. *How Beowulf Can Save America: An Epic Hero's Guide to Combatting the Politics of Rage.* New York: Discovering Oz Press, 2012.

33. Shakespeare, William. *Hamlet, Prince of Denmark.* In *The Bedford Shakespeare.* Boston: Bedford, 2015, 2.2.540-41.

34. Poulet, Georges. "Criticism and the Experience of Interiority." Translated by Catherine and Richard Macksey. In *Reader-Response Criticism: From Formalism to Post-Structuralism.* Edited by Jane P. Tompkins. Baltimore: Johns Hopkins University Press, 1980, 43.

35. Tolstoy, Leo. "What Is Art?" Translated by Aylmer Maude. New York, 1904; Project Gutenberg, 1998. https://www.gutenberg.org/cache/epub/64908/pg64908-images.html.

36. Shelley, Percy Bysshe. *A Defence of Poetry.* Poetry Foundation. https://www.poetryfoundation.org/articles/69388/a-defence-of-poetry.

37. Arnold, Matthew. "The Study of Poetry." Poetry Foundation. https://www.poetryfoundation.org/articles/69374/the-study-of-poetry.

38. Plato. *The Republic.* Translated by Benjamin Jowett. Oxford, 1888; *Project Gutenberg,* 2021. Book 10. https://www.gutenberg.org/files/1497/1497-h/1497-h.htm.

39. Gosson, *School of Abuse.*

40. Jack, Belinda. "Goethe's *Werther* and Its Effects." *Lancet* 1 (April, 2014): 18-19. https://www.thelancet.com/journals/lanpsy/article/PIIS2215-0366(14)70229-9/fulltext.

41. Young, Maya. "Tennessee pastor leads burning of Harry Potter and Twilight novels." *Guardian.* February 4, 2022. https://www.theguardian.com/us-news/2022/feb/04/book-burning-harry-potter-twilight-us-pastor-tennessee.

42. Murdoch, Iris. "Literature and Philosophy: A Conversation with Brian Magee." In *Existentialists and Mystics: Writings on Philosophy and Literature.* Edited by Peter J. Conradi. New York: Allen Lane, 1998. PDF.

1. Harari, Yuval Noah. *Sapiens: A Brief History of Humankind*. New York: HarperCollins, 2015, 25.

2. Ibid, 24.

3. Ibid.

4. Ibid, 25.

5. Ibid, 32.

6. Ibid.

7. Ibid.

8. Ibid, 37.

9. Ibid, 37-38.

10. Gottshall, Jonathan. *The Storytelling Animal: How Stories Make Us Human*. Boston: Mariner, 2012, 153.

11. Ibid, 153.

12. Ibid, 155.

13. Ibid, 147-48.

14. Ibid, 197-98.

15. Ibid, 198.

16. Brooks, Peter. *Seduced by Story: The Use and Abuse of Narrative*. New York: *New York Review of Books*, 2022, 3.

17. Borges, Jorge Luis. "Tlön, Uqbar, Orbis Tertius." Translated by James E. Irby. In *Labyrinths: Selected Stories and Other Writings*. Edited by Donald A. Yates and James E. Irby. New York: New Directions, 1962, 18.

18. Ibid, 14.

19. Fletcher, Angus. *Wonderworks: The 25 Most Powerful Inventions in the History of Literature*. New York: Simon and Schuster, 2021, 7.

20. Ibid, 26.

21. Ibid, 39.

22. Ibid, 36.

23. Ibid, 52.

24. Silko, Leslie Marmon. *Ceremony.* New York: Penguin, 1977, 2.

Plato

1. Plato, *The Republic,* bk. 10.

2. Ibid.

3. Plato. *The Ion.* Translated by Benjamin Jowett. Oxford; Project Gutenberg, 2008. https://www.gutenberg.org/files/1635/1635-h/1635-h.htm.

4. Ibid.

5. Ibid.

6. Coleridge, Samuel Taylor. "Kubla Khan." *Selected Poetry and Prose.* New York: Holt, Rinehart and Winston, 1951, 116.

7. Plato, *Republic,* bk. 2.

8. Ibid.

9. Homer. *The Iliad.* Translated by Robert Fitzgerald. Garden City, New York: Anchor, 1975, 475.

10. Plato, *Republic,* bk. 2.

11. Fielding, *Tom Jones,* bk. 9, chap. 5.

12. Homer. *The Odyssey.* Translated by Robert Fitzgerald. New York: Vintage, 1990, 145.

13. Plato, *Republic,* bk. 2.

14. Homer, *Odyssey,* 117.

15. Ibid, 201.

16. Annas, Julia. *Plato: A Very Short Introduction.* New York: Oxford University Press, 2003, 26.

17. Ibid.

18. Sidney, *A Defence of Poesy.*

19. Plato, *Republic,* bk. 10.

20. Ibid.

21. Ibid.

22. Ibid.

23. Plato, *Ion.*

24. Plato, *Republic,* bk. 10.

25. Ibid.

26. Ibid.

27. Ibid.

28. Plato, *Republic,* bk. 3.

29. Plato, *Republic,* bk. 10.

30. Ibid.

31. Ibid.

32. Ibid.

Aristotle

1. Aristotle. *The Poetics.* Translated by S.H. Butcher. London, 1895; Project Gutenberg, 2008. Section 10. https://www.gutenberg.org/files/1974/1974-h/1974-h.htm.

2. Hall, Edith. *Aristotle's Way: How Ancient Wisdom Can Change Your Life.* New York: Penguin, 2018, 189.

3. Ibid.

4. Aristotle, *Poetics,* sec. 4.

5. Ibid, sec. 7.

6. Ibid, sec. 4.

7. Ibid, sec. 9.

8. Hall, Edith. *Greek Tragedy: Suffering under the Sun.* New York: Oxford University Press, 2010, 65.

9. Ibid.

10. Hall, *Aristotle's Way,* 188.

11. Nussbaum, Martha. *The Fragility of Goodness: Luck and Ethics in Greek Tragedy and Philosophy.* Cambridge: Cambridge University Press, 1986, 378.

12. Aristotle, *Poetics,* sec. 6.

13. Hall, *Greek Tragedy,* 7.

14. Ibid, 6.

15. Ibid.

16. Aristotle, *Poetics,* sec. 13.

Horace

1. Horace, *Art of Poetry.*

2. Ibid.

3. Eyres, Harry. *Horace and Me: Life Lessons from an Ancient Poet.* New York: Farrar, Straus and Giroux, 2013, 16.

4. Horace, *Art of Poetry.*

5. Sidney, *Defence of Poesy.*

6. Swift, Jonathan. "A Full and True Account of the Battle Fought Last Friday, between the Antient and the Modern Books in St. James's Library." In *The Writings of Jonathan Swift.* Edited by Robert A. Greenberg and William B. Piper. Norton Critical Edition. New York: W.W. Norton, 1973, 383.

7. Horace, *Art of Poetry.*

Sir Philip Sidney

1. Sidney, *Defence of Poesy.*

2. Duncan-Jones, Katherine. *Sir Philip Sidney, Courtier Poet.* New Haven: Yale University Press, 1991, 295.

3. Gosson, *Schoole of Abuse.*

4. Sidney, *Defence of Poesy.*

5. Quote Investigator, https://quoteinvestigator.com/2015/09/16/history/#note-12001-7.

6. Sidney, *Defence of Poesy.*

7. Ibid.

8. Ibid.

9. Ibid.

10. Ibid.

11. Swift, *Battle of the Books,* 375.

12. Agbamu, Sam. "Blog: Whose Aeneid? Imperialism, Fascism, and the Politics of Reception." Society for Classical Studies. November 29, 2021. https://classicalstudies.org/scs-blog/samagbamu/blog-whose-aeneid-imperialism-fascism-and-politics-reception.

13. Sidney, Defence of Poesy.

14. Ibid.

Samuel Johnson

1. Johnson, Samuel. *Preface to Shakespeare.* London, 1765; Project Gutenberg, 2004. https://www.gutenberg.org/cache/epub/5429/pg5429.html.

2. Hunter, J. Paul. "The Loneliness of the Long-Distance Reader." *Genre* 10 (Winter 1977), 477-78.

3. Bate, W. Jackson. *Samuel Johnson.* New York: Harcourt, Brace and Jovanovich, 1975, 240.

4. Ibid, 296.

5. Johnson, *Preface to Shakespeare,* "King Lear."

6. Johnson, *Preface to Shakespeare.*

7. Bate, *Samuel Johnson,* 390.

8. Johnson, *Preface to Shakespeare,* "King Lear."

9. Johnson, *Preface to Shakespeare.*

10. Ibid.

11. Ibid.

12. Ibid.

13. Ibid.

14. Johnson, Samuel. "On Fiction." *Rambler* 4. In *The Norton Anthology of Theory and Criticism.* 2nd edition. Edited by Vincent B. Leitch et al. New York: W.W. Norton, 2010, 368.

15. Ibid, 369.

16. Ibid, 368.

17. Ibid, 369.

18. Ibid.

19. Johnson, Samuel. *Johnsonian Miscellanies*. Volume 2. Edited by George B.N. Hill. New York: Barnes & Noble, 1966, 251.

20. Johnson, "On Fiction," 369-70.

21. Johnson, *Preface to Shakespeare*, "Henry IV."

Romantics and Utilitarians

1. Coleridge, *Ancient Mariner*, 68.

2. Engell, James. *The Creative Imagination: Enlightenment to Romanticism*. Cambridge: Harvard University Press, 1981, 4.

3. Emerson, Ralph Waldo. "Poetry and Imagination." American Transcendentalism Web. https://archive.vcu.edu/english/engweb/transcendentalism/authors/emerson/essays/poetryimag.html.

4. Engell, *Creative Imagination*, 8.

5. Cited by Engell, *Creative Imagination*, 198.

6. Wordsworth, "Observations Prefixed."

7. Ibid.

8. Wordsworth, William. "Resolution and Independence." *Selected Poetry of William Wordsworth*. New York: Modern Library, 2002, 453.

9. Gilligan, Heather. "The most famous book about slavery has been rejected by black thinkers since it was published." *Timeline*. Jan. 11, 2017. https://timeline.com/the-most-famous-book-about-slavery-has-been-rejected-by-black-thinkers-since-it-was-published-b8dce54984c8.

10. Blake, William. *The Poetry and Prose of William Blake*. Edited by David V. Erdman. Garden City, New York: Doubleday, 1970, 95.

11. Wordsworth, "The World Is Too Much with Us," *Selected Poetry*, 515-16.

12. Coleridge, *Ancient Mariner*, 53.

13. Ibid, 58.

14. Ibid, 68.

15. Ibid, 69.

16. Ibid, 50.

17. Ibid, 69.

18. Glotfelty, Cheryll. "Introduction: Literary Studies in an Age of Environmental Crisis." In *The Ecocriticism Reader: Landmarks in Literary Ecology*. Edited by Glotfelty and Harold Fromm. Athens, Georgia: University of Georgia Press, 1996, xviii.

19. Berry, Wendell. *Selected Poems*. Berkeley: Counterpoint, 1998, 27.

20. Le Guin, Ursula K. "Introduction" to *The Left Hand of Darkness*. New York: Ace Books, 1969, vi.

21. Bentham, Jeremy. *The Rationale of Reward*. Classical Utilitarianism, bk. 3, chap. 1. http://www.laits.utexas.edu/poltheory/bentham/rr/rr.b03.c01.html.

22. Mill, John Stuart. *On Liberty*. London, 1859; Project Gutenberg, 2011. Chapter 1. https://www.gutenberg.org/files/34901/34901-h/34901-h.htm.

23. Dickens, Charles. *Hard Times*. Wordsworth Classics. Ware, England: Wordsworth Editions, 2023.

24. Swift, Jonathan. "A Modest Proposal." London, 1729; Project Gutenberg, 1997. https://www.gutenberg.org/files/1080/1080-h/1080-h.htm.

25. Swift, Jonathan. *Gulliver's Travels into Several Remote Nations of the World*. London, 1726; Project Gutenberg, 1997. Part 4, chapter 10. https://www.gutenberg.org/files/829/829-h/829-h.htm.

26. Wilde, *English Renaissance of Art*.

27. Mill, John Stuart. *Autobiography*. New York, 1874; Project Gutenberg, 2003. Chapter 5. https://www.gutenberg.org/files/10378/10378-h/10378-h.htm.

28. Ibid.

29. Wordsworth, "Ode: Intimations of Immortality from Recollections of Early Childhood," *Selected Poetry*, 525.

30. Mill, *Autobiography*, chap. 5.

31. Mill, John Stuart. "Inaugural Address Delivered to the University of St. Andrews." London: Longmans, Green, Reader and Dyer, 1867. Wikisource. https://en.wikisource.org/wiki/Inaugural_address_delivered_to_the_University_of_St._Andrews,_Feb._1st_1867.

32. Ibid.

33. Shelley, Percy Bysshe. "Hymn to Intellectual Beauty." Poetry Foundation. https://www.poetryfoundation.org/poems/45123/hymn-to-intellectual-beauty.

34. Mahoney, Mary. "When Love Stories Became Medicine for Warworn Soldiers." *Lady Science*, no. 57 (2019). https://www.ladyscience.com/when-love-stories-became-medicine-for-warworn-soldiers/no57.

35. Koch, Theodor Wesley. *Books in War: The Romance of Library War Service.* Boston: Houghton Mifflin, 1919, 146.

36. Ibid, 165.

Percy Bysshe Shelley

1. Shelley, *A Defence of Poetry.*

2. Hobbes, Thomas. *Leviathan.* London, 1651; Project Gutenberg, 2002. Chapter 13. https://www.gutenberg.org/files/3207/3207-h/3207-h.htm.

3. Shelley, *Defence of Poetry.*

4. Ibid.

5. Ibid.

6. Ibid.

7. Ibid.

8. Ibid.

9. Ibid.

10. Ibid.

11. Ibid.

12. Ibid.

13. Ibid.

Karl Marx and Friedrich Engels

1. Engels, Friedrich. "Letter to Margaret Harkness in London." April 1888. Marx/Engels Internet Archive. https://www.marxists.org/archive/marx/works/1888/letters/88_04_15.htm.

2. Marx, Eleanor and Edward Aveling. "Shelley's Socialism." In *The Real Percy B. Shelley.* http://www.grahamhenderson.ca/guest-contribution/shelleys-socialism-eleanor-marx-text.

3. Marx, Karl. "Marx to Ruge." In *Letters from the Deutsch-Französische Jahrbücher*. Marx/Engels Internet Archive. https://www.marxists.org/archive/marx/works/1843/letters/43_09.htm.

4. Marx, Karl and Friedrich Engels. *A Critique of the German Ideology*. Translated by Tim Delaney and Bob Schwartz. Marx/Engels Internet Archive. Part 1, section A. https://www.marxists.org/archive/marx/works/download/Marx_The_German_Ideology.pdf.

5. Ibid.

6. Defoe, Daniel. *Robinson Crusoe*. New York: Signet, 1961.

7. Watt, Ian. *The Rise of the Novel: Studies in Defoe, Richardson and Fielding*. Berkeley: University of California Press, 1957, 86-87.

8. Engels, "Margaret Harkness."

9. Engels. "Engels to Minna Kautsky," November 26, 1885. Marx/Engels Internet Archive. https://www.marxists.org/archive/marx/works/1885/letters/85_11_26.htm.

10. Ibid.

11. Lawrence, D.H. "Morality and the Novel." In *Study of Thomas Hardy and Other Essays*. Edited by Bruce Steele. Cambridge: Cambridge University Press, 1985, 172.

12. Murdoch, "Literature and Philosophy."

13. Engels. "Letter to Franz Mehring." Marx and Engels Correspondence. July 14, 1893. https://www.marxists.org/archive/marx/works/1893/letters/93_07_14.htm.

14. Gramsci, Antonio. "Critical Notes on an Attempt at a Popular Presentation of Marxism by Bukharin." In *The Modern Prince and Other Writings*. Edited and translated by Louis Marks. New York: International Publishers, 1972, 103-04.

15. Blake, "London," *Poetry and Prose*, 26-27.

16. Nye, Joseph. *Soft Power: The Means to Success in World Politics*. New York: Public Affairs, 2004.

17. Gramsci, "The Formation of Intellectuals," in *Modern Prince*, 118.

18. Jameson, Fredric. *Marxism and Form*. Princeton, New Jersey: Princeton University Press, 1971, 193; Eagleton, *Marxism and Literary Criticism*, 14.

19. Ibid, 7-8.

20. Ibid, 8.

21. Marx, Karl. "A Contribution to the Critique of Hegel's Philosophy of Right." Marx/Engels Internet Archive. https://www.marxists.org/archive/marx/works/1843/critique-hpr/intro.htm.

Sigmund Freud and Carl Jung

1. Freud, Sigmund. "Creative Writers and Daydreaming." In *On Creativity and the Unconscious: Papers on the Psychology of Art, Literature, Love, Religion.* Edited by Benjamin Nelson. New York: Harper and Row, 1958, 54.

2. Bettelheim, Bruno. *The Uses of Enchantment: The Meaning and Importance of Fairy Tales.* New York: Alfred A. Knopf, 1975, 8.

3. Rieff, Philip. *Freud: The Mind of the Moralist.* New York: Doubleday, 1959, 383.

4. Freud, Sigmund. *The Interpretation of Dreams.* Translated by A.A. Brill. New York, 1913; Project Gutenberg, 2021. Chapter 5, section D.

5. Ibid.

6. Marlowe, Christopher. *Doctor Faustus.* Norton Critical Edition. New York: W.W. Norton, 2005, 2.3.18-31.

7. Rieff, *Mind of the Moralist,* 69.

8. Freud, *Interpretation of Dreams,* chap. 5, sec. D.

9. Sophocles. *Sophocles I: Oedipus the King, Oedipus at Colonus, Antigone.* 2nd ed. Translated by David Greene. Chicago: University of Chicago Press, 1991, 52.

10. Rieff, *Mind of the Moralist,* 383.

11. Freud, "Daydreaming," 50.

12. Freud, Sigmund. "The Uncanny." *Norton Anthology of Theory and Criticism,* 840.

13. Freud, "Daydreaming," 48.

14. Ibid, 54.

15. Bettelheim, *Uses of Enchantment,* 5.

16. Ibid, 159-66.

17. Ibid, 164.

18. Kelly, Walt. *Pogo.* Billy Ireland Cartoon Library and Museum. https://library.osu.edu/site/40stories/2020/01/05/we-have-met-the-enemy.

19. Conrad, Joseph. *Heart of Darkness: A Case Study in Contemporary Criticism.* Edited by Ross C. Murfin. New York: St. Martin's Press, 20.

20. Freud, Sigmund and Josef Breuer. *Studies on Hysteria.* Translated by James Strachey. New York: Basic Books, 1957, 226.

21. Franz, M.-L von. "The Process of Individuation." In *Man and His Symbols.* Edited by Carl J. Jung. New York: Doubleday, 1964, 160-64.

22. Ibid, 168-70.

23. Ibid, 177-95.

24. Campbell, Joseph. *The Hero with a Thousand Faces.* Commemorative edition. Princeton: Princeton University Press, 2004, 57.

25. Ibid, 227-28.

Matthew Arnold

1. Arnold, "Study of Poetry."

2. Ibid.

3. Ibid.

4. Arnold, Matthew. *Culture and Anarchy: An Essay in Political and Social Criticism.* London, 1869; Project Gutenberg, 2003. Chapter 1. https://www.gutenberg.org/cache/epub/4212/pg4212.html.

5. Ibid.

6. Ibid.

7. Eagleton, Terry. *Literary Theory: An Introduction.* Minneapolis: University of Minnesota Press, 1983, 25.

8. Arnold, *Culture and Anarchy,* chap. 2.

9. Arnold, "Dover Beach." Poetry Foundation. https://www.poetryfoundation.org/poems/43588/dover-beach.

10. Arnold, *Culture and Anarchy,* chap. 2.

11. Cited by Eagleton, *Literary Theory,* 21.

12. Arnold, *Culture and Anarchy,* chap. 6.

W. E. B. Du Bois

1. Du Bois, W. E. B. "Criteria of Nego Art." *Norton Anthology of Theory,* 876.

2. Ibid, 875.

3. Ibid, 875.

4. Achebe, Chinua. "An Image of Africa: Racism in Conrad's *Heart of Darkness." Norton Anthology of Theory,* 1615.

5. Achebe, Chinua. *Things Fall Apart.* London: Heinemann, 1958, 3.

6. Du Bois, "Negro Art," 875.

7. Ibid.

8. Ibid, 876.

9. Hughes, Langston. "The Negro Artist and the Racial Mountain." *Norton Anthology of Theory,* 1195.

10. Du Bois, "Negro Art," 876.

11. Du Bois, W.E.B. *The Souls of Black Folk.* Chicago, 1903; Project Gutenberg, 1996. Chapter 6. https://www.gutenberg.org/files/408/408-h/408-h.htm.

12. McLeod, Melvin. "'There's No Place to Go but Up' — bell hooks and Maya Angelou in conversation." *Lion's Roar: Buddhist Wisdom for Our Time.* January 1, 1998. https://www.lionsroar.com/theres-no-place-to-go-but-up/?fbclid=IwAR0D 296pgWBXu2qkHRSGdkuiQk8enOPSjlNVNjj2Wgw2reQzOImUrEqnH40.

13. Ibid.

14. Sandefur, Timothy. "Robert Hayden, the Poet Who Would Not Be Canceled." *The Dispatch.* February 19, 2022. https://thedispatch.com/p/robert-hayden-the-poet-wh o-would.

15. McLeod, "hooks and Angelou."

16. Ibid.

17. Du Bois, *Souls of Black Folk,* chap. 6.

Bertolt Brecht

1. Hecht, Werner. *Brecht: Vielseitige Betrachtungen.* 2nd edition. Berlin: Henschelverlag, 1984, p. 218.

2. Marx, Karl and Friedrich Engels. "Theses on Feuerbach." Translated by W. Lough. Marx/Engels Internet Archives. Section 11. https://www.marxists.org/archive/marx/ works/1845/theses/theses.htm.

3. Squiers, Anthony. *An Introduction to the Social and Political Philosophy of Bertolt Brecht: Revolution and Aesthetics.* Amsterdam: Rodopi, 2014, 113.

4. Brecht, "Theater for Pleasure," 70-71.

5. Ibid, 71.

6. Brecht, Bertolt. "Appendices to the Short Organum," In *Brecht on Theater: The Development of an Aesthetic.* Edited and translated by John Willett. New York: Hill and Wang, 1964, 190.

7. Hecht, *Brecht,* 218.

8. Brecht, "Short Organum," 277.

9. Brecht, Bertolt. *Galileo.* Edited by Eric Bentley and translated by Desmond Vesey. New York, Grove Press, 1966, 115.

10. Brecht, Bertolt. *The Exception and the Rule.* In *Collected Plays III.* Edited by John Willett and translated by Tom Osborn. London: Methuen, 1997, 175.

Frantz Fanon

1. Fanon, Frantz. *The Wretched of the Earth.* Translated by Constance Farrington. New York: Grove Press, 1963, 240

2. Ibid, 236.

3. Ibid, 238.

4. Ibid.

5. Ibid, 239.

6. Ibid.

7. Ibid.

8. Ibid.

9. Ibid.

10. Ibid, 240.

11. Ibid.

12. Ibid.

13. Ibid, 239.

14. Ibid, 240-41.

15. Ibid, 241.

16. Ibid.

17. Ibid, 245.

The Frankfurt School

1. Marcuse, Herbert. *One Dimensional Man: Studies in the Ideology of Advanced Industrial Society.* London: Routledge, 2002, 65.

2. Horkheimer, Max and Theodor Adorno. *The Dialectic of Enlightenment: Philosophical Fragments.* Edited by Gunzelin Schmid Noerr and translated by Edmond Jephcott. Stanford: Stanford University Press, 2022, 94-136.

3. Marcuse, *One-Dimensional Man,* 65.

4. Flaubert, Gustave. *Madame Bovary.* Translated by Eleanor Marx-Aveling. New York, 1919; Project Gutenberg, 2000. Chapter 5. https://www.gutenberg.org/files/2413/2413-h/2413-h.htm.

5. Ibid, chap. 6.

6. Marcuse, *One-Dimensional Man,* 66.

7. Ibid, 65.

8. Ibid, 67.

9. Ibid, 80-81.

10. Jameson, Fredric. "Progress versus Utopia; Or, Can We Imagine the Future?" *Science Fiction Studies* 9, no. 2 (July, 1982), 153.

11. Jameson, "Progress versus Utopia," 153.

12. Ibid. 156-57.

13. Benjamin, Walter. "Theses on the Philosophy of History." In *Illuminations.* Edited by Hannah Arendt and translated by Harry Zohn. New York: Schocken, 2007, 263.

14. Ibid, 261.

15. Ibid, 251.

Twentieth Century Feminists

1. DuPlessis, Rachel Blau. *Writing beyond the Ending: Narrative Strategies of 20th Century Women Writers.* Bloomington: Indiana University Press, 1985, 1.

2. Ibid, 4.

3. Ibid, 2

4. Ibid, 7.

5. Gilbert, Sandra and Susan Gubar. *The Madwoman in the Attic: The Woman Writer and the Nineteenth-Century Literary Imagination.* New Haven: Yale University Press, 1979, 347-49.

6. Cited in DuPlessis, *Narrative Strategies,* 1.

7. Ibid.

8. Ibid, 4.

9. Modleski, Tania. *Loving with a Vengeance: Mass Produced Fantasies for Women.* 2nd edition. New York: Routledge, 2008, xxiii.

10. Ibid, xxi.

11. Ibid, 49.

12. Ibid, 58.

13. Ibid.

Hans Robert Jauss

1. Jauss, Robert. "Literary History as a Response to Literary Theory." Translated by Elizabeth Benzinger. In *New Directions in Literary History.* Edited by Ralph Cohen. Baltimore: Johns Hopkins University Press, 1974, 14.

2. Ibid, 19.

3. Kuhn, Thomas S. *The Structure of Scientific Revolutions.* 2nd edition. Foundations of the Unity of Science. Vol. 2. International Encyclopedia of Unified Science. Chicago: University of Chicago Press, 1970, 77-91.

4. Jauss, 20-21.

5. Flaubert, *Madame Bovary,* chap. 9.

6. Jauss, "Literary History," 38-39.

7. Dickens, Charles. *The Old Curiosity Shop.* London, 1840-41; Project Gutenberg, 1996. Chapter 72. https://www.gutenberg.org/cache/epub/700/pg700-images.html).

8. Jauss, "Literary History," 39.

9. "The Overton Window." MacKinac Center for Public Policy. https://www.mackinac.org/OvertonWindow.

Terry Eagleton

1. Terry Eagleton, *Literary Theory,* 31.

2. Ibid, 28.

3. Ibid, 23.

4. Ibid, 31.

5. Ibid, 34-35.

6. Ibid, 35.

7. Ibid.

8. Karlsson, Jonas. "The Dark Shadow of Faust: The Anti-Semitic Tradition of Reading Mephistopheles as the 'Jewish Spirit.'" *Austausch* 1, no. 1 (April, 2011), 52. https://www.psa.ac.uk/sites/default/files/Austausch,%20Vol.%201,%20no.%201,%20April%202011%20-%20Karlsson.pdf.

The Cultural Conservatives

1. Bloom, Allan. *The Closing of the American Mind*. New York: Simon and Schuster, 1987, 380.

2. Bate, *Samuel Johnson,* 240.

3. Ibid, 17.

4. Bloom, Harold. *Shakespeare: The Invention of the Human.* New York: Riverhead Book, 1998, 3.

5. Ibid, 5.

6. Ibid, 6.

7. Ibid, 4.

8. Ibid, 17.

9. Ibid, 13.

10. Ibid, 17.

11. Bloom, Harold. *The Western Canon: The Books and School of the Ages.* New York: Harcourt Brace, 1994, 18-19.

12. Ibid, 5.

13. Bloom, *American Mind,* 380.

14. Ibid, 381.

15. Ibid, 22.

16. Bloom, Allan and Harry Jaffa. *Shakespeare's Politics.* Chicago: University of Chicago, 1964, 104.

17. Ibid.

18. Ibid, 7.

19. Ibid.

20. Ibid, 6.

21. Ibid, 2-3.

22. Ibid, 3.

23. Ibid, 1.

24. Ibid, 2.

25. Hirsch, E.D. *Cultural Literacy: What Every American Needs to Know.* New York: Houghton Mifflin, 1987, 2.

26. Ibid.

27. Ibid, 85-87.

28. William Shakespeare. *Julius Caesar.* In *Bedford Shakespeare,* 4.3.218-224.

29. Hirsch, *Cultural Literacy,* 9-10.

30. Ibid, xiii.

31. Tran, Phuc. *Sigh, Gone: A Misfit's Memoir of Great Books, Punk Rock, and the Fight to Fit.* New York: Flatiron, 2020, 213.

32. Hirsch, *Cultural Literacy,* xiv.

33. Ibid.

34. Ibid, xvi.

Wayne Booth

1. Booth, Wayne. *The Company We Keep: An Ethics of Fiction.* Berkeley: University of California Press, 1988, 223.

2. Ibid, 174.

3. Ibid, 223.

4. Ibid.

5. Ibid, 271.

6. Ibid, 209.

7. Ibid, 281.

8. Ibid.

9. Ibid, 285.

10. Ibid, 488.

11. Ibid, 278-79.

12. Ibid, 3.

13. Ibid, 340.

14. Ibid, 282.

15. Ibid.

16. Ibid, 345.

17. Ibid.

18. Ibid.

Martha Nussbaum

1. Nussbaum, Martha. "Cultivating Humanity: A Classical Defense of Reform in Liberal Education." In *Norton Anthology of Theory*, 2308.

2. Ibid, 2306.

3. Ibid.

4. Ibid, 2307.

5. Ibid.

6. Ibid.

7. Ibid, 2308.

8. Ibid.

9. Ibid.

10. Ibid.

11. Ibid.

12. Ibid, 2308-09.

13. Ibid, 2327.

14. Ibid.

15. Ibid.

Recent Psychological Studies

1. Berns, Gregory S. et al. "Short- and Long-Term Effects of a Novel on Connectivity in the Brain." *Brain Connectivity* 3, no. 6 (2013). https://doi.org/10.1089/brain.2013.0166.

2. Murdoch, "Literature and Philosophy."

3. Paul, Annie Murphy. "Your Brain on Fiction." *New York Times*. March 18, 2012. https://www.nytimes.com/2012/03/18/opinion/sunday/the-neuroscience-of-your-brain-on-fiction.html.

4. Coleridge, *Ancient Mariner*, 53.

5. Paul, "Brain on Fiction."

6. Ibid.

7. Berns, "Effects of a Novel."

8. Goldman, Corrie. "This Is Your Brain on Jane Austen, and Stanford Researchers Are Taking Notes." *Stanford News*. September 7, 2017. https://news.stanford.edu/news/2012/september/austen-reading-fmri-090712.html.

9. Ibid.

10. Kidd, David Comer. "Reading Literary Fiction Improves Theory of Mind." *Science*. October 3, 2017. https://www.science.org/doi/full/10.1126/science.1239918.

11. Ibid.

12. Green, Melanie C. "Linking Self and Others through Narrative." *Psychological Inquiry* 18, no. 2 (2007), 100.

13. Ibid.

14. Ibid, 101.

15. Ibid.

16. Ibid.

17. Green, Melanie C. and Timothy Brock. "The Role of Transportation in the Persuasiveness of Public Narratives." *Journal of Personality and Social Psychology* 79, no. 5 (2000), 701.

18. Tangeras, Thor Magnus. *Literature and Transformation: A Narrative Study of Life-Changing Reading Experiences*. London: Anthem Press, 2020, 6.

19. Ibid, 191.

20. Ibid, 196.

21. Ibid, 191.

Has JANE EYRE Made the World a Better Place?

1. Scott, Eliza. Private family memoir. c.1920.

2. Ibid.

3. Ibid.

4. Ibid.

5. Gilbert, Nora. "A Servitude of One's Own: Isolation, Authorship, and the Nineteenth-Century British Governess." *Nineteenth-Century Literature* 69, no. 4 (2015), 460.

6. Bronte, Charlotte. *Jane Eyre: An Autobiography*. London, 1847; Project Gutenberg, 1998. Chap. 12. https://www.gutenberg.org/files/1260/1260-h/1260-h.htm.

7. Ibid, chap. 10.

8. Ibid.

9. Ibid.

10. Rigby, Elizabeth. "Vanity Fair–and Jane Eyre." *Quarterly Review* 84:167 (December 1848). http://www.quarterly-review.org/classic-qr-the-original-1848-review-of-jane-eyre.

11. Ibid.

12. "Elizabeth Eastlake." Wikipedia. https://en.wikipedia.org/wiki/Elizabeth_Eastlake.

13. Rigby, Elizabeth. *The Letters of Elizabeth Rigby, Lady Eastlake*. Edited by Julie Sheldon. Liverpool: Liverpool University Press, 2009, 1-12.

14. Ibid.

15. Miller, Lucasta. *The Bronte Myth*. New York: Alfred A. Knopf, 2004, 17.

16. Bronte, *Jane Eyre*, chap. 12.

17. Rigby, "Jane Eyre."

18. Miller, *Bronte Myth*, 21.

19. Ibid, 22.

20. Ibid, 34.

21. Ibid, 35.

22. Ibid, 33.

23. Waring, Kayla. "The Heroine vs. the Marriage Plot: How Film Adaptations Limit the Character of Jane Eyre." Senior Project, St. Mary's College of Maryland, 2017.

24. Gilbert and Gubar, *Madwoman*, 349.

25. Ibid, 359-61.

26. Lawrence, D.H. "Pornography and Obscenity." In *Late Essays and Articles*. Edited by James T. Boulton. Cambridge: Cambridge University Press, 2004, 242-43.

27. Bronte, Charlotte. "Editor's Preface to the New Edition of *Wuthering Heights* (1850)." In Emily Bronte, *Wuthering Heights*. Edited by William M. Sale, Jr. and Richard J. Dunn. 3rd ed. Norton Critical. New York: W.W. Norton, 1990, 322.

28. Rhys, Jean. *Wide Sargasso Sea*. New York: Norton, 1982.

29. Morrison, Toni. "Introduction" to *The Oxford Mark Twain: Adventures of Huckleberry Finn*. Edited by Shelley Fisher Fishkin. New York: Oxford University Press, 1996.

30. Morrison, Toni. "Unspeakable Things Unspoken: The Afro-American Presence in American Literature." *Michigan Quarterly Review* 23, no. 1 (1989). https://sites.lsa.umich.edu/mqr/2019/08/unspeakable-things-unspoken-the-afro-american-presence-in-american-literature.

31. "Theresa." Student essay. St. Mary's College of Maryland, 2014.

32. Ibid.

33. Bronte, *Jane Eyre,* chap. 24.

34. Ibid, chap. 27.

35. Ibid.

36. "Theresa," student essay.

Jane Austen on Pop Lit

1. Pope, Alexander. *The Poetical Works of Alexander Pope.* Vol. 2. *The Dunciad.* Book 4, ll. 651-56. London, 1743; Project Gutenberg, 2006. https://www.gutenberg.org/cache/epub/9601/pg9601-images.html.

2. Henry Fielding. *The History of Tom Jones, A Foundling.* London, 1949; Project Gutenberg, 2004. Book 4, chapter 1. https://www.gutenberg.org/cache/epub/6593/pg6593-images.html.

3. Booth, *Company We Keep,* 271.

4. Ibid, 203.

5. Ibid, 204.

6. Blumenthal, Paul and J.M. Rieger. "This Stunningly Racist French Novel Is How Steve Bannon Explains the World." *Huffington Post.* May 4, 2017. https://www.huffpost.com/entry/steve-bannon-camp-of-the-saints-immigration_n_58b75206e4b0284854b3dc03.

7. Ibid.

8. Raspail, Jean. *The Camp of Saints.* Translated by Norman Shapiro. New York: Scribner, 1975, 259.

9. Rogers, John. *Kung Fu Monkey* (blog). http://kfmonkey.blogspot.com/2009/03/ephemera-2009-7.html.

10. Sargent, Greg. "Scott Walker and the Hammock Theory of Poverty." *Washington Post.* February 3, 2015. https://www.washingtonpost.com/blogs/plum-line/wp/2015/02/03/scott-walker-and-the-hammock-theory-of-poverty.

11. Reynolds, Davis S. *Mightier Than the Sword: Uncle Tom's Cabin and the Battle for America.* New York: W.W. Norton, 2011, 117-67.

12. Reynolds, David S. "Uncle Tom's Cabin." In *Essential Civil War Curriculum* (website). https://www.essentialcivilwarcurriculum.com/uncle-toms-cabin.html.

13. Baldwin, James. "Everybody's Protest Novel." In *Notes of a Native Son.* Boston: Beacon Hill Press, 1955, 17-18.

14. Cited in Reynolds, *Mightier Than the Sword,* 259.

15. Gilligan, Heather. "The most famous book about slavery has been rejected by black thinkers since it was published." *Timeline.* Jan. 11, 2017. https://timeline.com/the-most-famous-book-about-slavery-has-been-rejected-by-black-thinkers-since-it-was-published-b8dce54984c8.

16. Austen, Jane. *Northanger Abbey.* London, 1817; Project Gutenberg, 2022. Chapter 24. https://www.gutenberg.org/files/121/121-h/121-h.htm.

17. Ibid, chapter 6.

18. Modleski, *Loving with a Vengeance,* 58.

19. Austen, *Northanger Abbey,* chapter 25.

20. Ibid.

21. Ibid, chapter 6.

22. Ibid, chapter 14.

23. Austen, Jane. *Sense and Sensibility.* London, 1811; Project Gutenberg, 1994. Chapter 10. https://www.gutenberg.org/files/161/161-h/161-h.htm.

24. Aligheri, Dante. *Inferno.* Translated by Henry Wadsworth Longfellow. Boston, 1867; Project Gutenberg, 1997. Canto 5. https://www.gutenberg.org/files/1001/1001-h/1001-h.htm.

25. Cowper, William. "The Castaway," Poetry Foundation. https://www.poetryfoundation.org/poems/44027/the-castaway.

26. Horace, *Art of Poetry.*

27. Austen, Jane. *Pride and Prejudice.* London, 1813; Project Gutenberg, 1998. Chapter 14. https://www.gutenberg.org/cache/epub/1342/pg1342-images.html.

28. Austen, Jane. *Sanditon.* Oxford, 1923; Project Gutenberg, 2008. Chapter 7. https://gutenberg.net.au/ebooks/fr008641.html.

29. Ibid.

30. Austen, Jane. *Persuasion.* London, 1817; Project Gutenberg, 1994. Chapter 11. https://www.gutenberg.org/cache/epub/105/pg105-images.html.

31. Austen, Jane. *Mansfield Park.* London, 1814; Project Gutenberg, 1994. Chapter 2. https://www.gutenberg.org/cache/epub/141/pg141-images.html.

32. Ibid, chapters 6, 45.

33. Ibid, chap. 16.

34. Austen, *Mansfield Park,* chap. 14.

35. Brown, Mark. "Not as good as P&P: Jane Austen mother's verdict on *Mansfield Park.*" *The Guardian.* December 1, 2016. https://www.theguardian.com/books/2016/dec/0 1/jane-austen-mothers-verdict-on-mansfield-park-british-library.

36. Austen, *Mansfield Park,* chap. 34.

Literature as Healing Narrative

1. Alighieri, Dante. *Inferno.* Translated by John Ciardi. New York: New American Library, 2009, 4.

2. Ibid.

3. Oliver, Mary. "The Lost Children." *American Primitive.* Boston: Little, Brown, 1978, 13, 15.

4. *Beowulf.* Translated by Seamus Heaney. New York, Norton, 2000, 95.

5. Ibid, 109.

6. Ibid, 118-19.

7. Ibid, 93.

8. Ibid, 97.

9. Ibid, 155.

10. Ibid.

11. Rutkai, Erica. "Blog: Befriending, Not Fighting, Grendel's Mother." *Better Living through Beowulf.* May 20, 2010. https://betterlivingthroughbeowulf.com/a-woman-w arrior-battling-grief.

12. Ibid.

13. Ibid.

14. Ibid.

15. Ibid.

16. Bates, *How* Beowulf *Can Save America.*

Assessing Literature's Personal and Historical Impact

1. Bates, *Better Living*.

2. Holland, Norman. "Unity Identity Text Self." In *Reader Response Criticism*, 122.

3. Ibid, 125.

Conclusion

1. Winterson, Jeanette. "Shafts of Sunlight." *The Guardian*. November 14, 2008. https://www.theguardian.com/books/2008/nov/15/ts-eliot-festival-donmar-jeanette-winterson.

2. Benjamin, "Philosophy of History," 261, 251.

3. Heaney, Seamus. *The Government of the Tongue*. London: Faber, 1988, 107.

4. Booth, *Company We Keep*, 223.

5. Rushdie, Salman. "Truth, Lies, and Literature." New Yorker, May 31, 2019. https://www.newyorker.com/culture/cultural-comment/truth-lies-and-literature.

INDEX OF AUTHORS AND TITLES

To contact Robin Bates for speaking engagements,
please email rrbates@smcm.edu.

Many Voices. One Message.

quoir.com

Made in the USA
Middletown, DE
03 September 2024

60219073R00236